JOY DAWSON

My Journey with Jesus

TAKEN FROM MY JOURNALS

Copyright © 2021 by Joy Dawson

Published by Joy Dawson
11141 Osborne Street
Lake View Terrace, CA 91342
www.JoyDawson.com

All rights reserved. No part of this publication may be reproduced, stored in a retrieval system, or transmitted in any form or by any means—for example, electronic, photocopy, recording—without the prior written permission of the publisher. The only exception is quotations in printed reviews.

First printing.

eBook edition created in 2021.

ISBN 978-0-578-95709-8

As a way of life, I used different versions of the Bible when having my daily devotions.

When writing this book there were times when I thought it helpful to state which version I had used when quoting a verse; other times I didn't think it was necessary, as evidenced in my journals.

The majority of verses quoted in this manuscript are from the Revised Standard Version of the Bible, copyright 1989, Division of Christian Education of the National Council of the Churches of Christ in the United States of America. Used by permission. All rights reserved.

Scripture marked AMP is taken from the Amplified ® Bible, Copyright © 1954, 1958, 1962, 1964, 1965, 1987 by The Lockman Foundation. Used by permission.

Scripture marked NIV is taken from the NEW INTERNATIONAL VERSION®. NIV®. Copyright © 1973, 1978, 1984 by International Bible Society. Used by permission of Zondervan. All rights reserved.nasb

Scripture marked NKJV is taken from the New King James Version. Copyright © 1982 by Thomas Nelson, Inc. Used by permission. All rights reserved.

Scripture marked KJV is taken from the King James Version of the Bible.

Scripture marked MSG are taken from THE MESSAGE, copyright © 1993, 2002, 2018 by Eugene H. Peterson. Used by permission of NavPress, represented by Tyndale House Publishers. All rights reserved.

John Dawson "TAKING OUR CITIES FOR GOD" How To Break Spiritual Strongholds" ©2001 by Charisma House, Lake Mary, FL. Used by permission.

Excerpt from "All Heaven will Break Loose" by Joy Dawson, copyright © 2014. Used by permission of Chosen Books, a division of Baker Publishing Group.

Dedication

To my two children and their spouses.

To my eight grandchildren and their spouses.

To my fifteen great grandchildren.

Acknowledgements

I want to give very high honor and express the deepest gratitude to those of you who have faithfully prayed for Jim and me over many years, and have supported our ministries financially. A few of you have consistently prayed and supported us for numbers of decades.... a priceless commitment which will have the appropriate rewards both now and in eternity.

While we have faithfully prayed for <u>all</u> your needs to be met in return, I am still believing God to reward you in ways that are beyond your comprehension. --- or mine!

I know I couldn't have done what I've done, in the power of the Holy Spirit, without your commitment to the Lord on my behalf. This includes everything to do with the writing of this book. Only God knows how much I needed you – BIG TIME!!

For some time, I have understood what Jesus said to His disciples in Luke 22:28 RSV "You are those who have continued with Me in my trials."

I want to make special reference to the very wonderful way that my daughter Jill and son-in-law J.B. have helped to meet my needs, especially since my beloved husband Jim went to be with Jesus in 2013, and my previously having had to give up my driver's license. Their rewards will be truly great.

I also want to express my love and gratitude to dear David Thompson for tirelessly putting all my handwritten scripts into the computer. There were times when I would bounce a portion of my script off on him, and ask for his perspective (as I used to do with Jim) and David was always willing to helpfully comply. He was a gift from God to me at a time of great need.

I am very grateful to my son John for the help he gave me in my lengthy and tedious job of editing this large manuscript.

My deep gratitude also goes to Layna Weintraub for her art work on the book cover, and for Michael Koulianos, who covered those expenses.

May God extravagantly reward each one of you as only He can, and as you so greatly deserve.

Psalm 115:1 Not unto us o Lord, not unto us, but Your name give glory, for Your mercy and for Your truth's sake.

The Forward

I've had my share of faith challenges over a long lifetime. But none of them compare to the one of writing this book. God alone knows I was out of my depth and totally cast on Him all the way through.

This project was never my idea or desire at anytime. It was surprising to me at nearing 92 years of age, that God would require of me to take on such a demanding project...and without my precious life partner of 65 years invaluable input and support.

My response was predictable. I had been saying "Yes Lord," to His orders over a long lifetime, and nothing was going to change that commitment.

However, I have never felt so totally inadequate to know what to report and how to report it; so I charged my faith batteries on my lover God's abilities to write it through me.

This was based upon 2 Corinthians 9:8 "God is able to make all grace abound toward you, that you, always having all sufficiency in all things, may have an abundance for every good work."

At times I would make up little songs to Him at the start of the day, like a little child. It never ceased to amaze and delight me how the rhymes and melodies spontaneously expressed the depths of my heart, to the only One who understood it!

For example:

"I don't know how to write this book,
But Jesus does, through me.
So when all the glory goes to Him,
The more fulfilled I'll be.
I cannot write this book to be
But the Great I Am is writing it through me
I don't know what I am to do
Jesus Christ alone will see me through
All the glory must go unto Him
Cos I thought I couldn't do it without my Jim"

It wasn't until March 23rd 2018, having written quite a bit of this book, that it dawned on me that God was actually answering my own prayers, through my doing so.

Ever since February 23rd 2013, when my precious sweetheart of over 65 years went to be with Jesus, I have fervently and frequently being praying the following prayer.

"Dear God, I want my **full destiny** to be fulfilled, as You alone know it to be. I will pay any price for this prayer to be answered. I don't want You or me to be disappointed when I stand before You at the Judgment Seat. Thank You that you will answer these heart cries, in Jesus mighty name. Amen."

Working on this book, while in a lot of pain from advanced osteoarthritis in both hips and my fingers, as well as a lot of insomnia, is part of the price.

I long for and pray that God's character of absolute justice will shine through these pages, and be a balancing factor in everything I've shared. One of my life verses is Psalm 147:3 "God is just in all His ways, and kind in all His doings." In times of pain and perplexity, I always come back to the truth of this verse.

By far my most passionate desire is that 100 percent of the glory will go to my precious Lord Jesus, as this book is read. My ultimate life verse is Romans 11:33 "For from Him and through Him and to Him be **all the glory,** forever and ever. Amen."

My earnest prayers are that the readers will more fully understand how incredibly awesome and wonderful Jesus is and have a heightened desire and experience to personally make Him known to others in the power of the Holy Spirit.

I also pray that they may have a greater understanding of God's character and His ways; specially the need to wait on God, listen to His voice, expect Him to speak in any of the many ways that He does, and then **instantly, joyfully, fully obey Him as a way of life**. That's fulfillment! Anything else is missing it.

My Journey with Jesus

Taken from my journals

Signs of my God ordained destiny showed up very early. My mother told me that when I was a baby of only seven months old, and being held in her arms as she was saying goodbye to guests, I waived my tiny hand and clearly said, "Tat-ah" (an English way of saying, "goodbye.") That I talked before I walked, was a sign of the public speaking gift that would be manifest years later.

On another occasion, I was about 18 months old and sitting in a high chair at the family dining table. My parents had a guest for the meal named Mr. Mace from England, who was highly esteemed among the Open Brethren as a deep Bible teacher.

In the middle of my dad's and Mr. Mace's deep theological discussions, my mother said that I clearly spoke out the words, "God's governmental dealings!" ---at which Mr. Mace turned to my father and said with astonishment, "Did you hear that child John? Did you hear that child?" I guess I overheard them use that term, but Mother never said that.

What amazes me is that "God's governmental dealings" are just another way of describing "The character and ways of God." And that's the basis upon which all my teachings, spoken and written are based, as I have often stated.

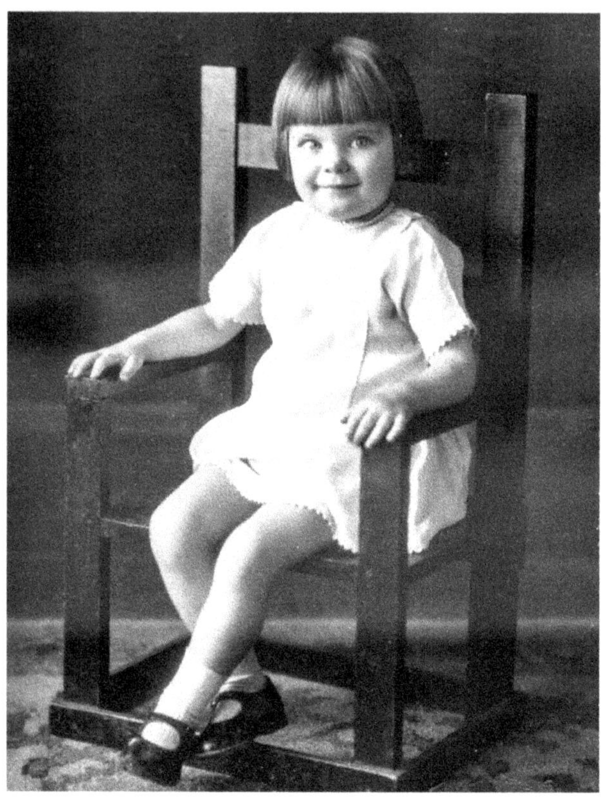

Joy at three years of age.

All through my normal happy childhood, I was aware of having a very sensitive conscience. It applied to little things, as I lived a very sheltered life. I see this as the sovereign, merciful hand of God upon me and I'm deeply grateful.

My loving and wonderful Christian parents in New Zealand greatly influenced my life as a child. My mother explained to me how I could become a Christian when I was five years old. That's when I confessed I was a sinner, invited the Lord Jesus to come into my heart and gave Him my life. I have never doubted the reality of that genuine conversion experience.

My father, John Manins, was a strong spiritual leader, Bible teacher, and evangelist among the Open Brethren. He pioneered Christian radio in New Zealand.

I need to explain here that the Open Brethren didn't believe in having a paid Pastor as the senior leader of a local church. They operated under the leadership of what they called the "oversight," who were several spiritually mature men who never received a salary.

My dad came into that category, so it necessitated his having to have employment to support his family. He worked for the Texas Oil Company as a salesman, from 9 a.m. to 5 p.m.

Consistently every year, he would come through as "the top salesman" and his employer would try hard to promote him to take a managerial position. But my dad just as consistently turned down the offers and the extra money.

His story was that to fulfill his spiritual calling and giftings as a pastor, evangelist, Bible teacher, and author, there were no other options at that time that he could consider. Of course this put a load upon him as a husband and father of 5 children that he was never meant to carry. It had its consequences.

I deeply respected my dad's priorities as it related to money, and it helped to shape my destiny. However, on Biblical standards, he should have been supported financially by members of the Body of Christ.

Galatians 6:6 "Let him who is taught the Word share all good things with him who teaches."

1 Corinthians 9:14 "In the same way, the Lord commanded that those who proclaim the gospel should get their living by the gospel."

My dad's passionate love for and study of the Word of God deeply impacted me, along with his genuine burden for lost souls.

The highlight of my week as a little girl was being allowed to go to church on Sunday nights, sit on the front row and listen to him preach the Gospel. He was an anointed, gifted, interesting speaker, and I joyfully listened with rapt attention.

I also loved to hear him tell the stories around the dinner table about how he had witnessed to individuals from all walks of life and led them to the Lord.

One time he picked up a hitch hiker out on a country road, witnessed to him, and the man genuinely responded. So Dad said, "Lets get out of the car and kneel down on the roadside with me and give your life to Christ openly, if you really mean business. The guy did just that. I loved it!

Another time he witnessed to a hitch hiker whom he had picked up, who gave his life to Christ during the ride. When Dad asked him about his life, he found out the guy was in need of clothing. Dad was on a pastoral visit to some house churches and had his only other suit of clothes that he owned with him. He promptly gave it to the new convert and trusted God to meet his own needs... which were real!

Later Dad would show us an expensive, warm overcoat (the New Zealand winters can be cold) that a wealthy business man had just given him.

My dad was gutsy! Where there was no way in a given situation, I would watch, fascinated, as he would try to make a way... and succeed... often.

Later, when Dad was debilitated with Parkinson's disease, he was forced out of all public ministry. When God in his sovereignty didn't answer our many fervent prayers for his healing; Dad would say with Job, "Though He slay me, yet will I trust Him."

I never once heard him complain. What a priceless legacy. My dad was my hero, and the Christian life was an adventure I wanted to pursue!

My dear mother was no preacher, but she had a great heart for the poor and needy and was **always involved** with helping them in practical ways. We called them; "odd bod's" who were always hanging around our home, because that is who mother specialized in ministering to.

She often said, "Don't trample on the daisies (the little unimportant people) while you're reaching for the dahlias (the important and influential people). Great wisdom.

She was a wonderful caring mother to her five children and then the same to her grandchildren. I honor her.

Both my parents were outstanding soul winners. As a result, sharing the gospel with others became as natural as eating and breathing, to this little girl. I led my first soul to Christ when I was ten. She was my best friend, and it was during a school recess.

Family Bible reading and prayer were daily events in my home, which often included my parents sharing remarkable answers to prayer which impacted me. Also, my Aunt Dahlia Manins was a single, Godly missionary among the Indigenous Maori and Immigrant Chinese minorities in New Zealand. She came to visit her brother John and family for extended periods of time. She was an intercessor of depth who loved me deeply and whose influence no doubt also contributed to my later choosing the call of God to make intercession part of my spiritual blood stream.

For years I went consistently to Christian youth camps, twice per year, and thrived on the holistic, vital programs.

Every summer holidays, Dad rented a beach house for four weeks at beautiful Browns Bay, north of Auckland. We reveled in swimming in the clear warm water at length and building amazing constructions in the clean white sand, by the hour. When the tide was out we would walk around the rocks exploring the next nearest beaches.

I had a wonderful holistic childhood, and am very grateful to be able to say with the Psalmist in Psalm 16:2 "The lines have fallen to me in pleasant places. Yes, I have a good inheritance."

I totally understand the justice of God, when He states in Exodus 15:2 "The Lord is my strength and my song and He has become my salvation, **my father's God**, and I will exalt Him." And in Luke 12:48 "To whom much is given, much will be required" The price to fully serve the Lord over my lifetime, has definitely been high. I was also given so many privileges. I get the equation!

I need to add here that at age 14, I was given my first lesson in dressmaking by a friend of Mothers. It was during a holiday weekend of three days. The kind lady started me off by showing me how to work a sewing machine, and then how to sew a strictly **tailored** set of pajamas--- which taught me all the basics. It soon became obvious that God had gifted me with a strong aptitude in this direction.

With so little money to buy clothes with then, and throughout my later life in New Zealand, this gift was a great asset. I made most of my own dresses, suits, and all of my hats. I have always had a flair for pretty clothes and still do! At 93 I still do most of the alterations of my clothing.

My mother, Grace Manins, consistent with her remarkable ministry of hospitality, often invited 17 year old Jim Dawson home for a meal after church, as he was boarding in the city away from home. Jim enjoyed interacting with my four brothers and with me their fourteen-year-old sister. He came from a strong Scottish Christian home in a country area, and was soundly converted at the age of seven.

One Saturday night, Jim walked me home from our church youth group. It was less than a mile. I vividly remember opening up my innocent little heart and sharing the high ideals I had for my future life. It was done naturally, with no ulterior motives or agenda.

Jim listened respectfully, and much later told me he never forgot it.

I thought he was a likable, handsome Christian young man. He was 17 ½ and I was 14.

When we got to the entry way of my home, to our surprise my mother was there waiting for us. Kindly but firmly she let us both know that I was far too young to have a boyfriend. I hadn't presumed I had one, but Jim and I sincerely submitted to her protective instructions. We were always in groups with others; and then Jim went on to date another girl!

A few years later I became a fanatic walker, and loved to walk the eight miles home from the center of Auckland City at night, after the last train car had stopped at midnight. I had to persuade my friend who I was with at the time, to do the same. Sometimes with a girl, sometimes with a boy.

On one such occasion, I had spent the whole day with a good Christian boy --- just a friend, going to a beautiful beach town. It took me a tram ride, a ferry boat ride across the harbor, and then a bus ride to get there. We spent the time swimming endlessly, and then hiking around the rocks to another whole beach area and then back again. After that we played tennis.

After a day full of activities, and being on the bus ride and ferry boat back to the city, I suggested that we skip the last tram ride that left at midnight and expend more energy with the 8 mile walk back to my home. Amazingly, he agreed. Around 1 am we arrived.

I then realized that he would have to walk several more miles back to his home. That thought had never occurred to me before. A brilliant solution emerged. "Have a loan of one of my brother's bikes." He agreed and took off.

I never thought any more about it, until 2 or 3 days later I heard my Dad telling my brothers that he would now have to notify the police about the stolen bike, as he had investigated every other plausible source as to why it was missing!

I readily confessed to being the culprit. The bike was finally returned, and life went on… with people around me having to cope with a teenager who was born in overdrive, with way too much energy, and obviously a lot to learn about the consideration of others!

Most of my teenage years were spent in the four years of World War II. These memories included having a large dugout air raid shelter in the middle of our backyard, and all our windows being blacked out at night. Also, my Dad had to bicycle nine miles to work and back each day, because of the gas shortages.

With New Zealand's entrance into the Second World War, Jim was conscripted into the military and was gone for several years. On his return he found I had grown into a young woman to whom he was attracted in many ways. I in turn enjoyed him as a good friend. We both knew that both of us had a heart after God... but there was nothing serious going on.

A few months later Jim joined the Navy and went on the famous New Zealand warship, the ACHILES. It went straight to Osaka, Japan. Only 3 weeks prior to its arrival, an atom bomb had devastated the entire city, just before the war ended. Jim said it was a very sobering and deeply impacting experience, to say the least, in the six weeks he was there.

Then they sailed on to England and Scotland where Jim had a great time meeting up with his Scottish relatives.

On his return six months later, Jim and I continued to be just friends among others.... until there came a time, when he indicated he was serious about our future together. I told him two things would have to happen. One, God would have to give me a deep-seated, unshakable conviction within my spirit that this was His will for me. Two, God would have to cause me to fall in love with him. As I sought God diligently for directions, He really did a number on me on both counts... big time! I came to the understanding that beyond a shadow of doubt Jim was God's choice to be my life partner, and I deeply loved him!

Just married February 28, 1948

Five months later on February 28th, 1948 when I was 22, and Jim was 25, we had a formal church wedding surrounded by family and friends. We then went camping for the first part of our honeymoon.

We soon found an old house for sale, on an amazing site, surrounded by beautiful native bush. It had a spectacular harbor view of 180 degrees. God made it clear to us both that it was for us to own.

Jim had to sell his car to make the down payment. I was so broke, I was still owing Jim 2 pounds when I married him.

With just a few tools, Jim built 2 built in wardrobes, and 2 frameworks for 2 sets of drawers that lined one side of our bedroom walls.

We had a few essential pieces of old second hand furniture; that was it…. with bare floors. The only toilet was called "the outhouse," because it was very much outside!

It took me 2 years working as a salesperson in a classy gown salon downtown, just to make the payments on the fridge we had bought on time payment. That was a lot of work with little to see for it, but I loved the job! I was a born salesperson, like my Dad.

We had the barest essentials of earthly possessions, but we couldn't have been happier. That's not a cliché; God surely knows!

Jim taught the boys' Bible class at the little Open Brethren church we belonged to, and I was the leader of the girls club, which met during the week. I taught them gymnasium, with some Bible teaching thrown in.

Early in our marriage we attended an Easter convention where an American pastor, Larry Love, was the main speaker. He spoke on the importance of intercession in the life of every Believer. I already knew that God worked in partnership with Believers' prayers to change other people's lives. But I did not have the Biblical understanding that **God requires our prayer lives to consistently include a broad spectrum of peoples in need.**

I returned from that conference with a powerful impression that I could do nothing less than obey what God had shown me. I heard the word of the Lord through this man of God and thanked him for it. I started by interceding regularly for missionaries from my denomination.

The first six months after I started disciplining myself, and earnestly praying for others as directed by the Holy Spirit, my spiritual maturity increased 100 percent. I was receiving God's heart and receiving God's mind for others and that was changing me. It was exciting. I would never be the same.

One morning, I walked out to the letter-box to get the mail. Walking back along the path to the front door I heard the Holy Spirit speaking to me in my mind. "*You belong to the nations of the world, and as a Christian you are responsible to be praying for the nations of the world.*"

This thought had never entered my mind. I had been praying for needy individuals, for unsaved friends, for missionaries. But for nations? I had never heard of anyone speaking of that before. I remember saying audibly, "You're right God, I'll start praying for the nations now."

As soon as I went into my house, I got down on my knees and said, "Which nation do you want me to start praying for, Lord?" I heard the Holy Spirit saying, "Afghanistan." I knew nothing about it except that it was near Central Asia. So I prayed for the Christians, and then the non Christians as best I knew how – which didn't last long. But I had started on a very historic journey.

Significant Changes

The tradition among the Open Brethren that Jim and I belonged to, was to feature the Lord's Supper, (Communion) every Sunday morning. This was followed by one or more bringing a Bible teaching –unannounced beforehand and which were usually elders.

They believed in the "priesthood of all Believers," not just clergy. Very scriptural.

Then on Sunday nights they had what was called, "The gospel meeting"; their evangelistic service.

Four years after marriage, to our happy fulfillment, our son John was born. He was sharp and abounding with energy. We enjoyed him greatly. This meant that Jim and I would take turns going to church, while the other one stayed at home with the baby.

One Sunday night I was taking my turn at attending the "gospel meeting". I was 26. It suddenly struck me that, as usual, in the small church we attended, there were only Christians there, listening to the gospel being preached month in and month out!

I thought, "This is ridiculous, there's got to be another way to reach lost souls!!" I then determined never to go back on a Sunday night to an ineffective tradition. I would ask God to show me what to do as an alternative. I had no idea how He would direct me. When I got home, I shared my decision with Jim, who listened quietly without any objections. The next Sunday night he went back, as usual.

The test was full on for me the following Sunday, as God had not yet revealed any alternative to me. I got suitably dressed, ready to be sent anywhere. Unwaveringly, I said out loud to God in Jim's presence, "I have no idea where to go, but I fully trust You to show me." I waited in silent expectancy for His orders. They came with clarity.

"Go down to the center of the City and join in with the "Open Air Campaigners". I then remembered that George Bremner was the leader of this evangelistic outdoors association. He too was a Brethren!

Jim made absolutely no sign of cautioning me or stopping me, so I was on my way in the car in obedience to God, with an expectant heart!

I was not disappointed. I stood under the night sky with a few other Christians near the Civic Center auditorium. The O.A.C. van had a platform that opened out. We sang and praised God to the sound of the piano accordion. A medley of non Christians were standing around listening with us. I kept saying enthusiastically to myself and to God, "THIS IS IT!" This was topped off with a clear presentation of the gospel by one of the O.A.C. staff.

When Jim heard my enthusiastic, positive report, he knew in his heart he too was to follow this new direction from the Lord, and he did. We had received an historic new direction for our lives. Believe me, nothing would ever be the same.

We were deeply committed members of this evangelistic association for years, witnessing for Christ in parks, at beaches, and in shopping centers. We loved it.

Children

When John was three years old, we were delighted to know we were going to have another child.

I need to explain something here. Growing up, I had one brother older and close in age to myself. Then another brother 3 years younger. Then another brother 6 years younger. Then another brother 12 years younger.

Growing up, I became aware that my mother was always hoping to have another daughter. While carrying her fifth child she actually named it, Esther Grace.....only to find it was another boy.

When my older brother married, he only had sons.

When I married, I very happily had a boy first. But when I was expecting my second child, I had a longing to have a girl.

So as not to disappoint myself--- after the long nine months of waiting, only to find it to be another boy, I decided to name the baby David and look forward to him as God's gift, which I totally did.

Jillian approximately 5yrs old and John approximately 9yrs old

When I was in the hospital, after hard labor, I heard the nurse say, "It's a girl." I immediately went into an almost delirious shock of unbelievable joy, and kept repeating over and over. "It's a girl! It's a girl!"

Later, when a late night nurse came and found that I was still awake, she wanted me to take a sleeping pill, reminding me that I'd given birth to an 8lb baby and needed rest.

My response was to turn it down and say, "Who needs sleep? I've got a baby girl!!" It was the fulfillment of a deep seated longing since childhood.

Of course we loved both our children equally and have had great fulfillment in seeing them become strong ambassadors for Christ with international ministries.

Again, all of God's grace and sheer goodness.

When John was five and Jillian was only one, Jim and I earnestly sought God to be filled with the Holy Spirit as commanded in Ephesians 5:18.

We were away on a summer vacation at Lake Taupo with my cousins, Mary and Frank Garratt from Wellington, who had already received this gift.

They were our closest friends. We often had great vacations together. Camping out at Algies Bay near the waters edge was a highlight. This continued on during their lifetimes. Mary was my cousin on my dad's side, and we had enough affinity to start "The Affinity Club" of all time.

When we were alone together at our peak moments of abandoned exhilarating joy, only God could understand us! We would laugh so intensely, only God could out do us.

Frank and Jim were very compatible at all times, while coping with us girls!

However, by far our greatest point of unity came from our mutually deep desire to know God more fully in order to make Him known to others.

Jim and I and our two children were camping out in our tent, at Taupo, when we asked Frank and Mary to pray for us to be filled with the Spirit, with the laying on of their hands on our heads. They prayed for Jim first who previously had deep heart preparation when alone with God. He sought God before I did, to obey God's command in Ephesians 5:18 "be filled with the Holy Spirit." When it came time to pray for me, the Holy Spirit convicted me that I prayed more often for other men of God than I did for my husband. I deeply repented with tears as I openly confessed this wrong priority. I then received the gift of the Holy Spirit's fulness, by faith. God really came through!

Consequently, I was given an intense desire to really **know God, intimately**, the author of the Bible. My times of witnessing to the unconverted became so much more powerful, and I had an **insatiable thirst for the Word of God**.

I asked God to teach me how to hear His voice with accuracy, so that I could fully obey Him. I also asked Him to tell me which book in the Bible I should be reading. The Holy Spirit answered both questions, by clearly speaking into my spirit, "Read the book of Isaiah." This started a chain reaction of being directed by the Holy Spirit to read many of the Old Testament books one by one. The results were electric.

This was new territory for me and I was totally fascinated by daily discovering fresh gems of truth! One day I was so excited, I phoned a friend and said, "Did you realize these amazing verses were in the Bible?" as I then repeated them over the phone.

I never attended Bible school, but I seriously studied the Word of God each day. The Holy Spirit soon instructed me to buy a large notebook and title it "*My Personal Concordance on the Character and Ways of God*". I obeyed.

Every day, when I came to a Bible verse that related to either of those two subjects, I would head up the page with the appropriate title and then write out the reference and the verse or verses and meditate on them, totally depending on the Holy Spirit's enlightenment.

For example, if there were verses about waiting on God, or obedience to Him, I would know they were some of God's ways. If they were about God's Holiness or His Justice, then they were parts of His character.

I soon observed that in relation to God's ways, I wrote down many more verses on **the fear of the Lord** than any other aspects of them.

I then applied what I was learning, to my everyday life, and I was being totally revolutionized! Over the many years of being in this School of the Holy Spirit and the Word of God, my future destiny was being shaped, and I was totally ruined for the ordinary.

Another Pivotal Change

At the time of the Charismatic Renewal sweeping the world, denominations had to choose whether they believed that the way the early church operated in the power of the Holy Spirit was for today, or it was no longer relevant.

The Hillsborough Baptist Church near us, was not only very strong evangelistically, but had followed the lead of the Baptist Union in New Zealand who openly identified with the fresh moving of the Holy Spirit. They declared that all the gifts of the Spirit are for us today.

At the same time the Open Brethren Assemblies in New Zealand took a united stand against this belief.

As Jim and I sought God for direction, He clearly led us to leave the Brethren Assembly and wholeheartedly join the Baptists. This was another pivotal and joyous turning point in our lives. Only those who willfully stay in a traditional mold, when God is urging them to do otherwise, become moldy. Think about that!

God's hand in blessing and expansion, was very evidently upon the Baptist denomination throughout New Zealand as a result of their taking this stand.

Our dear friend, Rev. Hayes Lloyd was a part of all this. In the opening chapter of my book on unity, titled "All Heaven Will Break Loose" I recount a dramatic story related to his leadership at that time.

Thank God my dear Dad took a bold uncompromising stand among his other Open Brethren Leaders, stating his strong convictions Biblically, that all the gifts of the Spirit are for to-day. He was a lone voice and paid a price to be so.

I was so proud of him.

**Joy Dawson "ALL HEAVEN WILL BREAK LOOSE" When We Make The Priorities Of Jesus Our Priorities" ©2014 by Chosen Books*

This paved the way for Jim and me to always be open to all the workings of the Holy Spirit that are consistent with Biblical teaching. Most of Jim's dear family remained in the Open Brethren all the days of their lives; which made it difficult for them to understand many of our choices. They don't believe in women preachers for starters. Jim was one of six children.

Muri Thompson, a young Maori evangelist, was often in our home when our children were young. He had a hole in his heart, which in 1956 was medically inoperable. His future was very bleak. Jim and I believed God had a plan to use him greatly in evangelism, and were praying for a miraculous healing. We were also praying that Muri would have the same conviction and faith.

One morning he shared with me that God had spoken to him in his daily reading of the Bible, from Isaiah 57:18 "I have seen his ways, and I will heal him," and verse 19, "Peace peace --- says the Lord; and I will heal him."

That was all we needed, so we arranged for a time that Jim would lay his hands upon Muri's heart, anoint him with oil and pray the prayer of faith for a total creative miracle! At the same time our two other evangelist friends, George Bremner, director of Open Air Campaigners, and Alan Williams, a radically converted seaman operating with the O.A.C. were interceding for Muri's healing in other places. And I was alone in my bedroom praying my heart out in faith.

Jim reported that he actually felt Muri's heart jerking around under his hands while he was praying for him, as Dr. God was performing His miraculous surgery!! This was very awesome to us both.

The proof of this was evident, as Muri was able to then do many things that were impossible for him before; like putting our 3 year old Jillian on his shoulders and running up a flight of stairs in a stadium. He went on to conduct Citywide Evangelistic Campaigns where many came to Christ.

I had the great joy of training my own gospel singing trio, of two girls and myself called The Melodaires, who sang at Muri's Crusades. Muri trained four young Maori men for the same purpose, called The Maestro's. They were so cool! Maoris were constantly in our home. We loved them dearly.

Muri was by far the most naturally gifted person musically we've ever known. **Without having any access to training at all**, he could play any musical instrument like a pro –including the large pipe organ in the Auckland City Town Hall. He came from very humble beginnings.

Jim and I hosted a prayer meeting in our home with our three evangelist friends every second Monday evening. They were George Bremner, Muri Thompson, and Allan Williams.

I found these protracted times of prayer for lost souls in our city of Auckland exhilarating as well as being serious business. One night I found myself praying, "Lord, show me my heart as You see it." Immediately the Holy Spirit reminded me of my bringing some sort of correction to one of the evangelists when we were alone. But I had not seen the un-dealt-with sin of pride in my own heart, while doing so. Immediately I sobbed uncontrollably and deeply repented before God. This became a pivotal turning point in my life.

Another night as the men were leaving, Alan Williams commented, "As usual we've had a fantastic time in prayer. It was just as great as when I am on my own."

This was a new concept to me. I realized that I didn't have to wait until I met with others to pray effectively **and at length**. The very next morning when I completed my necessary housework, I got down on my knees beside my bed, asking God to show me for whom I should pray.

He always came through, but to my chagrin I was finished in about fifteen minutes. But determined to obey what God had shown me I promised, "I'll be back tomorrow, God, same time."

I regularly went back to the place of prayer, submitting to the Holy Spirit, believing Him to come upon me, to enlarge my prayer life. Persistency, determination, and submission to the Holy Spirit paid off. There's no better Teacher.

Around about this time, David and Dale Garratt were gearing up to launch a very unique ministry called "Scripture in Song." As directed by the Holy Spirit, they would put to music numbers of selected Bible verses, and then sing them together as duets; to an instrumental background.

Dale has a particularly lovely, velvety smooth flowing recording voice and would often sing solo. This anointed ministry took off to have an international scope.

I had then and still have the deepest appreciation of this unique ministry. In recent years, almost on a daily basis, I've been playing a CD of a number of their songs in the mornings in my home. I sing along with them and always get spiritually refreshed. David kindly put together a powerful collection especially for me. Dale was one of my "Melodairs."

As I write this, they have just gathered for a 50th Anniversary Celebration for "Scripture in Song" in New Zealand, acknowledging all that was accomplished to bring glory to the Lord. They continued to make new recordings. Bring them on!

David Garratt is my second cousin, and a consistently strong man of God. His beloved wife Dale is therefore not a blood relative to me but it has sure felt like she was! Since my cousin Mary Garratt died, Dale has become the nearest thing to a sister to me. The bonding is unusually deep.

We both happen to have the same second name, Adeline! Dale is uniquely multi-talented.

One day, in the course of conversation about evangelism, Muri said to me, "There's something greater than evangelism!" I immediately enquired, "What's that?" He replied, "Revival." I said, "Explain."

He went on to tell me about sovereign outpourings of the Holy Spirit that have fallen upon Believers, where the unpredictable is the normal. Deep conviction of sin and then true repentance is followed by great releases of joy and praise and worship to God. The overflow results in large numbers of unlikely-to-be-converted-people coming to Christ.

Ivor Davis, a close friend of ours, belonged to the World Evangelization Crusade, known as W.E.C. He was a Presbyterian missionary overseeing this work in the Congo, Africa for years, and had just returned to Auckland, as the director of W.E.C. for the South Pacific region. Genuine revival had broken out on his African compound, first among the nationals, and later on among the missionaries (interesting order).

Jim and I were enthralled as he would recall the unusual, unannounced supernatural outpourings of the Holy Spirit and the inevitable radically changed lives among those who would cooperate with the Holy Spirit's workings. I was now learning some of the ways of God in revival.

God had given me the vision and increasing burden in prayer for revival, which I fueled by reading many books on the subject. This project has continued over my long lifetime.

I later learned what causes all this. "Desperate prayers." I got it!! My prayer life took on another whole dimension in depth and purpose, as I kept surrendering to the Holy Spirit.

By far the greatest revelation on this vital truth and the faith to believe for it among the nations, has come from the untold numbers of times interceding for it. It has also come from making an in depth study of all the Bible verses that are prayers asking God for revival and spiritual awakening, and then all the promises for us to believe that He will answer us. I have them written out on cards, for constant use.

If you are interested, D.V.D.'s and C.D.'s of my in depth teachings on this subject are available from my website, listed at the back.

The Holy Spirit enabled me to memorize countless Scriptures and where they are found; a valuable asset in the evangelism ministry I had, and for the Bible teaching ministry still to come.

Major Learning Curve

Jim and I became very aware that in order to fulfill the ministry purposes that were surrounding our home, we would need to have a larger one. God let us know this was from Him.

Each Saturday for months we would go in the car, house hunting for the right one, while praying for God's help. We also did everything we could to sell our home, and we came very close to doing that... but the deal fell through.

One Saturday, Jim and our children were in the car waiting for me to do our usual search. I was getting ready to join them, when thoughts came into my mind about stories I'd heard where missionaries would pray about a need and there would soon be co-ordination and fulfillment.

I then picked up my daily devotional, called "The Daily Light." It has nothing but Scriptures around a definite theme. Ones for the morning and ones for the evening. I thought maybe God had something to say to me.

Did He ever! Verse after verse was about waiting on God, and listening to His voice. I was convicted of our lack of seeking God for His directions as to **how** He wanted us to have the bigger home and quickly shared it with Jim.

As we then daily sought God diligently, He spoke to us clearly from His Word about demolishing parts of our old house, and building an enlarged new home right where we were.

"Enlarge the place of your tent, and let the curtains of your habitations be stretched out; hold not back, lengthen your cords and strengthen your stakes. For you will spread abroad to the right and the left…" Isaiah 54:2,3.

Our close friend, Allan Williams, who had been living north of Auckland, came down to visit us at this time. He said he had recently had a vivid dream about us. Our original home was being largely demolished and a larger new home was being built in its place. He asked if it made any sense to us?

Jim then showed him the architect's plans for the re-build, which included a downstairs guest room and bathroom.

Times Of Testing

The huge challenge facing us was that we now hadn't any money from the sale of our house, and no way of knowing how we could raise the finances to cover the costs of rebuilding the new one. This was a tough time for us!

After some time of uncertainty financially, God mercifully came through by causing an older Christian woman whom we knew, to loan us the needed money. God led us to a Christian builder and the project was finally underway.

After the builders had completed their lengthy project, I faced the additional financial challenge of furnishing the home with little money. **But I never let the lack of money hinder us from opening our home for ministry purposes, which continued unabated!**

Floor rugs had to wait; and there were times when all I had to cover the sliding glass doors in the living room at night, were bed sheets hanging from the wall above. It was many months before I was able to do the needed upholstery work on two of my living room chairs. This was dealing a death blow to any pride of ownership and decorating skills!

Small Beginnings

No wonder God says in Zechariah 4:10,

"Despise not the day of small beginnings."

My public speaking ministry started in the smallest possible way.

I was attending a small group of mostly young women Christians who met once a month in their lunch hour in downtown, Auckland. It was called the Christian Alliance for Women and Girls, known as the C.A.W.G. Both of my young children were in school at the time.

One of the older women asked me to speak to the group. When I asked God about it, He said, "Yes." When I inquired as to the message, He said, "Tell them about how I convicted you about your critical tongue, and also your lack of waiting on Me and seeking me for directions in matters large and small. Share how this has radically changed your life, through deep repentance." I said, "OK God."

When I got up to speak, I was so nervous, I had to hang on tightly to the small table in front of me, because I was shaking so badly.

I was all done in 15 minutes. When I sat down, I said to the Lord, "Well I've done what you told me to do, but I guess this will be the last time anyone will ask me to speak, because no one wants to listen to anyone that nervous!" I meant every word.

To my amazement, I was asked to speak again at a city church's womens meeting to a much larger audience. Upon inquiry, God confirmed this to be from Him. He then directed me to study a subject from His Word "The importance of the tongue," a truth that I had been living. I obeyed. When I spoke this time I had no nervousness, **And I have never experienced it since!** The rest is history.

This was the start of a consistent ministry speaking to women's groups from different denominations who were all over Auckland and surrounding towns and cities within driving distance. I always gave a clear presentation of the gospel, followed by a specific message from the Bible to the Christians.

Our destinies are only fulfilled to the degree that we obey the promptings of the Holy Spirit in matters large or small, as a way of life! There are no short cuts. No compromises. For the obedience to impress God, it needs to be instant, joyful, and whole. All else is disobedience.

I wonder how many readers of this book are obeying God's promptings, even as a way of life, but doing it in delayed obedience, partial obedience, or obedience with murmuring? ....and wondering why there isn't the assurance of a fulfilled destiny?

Severe Personal Testings

There came a time one morning in 1960 when I felt compelled by the Holy Spirit to totally relinquish Jim and both of my children into God's hands.... for Him to be glorified to the maximum through them, whether by life or by death. It was a sobering occasion, as I followed through in obedience, presenting them to the Father, one at a time. **I was to be tested!**

Jillian was five years of age, and was always promptly home at the same time early afternoon each day from our nearby school. (New Zealand was the safest place in the world, for children.) This day she didn't come home on time. I was being tested on the depth of my commitment. Would I ever see her again? I kept saying, "Your will, Your way."

It was with great relief when she arrived home with a perfect explanation of why she had been delayed. I had been given back my precious little girl. I thanked the Lord with a sense of great relief.

Sometime later, I was waiting for John to show up at his regular time from school. The time came and passed...no sign of him.

I kept my commitment, with trust in God's character, but I waited longer this time. Finally my beloved son John came through the door, and was being returned to me. Great relief and more deep thanks to God!

If Jim was going to be delayed from coming home from work, which was very seldom, he would always phone me and explain. This particular night he didn't show up at the regular time and there was no regular phone call, as I kept waiting and waiting, and wondering? ...but not going back on my commitment.

When he came through the door, I flung my arms around his neck and sobbed and sobbed with intense relief---unconcerned about why he'd been delayed. God had given me back my darling husband. I later explained to him all I'd been through on this important day with the Lord.

God's Provision

While attending a missions conference, the Holy Spirit impressed on me to give an amount of money to a Missions Organization. I responded that I had no money; but God's Spirit reminded me that I had a car.

I used this little old car to get to my speaking engagements and do the family shopping. If I sold it how was I going to function? Then I figured, "That was God's problem." So I told Him I would sell it.

John was about 12 years old and said to me, "I hope you've got your guidance right." I said, "You'll see!"

Jim was the sales manager for an expanding national Business. When he mentioned to one of his staff that we needed to sell my old vehicle, the man said he was looking for one like that for his son. He then stated the amount he was willing to pay for it. It was the **exact amount** of money God had told me to give to the missions organization. Wow! Only God could work that out!

The car sold on a Friday and I immediately wrote out the check for the Mission. Fortunately I didn't need a car until Tuesday because we'd all been away at a Teen Challenge workers Retreat over a long weekend.

On Tuesday morning, I was up to my dandruff with a lot of housework that needed to be done, when the phone rang. The woman on the other end of the line wanted to come for counseling.

Although I didn't want to stop all my work to counsel, I told the woman I would phone her back. I dropped to my knees to ask the Lord what to do. He told me to invite the woman to come. I obeyed.

In the kitchen over lunch preparations the woman encouraged me to attend a special meeting across town later in the week. I said, "That would be nice, but I don't have a car." The single woman exclaimed, "You don't have a car! So you're the one I'm supposed to loan my car to!"

She went on to explain that she was going away as a missionary (to the exact organization to which I had given the money) and had been looking for someone to use her car while she was away! God had now provided me with a much better car to use. The key to everything is instant, joyful, whole obedience to revealed truth.

God Unlimited

I believe there's an answer in the Bible for anything I would ever need to know. Consequently I often enquired of the Lord to speak to me from it when I had a specific need. Here's an example.

It was in the 1960s, during the major alterations that expanded our original New Zealand home. In due time, I was wondering what to do with the floor in the new guest room. Was I to cover it, or put floor rugs on it, or just leave it as it was?

I enquired of the Lord with my Bible in my hand. He answered me by opening it at 1 Kings 6, and my eye fell on verse 11. I read from there to the end of verse 15. I quote "...and he covered the floor of the house with boards of cypress." I left it as it was. It was good wood work.

The Massey Conference

It was 1961, during the early days of the Charismatic Renewal in New Zealand that God gave to Campbell McAlpine and Arthur Wallis a significant vision. Both men of God came from England and had prophetic teaching ministries and were close friends of ours.

The vision was to invite spiritual leaders from a broad spectrum of the Body of Christ to come together for a five day conference to hear "the word of the Lord" as directed by the Holy Spirit. They shared this with us and another Bible teacher friend, Milton Smith.

We then became the leadership team, who met together during the course of two years of preparation. We had vital times of intense intercession and fasting, with great unity of heart and a sense of Divine purpose. We sought God for His directions in all matters.

Our decisions were based upon our unitedly having "thus saith the Lord." Others were raised up to handle the logistical side.

The conference was held at a Massey University Campus, in the North Island, during the time when the students were away on vacation,

Invited leaders enthusiastically responded from throughout the nation, for what was to prove to be an historic, very unique five days in the presence of the life changing power of the Holy Spirit.

I have never experienced such a degree of the awesome sense of the fear of the Lord as was evident throughout that entire time. Bio Chemist and Bible teacher Winkie Pratney, who attended the conference, says the same thing.

In my book, "Intimate Friendship with God," * I recount a very humbling encounter with the Holy Spirit that took place there. It changed my life permanently!

Campbell, Arthur, and Milton were the three speakers, while Neville Winger was in charge of the men's counseling and I was appointed over the women's counseling.

The speakers were powerfully anointed, in a way consistent with their global vision to reach lost souls. Campbell emphasized interceding for the nations and being ready to be sent to anyone of them at any time at any cost.

I was asked to give a testimony at one of the sessions. I was directed by the Holy Spirit to humble myself and share that in my **earlier years** I knew nothing about waiting on God and had to be radically changed in that area of my life by obeying what the Word of God says about it. I also shared my **past** need to be changed from having a critical tongue, through repentance and submission to the Biblical standard.

Following every service people needed serious individual help for diverse needs. Those of us in leadership counseled them. As we

**Joy Dawson "INTIMATE FRIENDSHIP WITH GOD" ©2008 by Chosen Books.*

sought God diligently and obeyed His voice, the Holy Spirit came through powerfully for each one. What life changing testimonies followed for the glory of God!!

Arthur's emphasis was on God's ways in spreading house churches, as in China, and interceding for this multiplication everywhere.

At the close of the conference, Campbell asked us all to seek God if He would name any of the nations to which He may want to send us. I distinctly heard, "America and Brazil." I pondered it in my heart and shared it only with Jim.

A strong sense of God inspired unity pervaded this diverse group of leaders who had now encountered God's Holy Spirit in new dimensions… together. No wonder "God commanded the blessing" as promised in Psalm 133:3.

Teen Challenge Auckland

Initially, the Holy Spirit moved upon Jim's and my heart to start the ministry of Teen Challenge in Auckland. We then approached Neville Winger, asking him to seek God about joining us. His answer was, "Yes."

Then later, Wyn Fountain, joined us; and later still, Graham Braddock took over the leadership of this vital ministry.

Jim and I would take turns in going down to minister on Saturday nights in the below-the-street level place we worked out of. We made sure there was always someone interceding in the prayer room, off the kitchen. We had sandwiches, tea, and coffee available.

One of us was always at home, so that we could be available to our children--- even into their teenage years.

One Saturday night, Jim was down at Teen Challenge, and I was at home. It was very late and I was sitting up in bed praying, when suddenly I cried out loudly and passionately to God, "Put our whole family in world evangelization." I was sobbing my heart out.

The next thing I knew, I found myself on the floor beside our bed. When I got back up, I said out loud, "Could a prayer be that intense and strong and not have come from God?"

I hadn't the faintest idea how this engagement with other nations could ever eventuate! My husband was a business man in his forties. We had two teenagers and we were living in a small nation at the ends of the earth. We had no way to make it happen financially.

God must have thought, "That desperate prayer is enough to work with!" The rest is history.

A Trophy From Teen Challenge

A good example of worthwhile ministry at Teen Challenge was a young man named Michael Flynn. The first time I met him he was seeking spiritual help. I unhurriedly explained the way of salvation to him. He was very responsive to truth. Then he explained to Graham Braddock and myself that he had been a satan worshiper, but now wanted to become a Christian.

As we were carefully leading him through what it meant to commit his life fully to Christ, there came a real battle with demonic forces.

Michael said doubts came into his mind and my voice started to irritate him, while his body twitched all over and he became nauseated.

I did strong spiritual warfare, as I took authority over the enemy. I quoted Revelation 12:11, "in the name of the Lord Jesus, and in the power of the Holy Spirit. When I commanded the powers of darkness to loose their grip upon his mind, body, soul, and spirit,

Michael said he felt a strong pulling feeling going away from his body and that he was now free. Praise the Lord!

We then counseled him to ask for the Holy Spirit to completely fill him, according to the command in Ephesians 2:20. As we did, we laid our hands on his head and asked in faith for this to take place.

God completely met this dear young man's deepest needs. That was a Friday night. He readily accepted my invitation to come and spend the weekend in our home.

The next night Jim took Michael back to Teen Challenge where he freely testified to others about his conversion to Christ. That's when Michael became aware that God had delivered him completely from the craving to drink gin. He'd been consuming eight glasses per day for a whole year.

This started a very meaningful journey as we closely discipled this new convert over many months from our home. It also involved getting him a room at the Y.M.C.A. and helping him find employment. He freely gave his testimony wherever given the opportunity.

It also meant looking after him at our home when he was not well; and later, when he had an accident at work and had to have seven stitches in his leg, and then needed to recuperate.

There was a brief time when he was subtly attacked by demonic forces related to a relationship. But because Michael was always teachable and honest with us, Jim was able to counsel and pray him through it. The enemy lost on the first round! Hallelujah!

I have reported this conversion in such detail so that it can be used of God to help others.

It is important to remember:

1. Don't underestimate the potential of anyone who is seeking truth with the worst background.

2. Don't shortcut the process needed to bring them to freedom when leading them to the Lord for conversion.

3. Be prepared to disciple them toward the fulfillment of their God ordained destiny at any cost.

4. Obey whatever God tells you to do during this privileged process.

5. Rejoice in the fulfillment of the promise
   Proverbs 11:30 "He who wins souls is wise."

Michael kept on ministering to others at Teen Challenge while pursuing the deepening of his relationship with the Lord. One day while at our home, he told me that after a time of seeking God in relation to his future, that he was given a desire to go to night school and study Hebrew next year. This was in November 1969. We loved him dearly and delighted to see him heading for his God ordained destiny.

Prison Ministries

Another very fulfilling ministry outreach was going on many Saturday afternoons to the highest security prison in Auckland --- the Mt. Eden Jail. Little Jillian always came with us.

We had asked to be able to visit the worst prisoners who had no one else to visit them. We were recommended by one of the Chaplains, and then given permission by the authorities.

It's hard to describe the joy of those two years. We made close friendships with men who were ready to hear about the love and mercy of a holy God who was waiting to forgive them, cleanse them, and give them a whole new life through making Jesus Lord of their lives.

One of these was Des Bovey who was a pedophile. (Back in those days, he was disdained even by other inmates and had no visitors.) He was completely transformed by the power of the gospel and never looked back.

When he got out of prison he came and visited us in our home several times. Years later, when we lived in Los Angeles, the phone rang at 2:30 A.M. It was Des, greeting us warmly from New Zealand, reporting he was still going strong for the Lord. Hallelujah!

Another prisoner was a young married man with a child, who we were able to lead to Christ. When he finished his four years sentence for major armed robbery, he came straight to our home, as Jim was making arrangements to get him a job.

I thought he'd be longing to eat the beautiful dinner I had prepared, but he kept staring at our fabulous view, as though mesmerized! He was another great joy to us, with a totally changed life.

On some weeknights we would join all the prisoners for special occasions. That's when we would meet our dear friend Sonny --- a delightful inmate, who was put in charge of the other prisoners and very popular with everyone.

Unfortunately, he didn't respond to the gospel. When he'd be released from serving a sentence, Sonny would immediately commit a crime so that he could be arrested and be sent right back to prison. He was what they called, "Institutionalized." How very sad. He didn't know how to cope with the real world. He didn't surrender to the One who would have enabled him to overcome this insecurity. Sonny was a great disappointment. He was an influencer of others, with real potential for Kingdom purposes. Such is the free will of man!

Prior to one of the two Billy Graham Crusades that were held in our city, just one other woman, Joyce Mitchell, along with myself were assigned by the leadership to organize the establishment of one thousand new prayer meetings, without any other assistance. We were given one year to accomplish this task.

By God's enabling grace and a lot of work, we made it through. This included traveling among them and conducting training sessions related to having effective intercession. The genuine love and strong team work between us greatly contributed to the whole task being a privilege and joy. Knowing that thousands of lives would be affected for eternity was the ultimate driving force.

In the midst of all this evangelistic involvement I had another life changing encounter with the Holy Spirit.

During the course of one week, I noted that I had been convicted by the Holy Spirit three times for the sin of pride, for which I had repented. I then concluded there must be a root of pride that needed dealing with, that I couldn't see.

2 Chronicles 4:30 says "You alone know the hearts of the children of men." That meant God was the only one who could reveal this to me. I determined to seek Him with all my heart until He answered me. I locked the front door, took the phone off the hook, and got down on my knees in front of a chair in our living room. Three times in faith I said with intensity, "I will not let you go God until you reveal this to me." I waited expectantly, but nothing happened!

I pressed in again with weeping, pleading with God to show me my heart as He sees it, saying repeatedly, "I will not let you go!" I waited again --- but nothing happened!

I then started to think about Moses when he was desperate before God in intercession for the Israelites. He pleaded God's character back to Him in the situation, and it brought results.

So I cried out in desperation again, "You are a faithful God. You started all this conviction and You need to complete Your purposes. I plead Your faithfulness back to You as a means for meeting my needs." And three times more I repeated, "I will not let You go!" Then it happened.

The Holy Spirit revealed to me that when I was reporting back to Hayes Lloyd, my Baptist Pastor, (at his request) what God was doing in our evangelistic outreaches, I had mixed motives. Some were pure and others were based in pride. I had wanted the Pastor to be impressed with how God was using me! When I saw this root of pride as God sees it, I wept and wept with deep repentance and brokenness before Him, a holy God.

Then He told me to go to Hayes and tell him everything God had shown me, and ask for His forgiveness. I did, and he graciously received me. This was the restitution I needed to make. **I would never be the same.** Thank God!

In writing this manuscript, I have had serious work outs with the Holy Spirit in the endeavor to make sure that my passion is that God alone gets ALL the glory, ALL THE TIME. Amen."

Prayer Partners

In one of my morning prayer times, God impressed upon me to call Shelagh McAlpine, (Campbell McAlpine's wife) and ask her to become a prayer partner. Shelagh agreed. She had four children and I had two, and we arranged our schedules so that we could meet on Thursday afternoons to pray for the nations.

Among the many that God directed us to, the nation of China was laid particularly heavily upon our hearts. We interceded, only by the Holy Spirit's promptings, every Thursday afternoon for two years.

On the day before the McAlpine family left to return to England by boat, we prayed for the nations surrounded by many cardboard boxes. At the close, the Holy Spirit directed me to lay my hands on Shelagh's head and ask that she would be mightily used by God in ministering among women. Although I believed for it, neither of us had a clue what that meant at that time!

Not long after, Shelagh wrote me from England about how God had directed her to start up a ministry called "The Lydia Movement". It consisted of groups of women from all walks of life interceding together in homes, for the nations of the world as God directed, accompanied by Bible teaching. Later, they had their first conference in Worthing, England, and I was their speaker. It coincided with my first overseas ministry trip.

For many years I continued to teach at their annual conferences throughout America, England, and Scotland, which was always a joyous privilege. Today, the Lydia Movement is still thriving among women in more than 50 nations.

A branch movement called Ask Network International sprung out of it, and is also being greatly used of God to promote intercession for the nations with relevant Bible teaching. To God be all the glory.

After Shelagh left, I began praying with two other close friends, Dorothy Leonard and Hazel Elliot. We met for years every other week, from late morning until late afternoon, waiting on God, listening, praying as He directed for peoples and many nations.

Out of those times, I eventually wrote, "The Ten Principles for Effective Intercession," which have been distributed and taught all over the world, on cards, in magazines and books.

Remarkable Revelations

We three partners saw many miraculous answers to prayer. During the uprising in the Congo during the sixties, we were directed to pray for a woman missionary who had been reported missing and presumed murdered.

It was a real step of faith just to speak her name, let alone continue in prayer for her. However, direction to pray for her life to be spared, and for her protection came to us from specific Scriptures quickened by the Holy Spirit, as we continued to diligently seek God.

We believed the missionary's life would be saved. Even after the press announced her death, we continued to wait quietly for a reversal of the news. I shared this with my family by faith. Weeks later we learned that the missionary had been rescued by three nuns who had hidden her and cared for her until she could be returned to her co-workers. The woman's rescue had occurred **the very day we were interceding for her deliverance.**

In Jeremiah 33:3 God says, "Call to Me and I will answer you, and show you great and mighty things which you do not know."

When we wait on God and listen to, and then obey His directions when interceding for nations and peoples, we can expect to receive remarkable revelation, according to this truth.

This happened again with my two intercessor friends and me.

One of us spoke out in faith that we were to ask God to come with a mighty visitation of the Holy Spirit upon the Roman Catholics **worldwide**, so that they would be filled with the Holy Spirit according to Ephesians 5:18 and that the gifts of the Spirit would operate freely in them and through them to many others.

This concept totally amazed us, especially knowing that one of my intercessor friends had been a Roman Catholic for many years of her life before becoming an Anglican. Consequently she knew that only a sovereign act of God could produce such a thing! We asked

God to confirm this impression if we were on the right track. He did. We then prayed in full faith.

To our further amazement, the Holy Spirit then directed us to pray for the same mighty visitation of the Spirit to come upon Anglicans worldwide. Again, we fully discharged our responsibilities with fervent prayers, in full faith… accompanied by much awe and wonder!

We understood that God shares His secrets with those who keep them, so we only told our respective husbands. This took place in my home in New Zealand before the worldwide Charismatic Renewal was ever heard of. It was to those precise denominations initially, that God chose to feature the power of the Holy Spirit as written in the book of Acts, as being normal for all of Jesus' disciples today. To God be all the glory.

The worldwide Charismatic Renewal was very historic and life changing to multitudes. I have no doubt that God revealed these same secrets to other hidden intercessors somewhere in the world.

Our Home – Totally Available

I continued to regularly pray with and for others while I opened our home to guests, many of whom were spiritual leaders. Reverend Neville Horne was a Godly Baptist minister from Sydney, Australia who stayed with us, while having meetings in our local Baptist church.

He had been with me for an extended time in intercession one morning. Before he left for the meeting that night, I asked if he would like us to pray again. He looked at me kindly and said, 'Joy, I really think I've done enough praying for this meeting today!' Well he was probably right, but I was really sold on this amazing intercession trip!

Our home was always available to the Lord. This meant having many strategic meetings in it, with historic results.

For two years we had spiritual leaders from different denominations come to our home mostly by invitation only, on every alternate Friday night. We would start at 7 p.m. and they would leave around midnight and later. We always started on our knees, waiting on God in silence, listening to the Holy Spirit for His directions. There was no human leader.

It was refreshingly different and always so very vital, as hour by hour we were led to either worship and praise the Lord, or intercede for global concerns, or listen to a pertinent word from the Scriptures, or have communion, or wash each other's feet, or the gifts of the Spirit would operate, or just be silent as God's presence would be almost tangible. We all knew that we were being trained for genuine revival, with some being sent to different parts of the world.

Other times we would have meetings where International missionary statesmen would come and share to our packed out living and dining area. Historic things transpired. One of those times was when a prominent veteran Chinese leader came, and I introduced him to a New Zealand Bible teacher of depth, Keith Liddle. He was a close friend.

As they were shaking hands, the Chinese leader seriously invited Keith to come and teach permanently at his well established Bible School in Indonesia.

Keith and Bell Liddle, in their late sixties, had retired from business and had bought a choice piece of land overlooking a beach in New Zealand and were all ready to build and settle down… until this moment!! Keith immediately said he and his wife would seriously seek God. Within no time, they had heard from God and were subsequently on their way to what they said later, were the most rewarding years of their lives as missionaries!

An individual counseling ministry was another important part of my life in New Zealand. This included many spiritual leaders. Needy people would also come to my home by appointment, from far and near, to be set free with what the Holy Spirit of truth would reveal to me, as I waited on Him all throughout the many lengthy sessions.

Then there were times when "rough diamonds" from Teen Challenge would need to come home to have in depth counseling. There was never a dull moment.

Our children were raised with vital ministries all around them emanating out of our home. This was balanced by our having lots of relaxation and fun at endless picnics at beautiful beaches and parks; while camping out at every opportunity was a way of life. Jim had rebuilt a small trailer, and we had a tent.

To do all this, I was blessed by God to have the energy of at least several people, combined with the obvious enabling power of the Holy Spirit, and a wonderful husband.

Church Ministries

At the same time, Jim and I were also enthusiastically involved in all aspects of our vital Baptist church, which was open to the things of the Spirit. Jim was a respected elder and the boy's Bible class teacher; while I was an active choir participant.

It was during a missionary convention, that Jim had told God he was totally willing and ready for God to send him anywhere in the world at any time, under any conditions.

Grace Shaw, a missionary returned home from Africa, was a church member who had the vision for reaching out to unchurched women in our surrounding area. It was through renting a public hall once a month, and turning it into a "morning tea event", with a special woman speaker who would give a vital message.

A mutual close friend, Joan Brock, and I were deeply committed to this vision. My part was to go to the bare hall the evening before and set up all the round tables and chairs, and cover them with the lace tablecloths I had previously gathered from other church women.

My precious family would always willingly come and help me. Jim provided the sound system for the event, which I would be in charge of the next day.

The church women who attended, supplied all the delicious home baked goodies that went with the tea and coffee. Not surprisingly, the event was always well attended and vital.

Afterwards, there was the inevitable clean up, and the washing of all the dishes, and then the dismantling of the tables and chairs. I was always among the last to leave… This is not a complaint.

So why in the world am I reporting all this in detail??? Good question! Because in God's Sovereignty, I was never invited to be the speaker!

God was teaching me another lesson in servant hood; so that I would never forget the price that others would pay behind the scenes when, as a way of life, I would be one of the speakers, or <u>the</u> speaker. What a wise God!!

A Tough Assignment

I was on jury duty in New Zealand for three days in April of 1968.

Two men were on trial. On the first day, all the jury, including myself, believed they were innocent.

On the second day I was feeling the weight of my responsibility to only speak the truth as God knew it to be.

The only private place to seek God diligently was in the toilet area; so I went there and locked myself in one of them, with my Bible in hand.

The Holy Spirit directed me to Isaiah 66, verses 3 & 4. "These have chosen their own ways, and their soul delights in their abominations; I also will choose affliction for them, and bring their fears upon them; because, when I called, no one answered, when I spoke they did not listen; but they did what was evil in my eyes, and chose that in which I did not delight."

With the fear of God heavily upon me, I returned to my place. I bowed my head down on my arms on the table before me and silently prayed fervent faith filled prayers for the verdict to change. I made no argument. I just believed God for justice.

I kept this up for hours, before the changes came. Finally one by one each member declared their change of mind, including myself. The men were finally declared guilty.

All this was very intense, and I was thankful and wiped out when it finished! I serve an awesome God and give Him all the glory.

The Stage Is Set

Although I was regularly bringing the word of the Lord to women's meetings, the doors to meetings with men in attendance were closed to my gender. However, in 1967, a spiritual leader named Neville Winger, who understood my teaching gift and who believed I had messages both sexes should hear, invited me to speak at a summer Convention on the Great Barrier Island, attended by both men and women. It was off the coast of the mainland.

One of the speakers was Loren Cunningham, a young American who was the founder of a new and little-known ministry called, Youth With A Mission (Y.W.A.M.). Loren also became part of the conference leadership team consisting of Neville Winger the director, Milton Smith, and Jim and myself.

We met together daily to seek God as to who was to speak at each session. As there was genuine love and great unity between us, the directions came clearly. Providentially, Loren heard me speak.

At one session, I was sitting beside Loren, as both He and I were the speakers. I was to go first. During the worship, I clearly heard the Holy Spirit say these words to me, "The young man sitting next to you has a lot to do with your future." I am 10 years older than Loren, and I hadn't the faintest idea what that meant. Later I told only Jim about it, and then we both forgot all about it. I can't explain that phenomenon!

The conference had ended and the leadership team were sitting together at the top of a grassy slope chatting. Loren was in his little cabin down by the beach doing last minute packing, as the seaplane he had ordered was about to arrive to fly him back to the mainland. Most of the people were returning home the following day by boat, including our Dawson family.

Suddenly I heard the Holy Spirit give me an order: -"Go right now and ask Loren if he has sought the Lord if he is to return on the boat tomorrow." I understood the plane implications, and besides, I had **no desire** to question a man of God about his decisions!!

I quickly shared with the men what I had heard, and immediately Nev. Winger said, "Go straight away Joy." I ran down the slope as fast as I could and arrived at Loren's cabin, and gave the message. Loren humbly received it and sought the Lord, with the sound of the seaplane's arrival on the beach! He then said to me, "I'm meant to return tomorrow on the boat." --- to my great relief!! He then cancelled the flight and paid the pilot, as Loren was the only passenger.

Little did I know that my future destiny and my whole family's destinies hung on that one awkward act of obedience; as it was on the boat ride home that we invited Loren to stay in our home, which he gladly accepted. We later found out that he was planning to have a branch of Y.W.A.M. established in Auckland City.

We had many discussions and times of vital intercession about Kingdom related issues, in the four weeks he was with us. We shared together some of the many ways God speaks.

He was interested in the way I interceded for nations and cities, which was waiting on God, listening in silence, asking the Holy Spirit to give me directions, not praying until I heard, and then speaking out what He said in faith. We spent one afternoon interceding together for all the provinces in China, under the Holy Spirit's directions.

Before Loren left for the USA he asked for a cassette tape of any of my messages. I only had one, related to how to intercede effectively for others, including nations, which I gave him.

It was in the month of May in 1967 when the Holy Spirit spoke clearly to Jim and me from Ezra 8:21 "Then I proclaimed a fast there, at the river Ahava, that we might humble ourselves before our God, to seek from Him a straight way for ourselves, our children, and all our goods."

This resulted in our going away alone, with our car and little caravan, to an isolated place, for a three day fast from food, so that we could earnestly seek the Lord. Both our children went to Christian Retreats, as it was school holidays time; John with Neville Winger and friends, Jillian to a Christian children's camp.

We became aware that some kind of change could possibly be coming in the future, that related to our whole family. We needed to be spiritually prepared! Part of Verse 22 says, "The hand of our God is for good upon all that seek Him…" It was so for us.

As we diligently sought the Lord to speak to us as we read His Word and interceded for others, as always, He came through powerfully to help prepare us for the unknown.

Later, in 1968, Loren returned to Auckland, New Zealand with his wife Darlene. Loren was ministering around and further establishing a branch of Y.W.A.M. They stayed in our home, with the spectacular panoramic view!!

I shared with Loren and Darlene that there were times when in intercession, revelation had been given of specific missionaries both known and unknown to me, and their needs.

One example of this occurred when my Y.W.A.M. friend Reona Peterson (before she became Mrs. Jolly) and I were camping out at the summer Conference Center on the Great Barrier Island, where I first met Loren. We had decided to spend the whole night in intercession for whatever purposes God had for us. The agenda was entirely His. My tent was in an isolated spot surrounded by bush and a flowing stream, which meant we couldn't disturb anyone. Jim was at home working on building alterations.

As we worshipped God and then took authority over the powers of darkness in Jesus' name, and waited in silent expectancy, the Holy Spirit first revealed the name Mrs. Donahue. Then came the understanding that this was a single woman missionary ministering to many drug addicts in the city of Hong Kong, who were living underground. We were shown it was called "the walled city."

We were then directed to intercede for her specific needs, followed by fervent, faith filled, prayers for the conversions and total deliverances of the many addicts.

A week or two later, a New Zealand pastor friend of ours had just returned from a ministry trip overseas, and was speaking at a church that Darlene Cunningham had recently attended. He heard about our night of prayer and was very intrigued.

He had just come from being in Hong Kong and had spent time with Mrs. Donahue and had seen her vital underground ministry. He verified every word of what the Holy Spirit had shown us. What an awesome God we serve!

An Unexpected Announcement

At this time Loren told me that some pastors in the United States of America had invited me to come and minister in their churches. I seriously thought he was joking and told him so; then I emphatically replied, "They don't even know I exist!"

Loren then reminded me of my taped message he had taken with him a year before which he must have used and he then showed me a list of their names and addresses. "He must also have done some personal recommending I thought," to make sense of these sudden unusual circumstances--- of which God had never given me understanding ahead of time!!

Loren then invited me to teach at Y.W.A.M.'s first School of Evangelism in Switzerland. After much seeking the Lord for His answer only, both Jim and I were directed to tell Loren the answer was "yes, I was to go and teach," but I was **not to leave until a whole year later.**

Interspersed with a lot of other ministry responsibilities, 1969 was a year of diligently seeking God not only over which answers to the number of overseas invitations I was to accept, but the exact order in which the itinerary was to take place internationally.

The Holy Spirit responded by giving me detailed directions from God's Word, for **every single inquiry**. It was truly remarkable. I memorized every one of them.

The order of the seven nations that were involved was the U.S.A., the Bahamas, Switzerland, England, Singapore, Indonesia, and Australia.

God then gradually miraculously provided my seven-nation airline ticket, without my having said a word to a soul about this very real need.

The first gift of $100 came from our friend Allan Williams who was then a postman. This was very encouraging as this was the day I booked my round trip airline ticket by faith. Then a series of small gifts kept gradually coming in, until it was all covered.

Only then did I start to understand that for the last 13 years, God had me in His personal, intensive training course for an international Bible teaching missionary ministry.

Serious Research

I was being asked to teach the Word of God to both men and women. Because of some controversial Scriptures in 1Corinthians 14:34 and 1Timothy 2:12 related to women Bible teachers, Jim had been doing some serious initial research on this subject. While a measure of understanding had come to him, he was aware that he needed to dig deeper.

I had zero understanding and had decided that if I were asked by someone to explain them I would say, "I can't, but I believe God has already, or will raise up reputable men of God who will put God's answers into print."

What I did know, was that if we're submitted to the Holy Spirit and we love God's Word, and there are portions of Scripture that puzzle us; God will, in time, reveal to us that there is no conflict in His voice to guide us, and His written Word.

I also knew that I would always be submitted to the Godly headship given me on each occasion when I would teach God's Word.

Before I embarked on my three months of teaching God's Word Internationally, Jim had perfect peace and a deep conviction in his heart that I was totally surrendered to the Lord, and was living a holy life, in obedience to God in all things that I was aware of.

As a man who is called to love his wife as Christ loved the Church, Jim wanted me to be fulfilled, so he completely released me.

Before leaving on this long journey, God directed Jim to leave His employment. He obeyed. When his boss asked him if he had another job, Jim said, "No." I was so proud of the way Jim was willing to look foolish and irresponsible, while obeying God.

Then God opened up another job for Jim with more flexible hours, so that he could run our home and be responsible for our 2 teenagers; while I traveled in seven countries, speaking morning and night for six days a week. This meant a husband and father's marathon for Jim and a preacher's marathon for me.

My Commissioning

Prior to my leaving on my first missionary journey overseas, I was given a very meaningful farewell commissioning service at the home of our close friends, John and Dorothy Leonard. It consisted of key spiritual leaders and friends from different denominations, and my dear mother. My dad had recently died.

Following an unhurried powerful time in the presence of the Lord, partaking communion together, I was commissioned by spiritual elders and anointed with oil for the task ahead, accompanied by prayers and the laying on of hands. Ivor Davis of the World Evangelism Crusade, had a wonderful word from the Lord for me from Isaiah 42:6-20.

1. verse 6 "I have called you in righteousness"
2. "I have taken you by the hand"
3. "I have kept you"
4. "I have given you…as a light to the nations"
5. "to open the eyes that are blind…to bring from prison those who sit in darkness"
6. Verse 8 "…My glory I give to no other"

7. Verse 9 "Behold the former things are come to pass, and new things I now declare; before they spring forth I will tell you of them"

Then a warning comes in verses 18 and 19 for the servant of the Lord not to be blind or deaf and miss the purpose for which I've been sent. I must always speak out exactly what the Holy Spirit has given me to say and teach. I received all this with gratitude and in the fear of the Lord.

The 1970s

Romans 4:20 …He grew strong in faith as he gave glory to God.

The Big Adventure

I started out on January first, 1970, from the Auckland International Airport. The verses of Scripture that God gave me were Judges 6:12 and 14:

"The Lord is with you…go in this your might"

…and Psalm 71:16 "I will go in the strength of the Lord God and will make mention of His righteousness **only.**"

The tote bag I carried onto the plane, in addition to my handbag, exceeded the airline weight regulations. It included my Bible and some books.

I believed a verse God had registered to me in my daily Bible reading that morning. It was Proverbs 16:11:

"A just balance and scales are the Lord's; all the weights in the bag are His work."

Later, the airline officials overlooked the discrepancy and didn't charge me anything. Praise the Lord.

After I had gone away, Jim made a further study on whether a woman Bible Teacher can teach men. This eventuated in his producing an excellent, enlightening research paper that answered the basic questions. I was thrilled he did this, as I later learned a lot.

Not long after, comprehensive Biblical research by reputable male evangelical authors explained the **context** of the original texts, and further understanding of every scripture that has questioned the right of women to teach the Word of God to men.

For example, Loren Cunningham and David Hamilton's book, "Why Not Women," and Charles Trombley's book, "Who Said A Woman Can't Teach," and Gerald Derstine's book, "Women's Place In The Church." And there are more.

I stayed in the home of Pastor Scratch and Enid Scratch, in Redwood City, San Francisco, where they pastored a church. They were Darlene Cunningham's parents – dear people.

I taught a series of messages there on "What it means to seek God" and then "How to hear His voice on a regular basis." It was evident that the Holy Spirit did a life changing work in the peoples' hearts as they applied these truths.

Every morning I had to be driven to a Y.W.A.M. School of Evangelism, in San Francisco where I taught again…at length. Sirens screamed night and day, and cars roared around the location.

I was learning that this grueling schedule of teaching every morning and evening for six days was normal, and only the power of the Holy Spirit could get me through the inevitable times of real weariness, which He did!

Then came a Friday morning when I woke at 5:30 a.m. feeling very weary, with a sore throat, and a threatened cold coming on. I took action committing myself with my weariness and weakness into the Lord's hands, and then resisting the devil in Jesus' all powerful name.

I refused to allow the sin of self pity to take over, so I started singing God's praises and believed that as I did so, the joy of the Lord would be my strength. That is exactly what happened!

I then had my daily reading of the Scriptures, followed by more singing of God's praises from 6:30 a.m. to 7:30 a.m. By now I felt ready to face my day of teaching His people from His Word. All glory to Jesus!

I was seeking God which messages I was to give at the "Glad Tidings" Assemblies of God church in San Francisco. I had an impression I was to give a message on "The devices of satan and how to deal with him." When I asked God to confirm to me if this was correct, I heard Him clearly say, "Yes. Go to it girl." I loved that! And I did.

When I was taken to see the Stanford University south of San Francisco, I was impressed to go into the chapel and see that the truth of God's Word was actually <u>graven into the walls!</u> Praise God for that permanent powerful witness.

A huge highlight for me was when Winkie and Fay Pratney drove me through to Oakland to hear David Wilkerson speak. Ever since I had read his bestselling book, "The Cross and the Switchblade" in New Zealand, I had longed for this opportunity. Now it was actually happening.

I was very impressed with the spiritual impact, as I had expected it to be. After he had preached a clear gospel message, about three hundred people responded to the appeal for people to give their lives to Christ. All glory to Jesus!

I continued to teach the students at the School of Evangelism, who were responsive to truth. After I had taught them on "Ten of our automatic responsibilities in the ministry of intercession," I challenged them to be seriously praying among other things, for Russia to be opened to the gospel....as I had been doing.

A significant contact was made when Pastor Watson Argue Jr. and his wife Bonnie, the church music director, drove me 60 miles up the coast to Santa Rosa. I felt very bonded to them as we discussed spiritual things. It was the start of a deep friendship that lasted <u>many</u> years.... (until they went to be with Jesus.) Watson was known as J.R. He later conducted both our son's and daughter's weddings.

I gave a series of messages at their large thriving church, to which there was a deep response spiritually. I taught on "Waiting on God," "What to do when things go wrong," "How to hear the voice of God," and "The ways God speaks." Many stayed behind after the services with repentance and real brokenness, as they took time to listen to the Lord.

I was intrigued to find two whole rows, who were obviously hippies, sitting up the front of the church. They lived communally at a nearby Ranch.

After I greeted them warmly from my heart, they told me that they "dug" my message; and asked me if I'd like to visit them? I said I would, if I could. I loved this contact, but was only able to write a letter to one of them called Bud and enclosed the way of salvation with it, and then pray for them all.

My final teachings were on "The implications of obeying and disobeying God's voice."

I was due to fly back to Los Angeles on an evening flight, when I discovered that all the night flights had been cancelled due to heavy fog. As I sought the Lord about this, He assured me that I would get a flight out at midnight; so I went to the airport with my friend J.R. and waited and waited in full faith. There were no other passengers in sight. Finally a plane showed up, right at 12 midnight. I took off as my God lifted the fog over the LA area. I serve an awesome God!

Ministry In The Bahamas

One of the seven parts of the world where God first launched me into a teaching ministry in 1970, was the Bahama Islands.

Rev. Leonard Ravenhill had invited me to come to Nassau, and speak for a week. We had gotten to know him when he came to Auckland, New Zealand prior to this time.

The meetings were held in a large home of a millionaire. Another wealthy family were housing Leonard and his wife Nancy.

Leonard was internationally well known as a fiery feisty prophet, with an unusually strong prayer burden and vision for world revival. He had written powerful books on the subject. Many lives had been impacted by them including mine, especially the one titled, "Revival Praying".

I understood the privilege of this assignment, regardless of the very grueling schedule. He was a veteran on the spiritual international scene. I was just the new girl on the block.

Recently, I discovered a book with a carbon copy of a lot of long letters I had written to Jim, over those first three months away from home. I'm going to quote from some of them now in relation to the week in Nassau.

"To spend a week under the same roof as Len Ravenhill is quite something experience-wise. He's a remarkable man of prayer, who is convinced a worldwide out pouring of the Holy Spirit is the only hope for the world, so he spends many hours in a day praying for just that.

As you know, the interesting and unusual stories Len tells of peoples' lives and how he's seen God work are legion. The repertoire is unending and told in a way which is humorous and unique.

During the course of the week he kept telling me it was thrilling to him, and a great encouragement, that so very much of what I was teaching was just exactly what he believes and teaches in many areas of truth.

He'll never know how much his constant murmurs of "Yes" and "Amen" and "Mmm" encouraged me enormously as I was speaking!!!

I spoke for 6 out of the 7 mornings I was there and 7 out of the 7 evenings, with a lot of counseling in addition. But because I'm sure I was doing what God directed me to do, I have experienced the supernatural energy necessary to keep going.

Len Ravenhill has prayed some tremendous prayers for me and for the Y.W.A.M. students I will be teaching in Switzerland this coming month. I am daring to believe that the need of the hour, and the greatness of God, warrants their being answered.

You will recall, I expressed to you months before I left home, that I had a definite impression I was going to lead some very wealthy person to the Lord while in the Bahamas; and that there was some real significance about this case in the powerful influence this person would have on many.

I experienced the most wonderful fulfillment of this in detail. When I got to Nassau and the meetings had been going for several days in a millionaire's home, I completely forgot about this impression. It wasn't until beautiful Virginia Maura was kneeling beside me weighing up the implications of becoming a real Christian. I remembered and marveled and stood in awe of God and His amazing ways and knew SHE WAS THE ONE.

I made it very clear to her that Lordship to Jesus means the total surrender of our wills to Him. He becomes the boss. She looked intently into my eyes and said, "Joy, this is a big deal!" I said, "Yes, it is the most important deal you'll ever make." She then repented of her sins, asked the Lord Jesus to come into her heart, thanked Him for His forgiveness and the price He paid to give her eternal life by dying on the cross. She surrendered everything to him.

Virginia used to be a well known dancer at the British Colonial Hotel. At the time of her conversion she had been living constantly on tranquilizers for the past 4 years! She's a born leader, has a wide sphere of influence among her wealthy kind and is an all or nothing at all style of person. Praise God.

It has been verified by more than one who was in the meeting on Saturday night that I had <u>2 multi</u>-millionaires and 2 millionaires in the audience. This of course doesn't cause me to give any change whatever in the message God has laid on my heart--- but it is interesting! That was the night I felt compelled to stop right in the middle of the message "Intercession --- what it is and what it does," --- and call the people to pray for those suffering for Christ behind the Iron Curtain.

I haven't really told you anything of the extent of the moves of God's Spirit in Nassau, because I felt a reticence having been so involved, but I have given every vestige of the glory to the only One

Who could do it anyway. And when I think how you and others have prayed, perhaps I owe it to you to at least tell you that each person who has spoken to me personally, has acknowledged that they will never be the same again. They were hungry, prepared hearts, so of course God has met them. **The more I see God move, the more determined I am not to touch the glory.**

It's been something to see these cultured, wealthy people having real brokenness, with open confessions and weeping as God has dealt with them during the messages, and then poured their hearts out afterwards. Their honesty has been WONDERFUL. They didn't resist Him when God had said, "Humble yourselves." No wonder they're changed.

A highlight was to speak at a Bahamian church_on Sunday morning. All were Afro Bahamians people. God had been telling Len all day Sunday that He was saving the "good wine until the last," and was that ever fulfilled. I spoke on "How to become an Intercessor and remain one" --- for over an hour. There was not the slightest sign of restlessness.

These people were HUNGRY. Then we went to prayer. The big lounge was packed out with an overflow in the large foyer. That meeting went on for another 2 hours; and then no one wanted to leave. God moved among His people, and when that happens no-one is conscious of the clock.

The next day, my dear friend Len handed me the following poem he had just written, as I was leaving to go to Switzerland. It blew me away then, and still does today!

Dear Jim, "we lost" our Joy today
She took a plane and flew away
After some wondrous holy days
In which she taught us God's dear ways.
At times our hearts did deeply yearn
At other times they'd burn and burn,
At His great Truth alive unfolding
Left us in awe and still beholding

His works to men,…just mortal men,
So we could cry, "do this again"
As we proclaim Thy blessed story,
Come, come, Oh Lord in All Thy glory
Let the prophetic word be heard,
Let hearts of flesh through Thee be stirred
Let men unknown, be known to Thee
Stride forth with Holy majesty
To say with power, "thus saith the Lord"
And millions bow before the Word.
Joy preached with power, brought inspiration
Dug deep in truth, brought revelation.
Dispelled much doubt, banished great fears
Brought Holy laughter…Holy tears.
God showed us that through gracious Joy
We could have "gold" without alloy
In her the meekness of the Son
(But not too "holy" to have fun).
A woman zealous and with heart
Wedded to Him and yet so smart
Even in dress as well as love
Just moved by Him who dwells above
In her we saw a soul ablaze
Wedded to God in all His ways
Intent to please the Lord in all
And travail though the heavens fall
Content to grasp no earthly prize
But wait for "pay day" in the skies
Now Joy has gone to Switzerland
Under the power of His hand
Carrying a treasure more than gold
And from it bringing new and old
Foundation Truths, those souls to gird
From the vast ocean of His Word.
We thank you Jim, and children too

For sparing Joy, to tell the true
Unvarnished facts of God's great dealing
With sweetness in itself appealing
Take heart because our blessed Lord
Says those at home get great reward.

Len Ravenhill
4th February 1970

Learning God's Ways

It was February 8th of 1970, and I was at Chalet et Gobè, Lusanne Switzerland, teaching at Y.W.A.M.'s School of Evangelism.

On a Sunday about 5 p.m. I started to feel ill. This increased with intensity until I was having severe pains in my stomach like food poisoning or gall bladder pain. I was writhing in pain on my bed.

I asked God to convict me of any sin, should this be the cause. He did. He revealed to me the pride of my heart because of the many close friendships with men of God that I had. He also said that I talked too much about myself!

Just that day I had received personal letters from two Pastors, and from Jim.

I deeply repented of the worst sin of all. Pride. I confessed it openly, before three mature young women who had been praying for me. As I did this, the pains subsided, until I was completely well again. Thank You Jesus.

Psalm 107:17 clearly states, "Some were sick through their sinful ways, and because of their iniquities suffered affliction."

David says in Psalm 119:75 "I know, O Lord, that your laws are righteous, and in faithfulness You have afflicted me."

My book, "Some Of The Ways Of God In Healing" * has a lot more on this subject.

Seeing The Sights

It was Saturday March 14th in 1970 and I was in England, being driven by car to London, coming from the south. My friends took a lovely country route with beautiful scenery, before arriving at St. Paul's Cathedral. I was very impressed as we walked through it.

Then we saw a demonstration and a march at Trafalgar Square surrounded by mounted police. At the same time people were standing on the steps at Trafalgar Square, behind a microphone sharing their thing.

Right in the middle of the street a weirdo funny man about forty-five, dressed in short striped under pants, and a bowler hat, was tap dancing and acting. Crowds of people were watching his performance. It was hilarious!

From there we saw the Piccadilly Circus, Big Ben, the Thames Bridge, the Tower of London, Buckingham Palace, Parliament Buildings, and the Post Office Tower.

I really loved it when we went two stops on the underground tube train. We then saw St. James Park, and the Whitehall, where they have the trooping of the colors.

This was all very impressive.

* *Joy Dawson "SOME OF THE WAYS OF GOD IN HEALING" ©1991 by Y.W.A.M. Publishing.*

An Enlightening Flight

On Route to Singapore, following our brief look at London, there were some interesting challenges.

All passengers were told to wait in the plane at the Vienna Airport. We were there for two hours. We were told, "There was trouble in the Middle East." The air stewardess nodded in agreement, when I asked if it were to do with the hijacking of planes?

So I did spiritual warfare, taking authority over satanic forces with the Word of God, and noted that my daily Bible reading was in Psalms 69-71. Psalms 70 and 71 were very reassuring! Praise God.

In the middle of the night, we touched down in Arabia at Bahrain, and were there for 1½ hours. It felt very strange to be in this place. I interceded for this nation.

We had another stop over at New Delhi, India. I saw many men and women working in the heat at the side of the tarmac. Men were cracking stones with mallets and women were carrying large baskets on top of their heads, presumably with stones in them. They then walked in relays, delivering them to another place. I had never seen anything like this. The situation looked grim!! We then stopped in Bangkok, before arriving in Singapore.

As I was being driven by my host through the city, I was amazed at all the little shops that were open at night, and restaurants all open to the road, with people cooking all out in view on the foot path it seemed. My host said this was normal; and there's no law about closing time. There were crowds of people everywhere in DENSE HUMIDITY.

Ministry In Indonesia

I was in Indonesia in March of 1970, speaking daily at a Bible School directed by American missionaries Claude and Wilma Rediga.

The students were receptive to the numbers of new concepts of Biblical truths they were hearing, for which I was thankful. I was very bonded to the Rediga's and had an ongoing friendship with them.

I would diligently teach throughout the day with interpreters, and with perspiration running down my back. It was extremely hot and humid. This was followed by at length counseling one of the needy interpreters. I wept and prayed with this precious medical student like he was my son. He came from a very sad background and needed an expression of the mother heart of God. All very exhausting, but fulfilling.

The Ridiga's and I shared one small fan at night by taking turns to have it!! I was acutely aware I was on a missionary journey.

Every morning at 6 a.m., I would see all the windows barred up in the surrounding houses, with sounds of blaring wirelesses and dogs barking loudly all over the place. The people were small and thin. I interceded for God to move powerfully among them.

One day, after speaking to the students in the morning, my interpreter took me to Dr. T. Marbun's group. They must have been all non Christians, as my diary records that this was a <u>unique</u> and wonderful opportunity to share the gospel.

I spoke from 1 Timothy 1:2 "I know whom I have believed," and then went through the steps on my "Committal of life to Christ" card. I answered all the questions that followed. I left six of the cards with Dr. Marbun, who said he was going to have them printed in Indonesian.

I also recorded that "this assignment was definitely a takeover by the Holy Spirit, as I was right out of my depth in this whole deal, but I believed, He would." All glory to Jesus.

I later received a gracious letter of gratitude from Dr. Marbun. I regret that I can't remember what kind of unbelievers he was leading.

I arrived at Djakarta Airport at 2:45 p.m. to start my journey home. I left the airport 13¼ hours later at 4 a.m. What a night! My plane was delayed.

There were several weird looking men in the waiting room during the long night hours besides myself, which prompted serious prayer. God answered with the arrival of a courteous, well-dressed fine-looking man who came and sat in a seat near me. He was an Indonesian who spoke perfect English. He couldn't have been more helpful to me, and we intermittingly chatted away until I finally left for my plane to Sydney which was then 21 hours in flight.

Only God knows how I needed that person.... whoever he was!

I have since seriously wondered whether he was an angel in disguise! He certainly fitted the criteria. He never talked about where he was going or where he came from!

Thank You FATHER GOD, for looking after your little girl Joy!

I finally arrived in Pastor Howard Carter's home in Sydney, Australia. While having my Bible reading that night in 1 Samuel 20, I realized that this was exactly the chapter the Lord had directed me to read, four months ago, when directing me that I was to leave Indonesia and come on to Sydney. How amazing that this chapter should be in my daily normal Bible reading on the exact day I arrived here!!!

Very unusual difficulties had arisen in getting planes into New Zealand's Auckland International Airport, so I was delayed several days before I could finally get home. It was very thrilling when I did. Believe me!

A "Waiting" Marathon

One week after arriving home I received a letter from Loren, asking me to return to Switzerland next year to teach again at his School of Evangelism for 3 weeks. As I sought the Lord, His answer came from my "Daily Light" devotional. It was Exodus 4:12 "Now therefore go, and I will be your mouth and teach you what you will speak."

Verse 18 says, "Go in peace." The next day it was clearly confirmed from Psalm 71:16 "I will go in the strength of the Lord God: I will make mention of Your righteousness, even of Yours only."

The next day I received a letter from Pastor Scratch in San Francisco inviting me to come and minister again in his church and beyond. He wanted to set up an itinerary of speaking engagements for me, but I had no witness in my Spirit that this was right, and turned it down. Later, when they moved to pastor a church in Seattle, I was directed by the Lord to accept their invitation to come and teach for two weeks.

At this point, I sought God to know which month I was to depart from New Zealand again and the answer came from Ezra 8:31, "They departed in the first month."

When I enquired which of the above nations I was to go to first, God made it clear that it was Switzerland.

Whenever I enquired of God how long I was to be in America, and how long away from home, the answers were always "to wait on Him and trust Him." So I did.

Then when I received an invitation to speak at a winter conference that Bethany Fellowship in Minneapolis was sponsoring, and sought God for an answer, it came in Psalm 38:15 "Lord, I wait for You; You will answer, Lord my God." God also continued to speak to me from 1 Corinthians 16:9 "a wide door for effective work has opened to me, and there are many adversaries."

Many weeks went by, and I was still waiting on God!

One night, I awoke somewhere in the early hours of the morning with a strong impression on me that God hadn't spoken to me at all about the next ministry trip overseas. I was disturbed, so I immediately resisted the devil in the name of the Lord Jesus in a whisper, so as not to disturb Jim. I then quoted Acts 27:25, "I believe that it shall be exactly as it was told me by the Lord." Peace came and I went to sleep!

A week later, when awake in the night, the enemy came again with the same tactics, trying to convince me that the ministry trip overseas was a total farce! Again I did spiritual warfare, and silenced him.

Around this time, Jim and I had a serious time of seeking God together from 9:45 a.m. to 3:45 p.m. asking Him to speak to me in whichever way I needed it most. He answered by saying, "The book of Zephaniah." As I read it, chapter 3 and verse 8 was quickened to me by the Holy Spirit. "Therefore wait for Me," says the Lord, for the day when I arise as a witness." As I read on, verses 14-18 were so very encouraging!!

"Sing aloud, O daughter of Zion; shout, O Israel! Rejoice and exult with all your heart, O daughter of Jerusalem! The LORD has taken away the judgments against you, He has cast out your enemies.
The King of Israel, the LORD, is in your midst; you shall fear evil no more. On that day it shall be said to Jerusalem: "Do not fear, O Zion; let not your hands grow weak. The LORD your God is in your midst, a warrior who gives victory; he will rejoice over you with gladness, he will renew you in His love; He will exult over you with loud singing as on a day of festival."

I obeyed verse 14, and had a meaningful time of audible praise to God. I then enquired of the Lord for anything more He had to say to me. He spoke "Luke 4" into my spirit. Verse 43 was extremely significant.

"I must preach the good news of the Kingdom of God to the other cities also, for I was sent for this purpose."

The next morning I woke with a wonderful sense of well being and freedom that the Lord was with me, and that the enemy was defeated in his insidious efforts against me regarding this ministry trip overseas.

In my daily reading of the Scriptures, Psalm 97:10-12 were particularly pertinent and encouraging. Praise God! "The LORD loves those who hate evil; He preserves the lives of His saints; He delivers them from the hand of the wicked. Light dawns for the righteous, and joy for the upright in heart. Rejoice in the LORD, O you righteous, and give thanks to His holy name!"

More weeks passed and I kept emphasizing the fact that God was working on my behalf, as I kept waiting in faith.

Another month passed and I was asking God to do a deeper purifying work in my life. I also asked if there was any act of obedience that He required of me that related to my next trip away.... or do I just remain "waiting on Him" for the rest of the itinerary.

Psalm 130:5 was in my daily reading of the Scriptures, "I wait for the LORD, my soul waits, and in His word I hope."

I worshipped my lover God and thanked Him from a very grateful heart for the clarity of speaking to me again and again!

Big Transition

Ever since I returned home, Jim and I had been stirred in our spirits about his leaving secular employment, relinquishing all our financial securities, house, car, family, and friends and joining

YWAM as unsalaried missionaries and going to the United States—all of this with two teenagers!

We knew of no ongoing financial support for us whatsoever. We simply knew the character of God and the promises from His Word. It was absolutely crucial that we have God's clear directions, from the Bible, if this in fact was His will for us as a family.

At this time, for three whole weeks I kept hearing in my spirit a verse of Scripture I had memorized. It was, "It is God Who works in you both to will and to do for His good pleasure" (Philippians 2:13). At first I wondered why these impressions persisted, until I came to the understanding that it was God's way of saying to us that it was God who was stirring us, putting these thoughts and desires into our hearts, preparing us to take the big step of obedience and faith to become lifetime missionaries to the nations.

Also, one evening when we were having our daily family worship time after the evening meal, Jim was clearly directed by the Lord to read through Luke chapter 5.

When he came to the words, "Do not be afraid. From now on you will catch men. So when they had brought their boats to land, **they forsook all and followed Him**" (vv. 10–11), we had the strongest witness in our spirits that God had given us His mandate from His Word.

Another Scripture that stood out, or seemed to light up every time we read it, was, "**In You they trusted, and were not disappointed**" (Psalm 22:5 RSV).

During that same 9 month period, invitations came from five nations for me to come and teach the Word of God again.

Once again I had to seek God diligently to receive His answers for each individual request. This was always time consuming, but there were no alternatives. The sin of presumption wasn't an option.

Again, I was directed by the Holy Spirit to leave on the first day of the month. This time it was 3 ½ months that I would be away.

These long stretches of being separated from each other were anything but easy for both of us, and were only possible through God's amazing grace.

Jim was an amazingly releasing and supportive husband and intercessor, who paid a big price to be so. He was an equally outstanding father whom God could trust with the inevitable challenges of being responsible for two teenagers without my participation, during these extended times. Jim's reward will be great in eternity. I've always said that I could never have done what I've done, without him.

Before I left on this long journey, God directed Jim to leave His employment. He obeyed. When his boss asked him if he had another job, Jim said, "No." I was so proud of the way Jim was willing to look foolish and irresponsible, while obeying God.

Then God opened up another job for Jim with more flexible hours, so that he could run our home and be responsible for our 2 teenagers one more time.

Then the Lord stirred both of our hearts for Jim to leave secular employment and to join Y.W.A.M. as unsalaried missionaries.

When I finally returned home, we continued to seek God diligently regarding our directions for the future.

The Holy Spirit spoke remarkably to Jim from his daily Bible reading, on the first day after receiving his last pay check. It was Haggai 2:18-19 "Consider now from this day forward, from the 24th day of the ninth month… from this day I will bless you." **It was exactly the 24th of September** when he was reading this!! Verse 4 says "Be strong and work for I am with you, and verse 8 says, "The silver and the gold are Mine says the Lord of Hosts.

God was saying that He's not short of finances and would take care of us in our new walk of living entirely by faith. We believed Him!

Later, God spoke to me from my daily Bible reading in Genesis 12:1 & 5, "… Get out of your country, from your family, and from your father's house, to a land that I will show you." God also spoke to Jim from the exact same verses that are quoted in Acts 7:2-4, during one of his daily Bible readings."

In obedience to the Lord we notified Loren that God had called us into Y.W.A.M. This confirmed to Loren what God had been showing him about us, and said that Jim would become Y.W.A.M.'s first administrator. There was a small office in Los Angeles, with 2 on staff (one part time.)

Then came a real a testing of our faith. We had put our earthly belongings into boxes and sent them on ahead of us six weeks before we were due to fly to California. A friend was holding them in storage… but I need to back up!

For many weeks prior to this, the Holy Spirit had been repeatedly speaking to me saying, 'The stone is already rolled away,' **without any understanding of the purpose.** I just trusted the Lord that there would be one.

Later, I was sitting in a church service in San Francisco where I had been ministering, when a friend who was sitting in front of me turned around and just said, 'The stone is already rolled away.' I said, 'Thank you.' That's all! I hadn't said a word to **anyone** about what God was saying to me.

I suppose the man concluded I had complete understanding of what that was about. I had none, other than God had spoken AGAIN. Back in New Zealand Jim and I continued on with the many tasks related to the big transition ahead.

The final official thing to be done before leaving New Zealand was to go to the customs and immigration official to get our clearance papers for living in California. Jim and I were both sitting in his office as he was carefully checking our application papers and then the requirements, according to his records.

Jim explained that as a family of four, the purpose of our going was solely to do missionary work. I sat quietly listening in perfect peace and expectancy… when the unbelievable happened!

The official said with conviction, 'I'm sorry, but according to my records you do not have the needed qualifications to live in the United States.'

We also explained that all we owned was in boxes and had been shipped 6 weeks prior to Los Angeles. The understanding official 'got the picture' and went back to further check through his records.

I was as relaxed as a poached egg and kept repeating silently, in faith, what I had heard the Holy Spirit say for many weeks.... But AT LAST WITH UNDERSTANDING.... 'The stone is already rolled away.' That means there is no problem here in God's reckoning. Hallelujah! **I did nothing but thank Him**.

After some time, the official said, 'I think I've found something that may work. There's a clause that says if you are a pastor of a certain number of people, you can qualify. Can you meet that requirement?'

Jim answered that he was part of a working eldership team at our Baptist church and would ask for their verification of his level of responsibility. He did, and they cooperated. Then they officially, gladly commissioned him as a pastor. God is always on time, even if it's at the eleventh hour!

All this meant leaving all financial securities: our home, family, and friends with our two teenagers to go to Burbank, California where Y.W.A.M. was based, without **any promised financial support from anyone**.

All this proved again to me that when God requires us to walk out into the unknown, uncharted waters, all we have to be sure of is the following truth. A bond slave of Jesus Christ has only two rights. One, is the right to know the instructions clearly. Two, is the given strength to carry them out. We believed that and lived by it.

It reminds me of the quote I saw, "Two kids went to The Fair and one said, 'I've got 2 whole dollars. What have you got?' The other replied, 'I've got Daddy – He's got everything.'"

Three weeks before our leaving for America, John returned from a brief but historic trip to the Great Barrier Island, where he had a serious life changing encounter with the Lord.

Subsequently Neville Winger commissioned him into his life's calling as a missionary, and then prophesied into his future – all of which has come to pass, and so much more.

This brought great delight to us, and great praise to God.

The Orama ministries that flowed out of Karaka Bay on the Great Barrier Island, led by Neville Winger, will forever be an integral part of our family history, with the best of wonderful memories. Our best family vacations when the children were younger were spent there.

Just prior to leaving N.Z. to live in Los Angeles.

July 1972

On the Sunday night, just prior to our family leaving to live in America, our pastor handed over the Sunday evening service to us. Jim shared meaningfully and briefly and then announced I would be bringing the message.

I mounted the steps of my home church for the first time ever, and spoke on "Seeking God," "Why we seek Him," "When we seek Him," and "How we seek Him."

We went with their blessing but no mention of financial support. Our faith was totally in the Lord, and that was fine with us. The last thing a few friends who came to see us off at the airport saw of me, was throwing one of my shoes in the air, catching it, and shouting, "Hallelujah." I was off on the adventure of a lifetime---following Jesus!

We flew to Honolulu and stayed the night, before flying on to arrive in San Francisco. We were then driven by car to Santa Rosa as I was scheduled to speak the next day, Sunday, at the Christian Life Center. My friend Watson Argue Jr. was the pastor. We had just enough money to purchase a second hand car, so that we could then drive down to Los Angeles.

We arrived on the 15th of July, 1971, in a heat wave. We went straight to a small house in Altadena, which we had previously arranged to rent.

Quickly John went into a summer of service outreach and preparation for a School of Evangelism in Lausanne, Switzerland, having recently received his calling to missions in New Zealand.

When Jim tried to open some of the windows to get some air, he found that they had been painted in; so his first job was trying to scrape them open!

There was no air conditioner and no fans. It was so unbearably hot, I soon worked out that the only way to cope was to spend extended times at the nearest supermarket each afternoon.

We had signed on as missionaries and this was part of the package. Nine months later when our New Zealand home sold, we were able to put down a small deposit on what became our own home. This was just prior to when all the prices of homes skyrocketed.

Jim initially took on the administrative role of Y.W.A.M. with two office staff, while I continued traveling and teaching frequently, but only as God directed. Jillian initially worked in Jim's office, before leaving for a summer of service outreach in England with Y.W.A.M. She was only 16.

My ministry of international Bible teaching expanded in the years ahead. I traveled frequently, often alone, to difficult places like Afghanistan, Indonesia, Calcutta, India, Egypt, etc.; eventually to fifty-five different nations.

God directed the majority of my teaching to spiritual leaders both in Y.W.A.M. and at many inter-denominational leadership conferences worldwide. Loren Cunningham had released me right from the beginning to minister to the Body of Christ wherever I was called of God. This also included speaking to the churches of many different denominations.

Soon after we lived in California, God blessed me by giving me another wonderful prayer partner, Virginia Otis. Intercession was unhurried serious business with us. We always waited on God for His agenda, and then unitedly followed through, as He shared it with us.

Virginia also became one of my dearest, most longstanding, trusted friends. She is to this day an encouraging, faithful intercessor for me, for which I am deeply grateful.

A Strategic Nation

When God decides to give any of His children significantly broad platforms of influence for the extension of His kingdom, His testings and trials beforehand will inevitably match them.

It is a principle throughout the Bible. Moses, Abraham, Joseph, Daniel, David, and Paul are classic examples. It's no different today.

In the early seventies in the early days of Y.W.A.M., Loren asked me to seek God if I was to go and teach at Y.W.A.M.'s first School of Evangelism in Seoul, Korea. God confirmed that this assignment was for me.

My dear friends Jimmy and Jannie Rogers were the leaders of this school and were doing their best in this pioneering stage of our Mission.

On arriving, I found there were only 3 Korean young men in the school and one other English speaking couple. The living conditions were very primitive. We were housed in an old dilapidated building, where the only means of keeping clean was to stand under a broken shower with a trickle of cold water. The room I was assigned to, had only a mattress on the floor. That was it! The temperatures were well over 100 degrees F, and the humidity was intense.

I diligently taught every morning and evening during the week for the two weeks I was there. I freely admit I was not "fully counting it all joy when in various trials" as we're admonished in James 1:2. I was tempted to count the days to when they would be over. The tests of God were on and by God's grace alone I almost passed them, as I don't remember complaining.

It turned out later, that one of those Korean's became the leader of that school.

Little did I know the major role the nation of Korea was going to play in my future destiny.

David Ross was an American missionary called by God to Korea, who was drawn to Y.W.A.M.'s vision, "To Know God and to make

Him Known." He had laboriously studied the Korean language, which is a challenge to most to learn, until he was baptized in the Holy Spirit. That's when God supernaturally "gave" David the language and from then on, he spoke it like a native, later becoming one of the top 3 best interpreters for the nation!

God had opened up a strategic door of opportunity for David to regularly speak to a large group of Christian Korean University students. When Loren and I were next in Korea, we accepted his invitation for us to address them, with David as our interpreter.

It was thrilling to bring the word of the Lord to these enthusiastic-to-learn young people. They were eager to learn about a global vision and how they could be a part of it, and to understand the character and ways of the One who says, "Go."

At that particular time in the seventies, there were very few, if any, Koreans going overseas as missionaries. God was about to radically change that statistic!

I had spoken one evening under a strong anointing of the Holy Spirit, a forceful message on "God will always make a way to those who believe and obey." This became an historic message with a strong emphasis on fearing God in every situation and not men.

An 18 year old student was stirred by the Holy Spirit as he had listened to Loren give a powerful message, and then share that Y.W.A.M. was having a three-month course in discipleship training for Koreans in New York. The student longed to go.

But he had to face the formidable facts. By law, no-one could apply for a visa to go overseas if he hadn't spent time doing army duty ---- or if he was a student! That ruled him out on both counts!

Undaunted, the student obeyed God's promptings and went and filled out the application forms and handed them in. When the official looked at him and the forms, he asked if the student was aware of the restrictions clearly stated. The student said he was very aware of them and declared he was a student and had not done military training.

The somewhat-irritated official asked the obvious question. "Then why on earth are you making this application at this time?" With quiet authority the young Korean Christian simply said, "Because I fear God, and He has told me to go to New York for missionary training." The stunned official paused, and then said the unheard of: "Then in that case, I'll grant you a passport," and proceeded with the processing of it. Hallelujah!

God's Word works! What is impossible to man is easy street for God. The "adventure" part of what I'm teaching in this book only happens when we obey God's voice. And believe me, it's some adventure.

It is the most challenging and at times the most difficult. It is also the most exciting, the most rewarding, and the most fulfilling adventure known to mankind.

All this started up a chain reaction in the Spirit realm as many thousands of Koreans have since been in missionary training in Y.W.A.M. alone, and Korea is now one of the largest sending forces of missionaries in the world.

An older spiritual leader who had been listening to Loren and me teach, invited us to return to Seoul, Korea and share our vision of fulfilling Jesus' mandate in Mathew 28:19, 20 with a lot of pastors that he could bring together.

God directed us to go back and teach some more; opening up the opportunity for us both to reach a higher level of influence in the nation, at a later time.

Again later, David Ross invited Campbell McAlpine and myself to return and speak to a large contingent of pastors from all over Korea. This was a great privilege and an equally great responsibility. We spoke every morning and evening from Sunday through to Friday, with times of application following messages. The power of the Holy Spirit was very evident, and we were both exhausted!

Those many pastors and spiritual leaders were hungry for the deeper things of God and time was not an issue to them.

At the call of the Lord, I traveled to Korea eight times for ministry purposes before I had to stop. The severity of my back pain cancelled that out; along with the need to concentrate on my book writing ministry.

It is significant to share that the Koreans, after having my first book translated in their language, "Intimate Friendship with God --- through understanding the fear of the Lord," kept urging me to write another book. This became a pattern which they kept up after my writing each of the seven books that followed. To this time of writing more of my books keep selling in Korea than in any other nation that I know of.

I understand the Apostle Paul's testimony where he said he had "learned to be abased and to abound and in all things to be content" Phil 4:12. My dear friend David Ross consistently put me up in the spacious and conveniently situated Chosen Hotel in the center of the city. My gratitude has always been deep to him for this, and for being the best interpreter I've ever had. He and his wife Ellen, later joined Y.W.A.M. and became the directors over our Korean ministries in America.

To this day, there is still a continuous stream of Koreans attending courses at Y.W.A.M.'s University of the Nations Campus in Kona, Hawaii. They have schools specifically tailored to Korean needs. Even campus events that serve the youth of many cultures are always translated into Korean.

"To God be the glory. Great things He has done."

**Joy Dawson "INTIMATE FRIENDSHIP WITH GOD" ©2008 by Chosen Books*

A Unique Privilege

On three different occasions in the seventies, I had the great and unique privilege of speaking at the enormous Yoido church in Seoul, Korea. Dr. Yonggi Cho was the pastor. No other woman, I was told, other than his mother had been given that privilege. I took these strategic ministry assignments very seriously. At that time, and for many years following, it was the world's largest church.

Each time I spoke, Pastor Cho interpreted for me. It was a joy to get to know this mighty man of God.

Loren Cunningham was also a speaker on each occasion that I spoke.

I noticed my diary reference to Dr. David Yonggi Cho in February 2012. It was related to his speaking at a conference in Chicago. I quote, "He spoke at night on the reasons why he prays three hours per day minimum. It was dynamic, very interesting and challenging." As I write this in 2019, it is still challenging!

Unusual Tests

It was early in the 1970's when Pat Boone and George Otis Snr. teamed up to lead a tour group of 1,000 people to go to Israel. When there, it took a fleet of buses to accommodate them. George very kindly invited Jim and me to go, and I was to speak to the whole group when they were all back at the hotel during one evening.

One afternoon the tour group had climbed up to a high point, which George had explained was where Paul had spoken on Mars

Hill. Without giving me any notice ahead of time to prepare, he came up to me and simply said, "You are on in a couple of minutes to explain the Biblical significance of all this. You have 5 minutes to speak," and he walked away.

My mind went totally blank in shock, and all I could do was to turn to Jim and say in desperation, "Pray for me!"

I then stood in front of this large crowd from all walks of life and beliefs, and whispered to God, "I don't know what to say right now. I am totally cast on You."

And then it happened! I opened my mouth and clearly uttered the flow of words which came effortlessly through me, and continued on until it was time for me to stop.

As soon as I returned to Jim, I said, "What on earth did I say? I can't remember a word! What was it like?

He assured me it was exactly according to the Biblical account in Acts 17 with the appropriately significant comments that effortlessly followed. I still couldn't recall **any of it then, nor have I since**!

Psalm 81:10 "Open your mouth wide and I will fill it," was all I could think of to explain those emergency moments. What an amazing, faithful God!

In the school of the Spirit, where I majored on studying the character and ways of God, I learned that I could always trust God to come through for me regardless of the circumstances, provided I was in His perfect will. That's why **I didn't** say to George, "I can't do this without being given some time to prepare."

Little did I know then that there would be numbers of other times when I would be **absolutely right out on a limb**, as God was testing me. Would I wait, and do only what God directed me, or to save face, would I do my thing? By God's grace I always chose the former.

Meeting Brother Andrew van der Bijl

When in New Zealand in the sixties, Neville Winger gave us a cassette tape of Brother Andrew speaking somewhere in the world. The enormous challenge was our being able to hear any of it, regardless of the different ways we tested it. It had to be the worst recorded message ever. No exaggeration!!

I decided this was no problem for God to fix. Believing Psalm 37 verse 5, had become a way of life to me. "Commit your way unto the Lord, trust also in Him and He will act." The word commit, in the Hebrew language means "throw." So I lifted up the useless tape in my hand and said to the Lord, "Before I throw this to you, I trust in Your total ability to catch it. I am also totally convinced that you will go into action to solve this problem, according to Your Word." I then threw it into the air.

As I walked away from it, I said, "Thank You Lord that you are fixing it."

When I put that tape back in the cassette player, the whole message was crystal clear with the volume just right. I shouted praises to my magnificent Master for this obvious miracle.

Years later, I was able to tell Loren about this radical Dutch man who was risking his life smuggling Bibles into nations where it was forbidden to own a Bible. Loren then invited Brother Andrew to teach at Y.W.A.M.'s School of Evangelism in Switzerland, which he accepted.

As I had been teaching for weeks at the same school, I was assigned to go with the driver to the Geneva airport to meet Brother Andrew. This gave me an hour of interacting with him, on the way back.

I shared about the past 3 weeks where the Holy Spirit had been doing a deep work among the students, as I had taught them to diligently seek God for a revelation of their hearts as only God sees them, according to 2 Chronicles 16:9.

This resulted in genuine brokenness before the Lord, and then before the others, as they humbly testified to the radical changes that had taken place in their lives. I shared that many tears had flowed during this time.

Brother Andrew got the picture, that these 75 students were very serious about their journey with Jesus.

When we arrived back at Chalet à Gobet, the hotel that Y.W.A.M. now owned, I was amazed to hear loud, exuberant peals of laughter coming from the classroom that Saturday afternoon. I was informed that all the students were having "a fun time." (Loren had forgotten to tell me about it.)

I managed to introduce Andrew to Loren. Then we cautiously opened the classroom door to discover young Dennis Lyndsay, doing an hilarious "performance" with 2 large fake teeth stuck in his upper mouth. Some of you must be thinking, "You can't be referring to Dr. Dennis Lyndsay, the present Director of Christ For The Nations Institute in Dallas, Texas?"

Yes, that's exactly who I mean! He's always been a dear friend of mine.... then and now.

I tried to apologetically explain to Andrew this was all new to me in a Y.W.A.M. training course setting. I will never forget his response, "For every repentant tear they've been shedding, they need this kind of laughter." What wisdom!

Loren made a fun night part of the new curriculum, and Andrew became a regular teacher in some of Y.W.A.M.'s training schools.

Just Having Fun

In the 1970's I was invited by my good friend Stewart McAlpine to speak to a group of Christian students at Cambridge University in England. Stewart was a student at the time. He is the eldest son of Campbell and Shelagh McAlpine and I had known him since he was a boy, when they lived in New Zealand.

God directed me to accept, and I ministered among them for a few days, being very aware that they represented future leaders in society. I remember one of the subjects I taught was on The Fear of the Lord, which I emphasized is the beginning of all knowledge and wisdom according to the Bible.

One afternoon, Stewart and a friend took me on a tour around this famous place representing high degrees of academia. In the 1970's it was evident to me that formality and the future upper crust of society were flourishing here.

With this backdrop I thought I'd have some fun! We had arrived at the Maudiline Courtyard right in the Center of the University. It was manicured to perfection. Not a blade of grass was out of place.

At any moment any of the professors could appear as they would be going to their next assignments. I was well aware of the formal facts.

That's when I decided to do three cartwheels on end. (I used to do a lot of gymnastics.) It was worth the risk, to see the look of disbelief and total shock on the face of Stewart's colleague!

I've often thought that a bit of history could well have been made that day.

The next afternoon, I was out on the Thames River with five of the male students who had heard me teach very seriously from the Word of God.

We were in a punting boat. I asked if I could take over with the one oar they were using to navigate. Permission granted, I maneuvered the boat to one side of the river bank, and then quickly jumped out, taking the oar with me and pushing the boat into the river with it.

I thought it was great fun seeing them let loose on their own... without their oar!

I can't remember how, but somehow they finally managed to get near enough to the bank for me to hand them the oar again.

Only God knows the intensity and seriousness of the multiplied hours of preparation that went into every message I spoke. And only God knows how I needed to "let my hair down" occasionally.

Punting on the Thames River, alongside Cambridge University, England.

I returned to the heart of London to speak at the prestigious Westminster Chapel on Saturday. Shelagh McAlpine was leading a vital national conference of women from the Lydia Prayer Movement and had asked me to teach all day, which was a great privilege and joy. God answered many prayers and moved in power among us.

It was a unique privilege for me to be speaking from the preacher's high pulpit that Rev. Martin Lloyd Jones, the famous British preacher had occupied for so many years. Dr. R.T. Kendell followed him as the pastor, whose writings I later deeply appreciated.

At the end of the day I had to change into travelling clothes because I was going to the airport to catch a plane for the long trip to Calcutta, India that evening.

Stewart took advantage of this. He saw I was in my slacks, so right outside the back door of the Westminster Chapel, on the sidewalk, he said, "Why don't you do a cartwheel here?" So of course I did. More fun.

A Castle For Sale

I had found that the more I spent time alone with God, listening quietly to His voice, the more familiar it became to the ear of my spirit.

I was in Lausanne, Switzerland again teaching at Y.W.A.M.'s training school. Don Stephens, the school director at that time, told me there was a castle in Germany that was for sale. Y.W.A.M. needed training facilities in Germany, so he asked me to seek God if we were to purchase it, as he was doing. I agreed.

He knew what I knew. We had no money; even for the down payment. No problem to God. Money never has been His problem. He owns it all.

Alone in my bedroom, I died out to all human reasoning and desires; resisted the enemy in the all powerful Name of the Lord Jesus, and simply thanked God that He would speak according to John 10:3,4,27.

I asked, "Lord do we buy the castle?" Very simply and quietly I heard in my spirit one word, "Yes." This was accompanied by a deep-seated conviction and peace I had long since come to recognize as God's confirming signal.

I shared my answer with Don, and it confirmed what God had said to him. Don then contacted Loren, the International director, who was in another country. He did exactly what we did and received the same answer. We then simply believed Psalm 32 verse 8 "I will instruct you and teach you the way you should go; I will counsel you with my eye upon you," ....to know what next steps we were to take.

How delightfully uncomplicated are the ways of God compared to the ways of men. There were no drawn-out committee meetings; no talking about the pro's and con's; no discussions about how and from where we would ever get the finances. We operated in the rest of faith, spoken about in Hebrews chapters 3 and 4. No sweat!

In 1972, the Olympic Games were held in Munich Germany, and Y.W.A.M. planned to have a big evangelistic outreach during them.

A lot of logistical preparation took place that Jim was heavily involved in, as many Y.W.A.M.ers signed up for the two weeks involvement.

As Y.W.A.M. had rented the castle in Hurlach near Munich, it became the main source of housing. It was relatively near the Games stadium.

More people than who had registered had turned up and we were packed in like sardines. Believe me! They were two weeks of "close fellowship". The Castle could comfortably house 250. We jammed in 900!!!

The plan was for half of the participants to be out witnessing at the Games one day, while the other half were in a large tent next to the Castle receiving in depth training; and then vice versa the next day.

Brother Andrew, Corrie Ten Boom, and Alan Langstaff spoke, but Loren and I shared most of the responsibility for those historic training sessions. Numbers of individuals have reported to me over the years that they were absolutely life changing days. All glory to Jesus!

For witnessing purposes, it is to our great advantage that we are multinational and non-denominational as a Missionary Organization. Only eternity will reveal how many souls were saved during this strategic time.

Those Olympic Games were truly historic internationally, as in the middle of it all there were fatal shootings of eleven Jews and one police officer by eight Arabs. Horrible and shocking.

However, God's Kingdom was truly extended through the many who had gone to Munich at that time for that sole purpose. God always wins, because He's always the Victor. Hallelujah.

The Castle which was up for sale, could be used as a training base for our varying schools that would be emerging, as well as for the needed staff and their families.

Loren shared publicly that God had directed us to buy the castle; and then said he would take up an offering from among us. That's when Brother Andrew very generously gave $10,000 for the down payment, for which we all heartily praised God and thanked His sensitive, obedient servant.

Loren then explained that there was still a need to have the payment that would be due next month. He then took up the offering and we all sought God what we were to give, believing He would direct us.

Obedience to the Lord by so many was evidenced by the amount that came in; much of it being sacrificial giving.

At the same time our dear 16 year old daughter Jillian who had just returned from doing a Y.W.A.M. summer outreach in England, was sitting in the back of the big tent, longing to participate in this time of extravagant giving. All she could do was to express this deep desire to God and say, "But I have nothing to give."

Almost immediately a lady walked to the back, and placed some money in her hand. Jill bounded to the front of the tent and put it in the money bucket.

Upon returning to her seat, another person reached down and put even more money in her hand. With joyful exuberance, Jillian rushed to the front and threw it all in the bucket. How that would have delighted God's heart. It did ours.

The point is that God will always give to those who want to give.

Fast forward now with me to 1989, years later. Jillian was married to John Bills, and they had two young children. They were unsalaried Y.W.A.M. missionaries living entirely by faith, who had spent a combined six years ministering to Cambodian refugees in both Thailand and Long Beach, California. This was followed by years of ministering to people with AIDS.

This family of four had a great need to have a home of their own, but they had no money to fulfill that need. That's when God miraculously stepped in! He had never forgotten the time that teenager had joyously given to His work at a time of her real financial need.

A woman friend of ours gave them a significantly large gift towards the purchase of a nice home God had directed them to own.

Then Jill did it again!

As the result of a deep desire, confirmed by the Holy Spirit, she gave away all of the money she earned from a small business which she operated from her home. It went in monthly payments to 10 indigenous missionaries in India. This brought her joy and deep satisfaction.

A remarkable girl, who learned to trust an extremely remarkable God.

Now back to the big tent in Munich.

Immediately prior to all this, I had come from being in Kabul, Afghanistan, where I was ministering to the very small church of Believers there.

I stayed in the home of a dear missionary. That city had to be the most bleak, dark, barren place on planet earth, at that time. No wonder it was the first overseas nation God called me to intercede for!

My Y.W.A.M. friends Floyd and Sally McClung were missionaries in Afghanistan, and had opened this door of opportunity for me. What a privilege.

I had been ministering in two other nations before this, so it was wonderful to be with all my family again.

A Vow Made And Kept

In 1973, two years after coming to America, I made a vow to God that I would spend a minimum time of one hour's intercession every week for the U.S.A., regardless of where in the world I would be. It is now 2019 at the time of this writing, and by God's grace I have kept that vow, and will continue to do so.

Because of the deep seated God given love for this nation, it hasn't been a burdensome commitment. Besides, this is where God chose to release my ministry giftings, and I will be forever grateful.

At the same time I have a great love and appreciation for New Zealand, and remain committed to consistent intercession for that very beautiful country.

I greatly appreciate the fact that my spiritual roots are found among the British commonwealth countries. They run deep. I am equally thankful for the American side of my life for its breadth of vision. A great combination!

Early Days Y.W.A.M. Los Angeles

This next story powerfully illustrates the faithfulness of God in the early days of Y.W.A.M. at the Lake View Terrace, Los Angeles, base.

John and his team had sent out fliers announcing an upcoming Discipleship Training School. There were no stipulations related as to how many would attend, although there was limited housing. In prayer, God had told them they were not to limit the number of acceptances. They said they trusted God to work out the logistics if problems arose! It stated there would be a three months training period followed by a two months evangelistic outreach overseas.

On the day of the arrival date, considerably more students showed up than they had housing for. They had beds for only seventeen. The overflow of 23 were standing around in the car parking area with their luggage, waiting for directions!! Additional housing was the glaring need--- but where? Only God knew!!

As John sought God for directions, He showed him to ask Jim to join him in search for the needed housing. Jim's white hair and lovely personality made him look like the mature and trustworthy man that he was!

They drove off in Jim's car, while Jim received clear directions from the Holy Spirit to "turn right and turn left" etc. etc. They soon came to a good looking street, when Jim heard clear inaudible directions, "Stop here and look up."

He saw a big home at the top of a lot of steps. The Lord said, "Go to this house and tell them your story of need." Immediately Jim obeyed.

Subsequently the man who came to the door and listened said, "The owner of this house needs to hear about this, I'll call her!"

When she came and heard Jim's explanation of the need and how he had finally arrived at her door, she burst out saying, **"So you are the answer to my prayers!"**

She went on to explain how she had fully prepared her home to become the place where a contingent of handicapped children would come to stay and get professional help, for certain periods of time. She also owned three guest cottages and the house next door.

However, her neighbors on hearing about this, clubbed together and submitted a petition which was granted by the city council stating that she couldn't go ahead with her plan.

She said she had just been informed about this and was asking God what she was to do with all the food stacked in the two large refrigerators and the beds that were all made up etc etc; What was His alternative plan for all her ministry preparations?

She then said, "Bring your overflow of students to stay here now! They will enjoy my big swimming pool in this L.A. heat." When Jim asked her about the financial costs, this dear lady replied, "Just give me whatever you can, when you're able." Later, God honored her trust and the Y.W.A.M. leaders' faith. All obligations were fully met.

"Jim rehearsed to John the incredible miracle that had just taken place. John jumped out of the car to see over the estate. The caretaker told them that it was once the home of a famous Hollywood film producer. In fact, just across the road and at the bottom of the hill was once the home of deceased Hollywood legend Cecil B. De Mille and was still owned by the De Mille Family.

Back in the car, they rejoiced and thanked and praised God as they went back to the Base. The staff and students were all in the parking lot waiting their arrival. When they shared the story the scene was wild. 'Grab your belongings, get in your cars and the Y.W.A.M. vans and follow us,' were the instructions.

These miracle houses were within easy walking distance of our new Y.W.A.M. Base. Only our Almighty God could have planned and coordinated so precisely this amazing answer to prayer. Hallelujah."

Every time I recall or recount this remarkable story, I am reminded of three things:

a.) God's unswerving faithfulness. It's part of His D.N.A.
b.) Humble servants of the Lord who obeyed His voice **as a way of life**, so that in a time of crisis they continued doing that, while operating in the "rest of faith" as described in Hebrews 3 and 4.
c.) The little song I've sung and believed since childhood: "Trust and obey, for there's no other way to be happy in Jesus, but to trust and obey."

An impromptu photo taken in Jim's Y.W.A.M. office in the 70's.

God Wowed Me

I have spoken at many Women's Aglow Retreats across America and Canada, as well as at some of their National Conferences. I have also had a close relationship for many years with the president, dear Jane Hansen Hoyt and her husband Tony, and with their wonderful assistant Kay Rogers. I thank God for them.

I had been speaking at a Women's Agow Retreat in Ottowa, Canada throughout the weekend. On Saturday night, after I had spoken, the Retreat leader took up an offering for me.

She and two other women in leadership counted it out carefully and realized it was short by $500 of the amount God had spoken to them beforehand to give to me, as they sought Him together.

They determined in their hearts to make up the difference, but didn't know how God was going to do it. They prayed in faith for God to come through.

Then they took the offering to the hotel manager and he counted it out and wrote the amount down on a piece of paper and locked the money away in a safe deposit box.

The next morning, (Sunday) the manager handed the money back to the Retreat leader, and when she counted it, it had multiplied overnight to exactly $500 more!!!

When the 3 women told me this story, I was then able to tell them that I was booked to fly out to minister in Asia in 3 days and was short of $500 for my airfares, but had told no one. Only God can perform this kind of unexplainable miracle. It is easy to give Him all the glory.

Romans 11:33 says, "…His ways are past finding out." I am in awe of Him…. again as I record it for this book. Psalm 115:1 "Not to you, but to Your name give glory, for the sake of Your mercy and Your faithfulness."

Brazil

In 1973 God directed Loren and me to speak at spiritual leadership conferences in numbers of nations. Loren always traveled with at least one male staff person, who would serve him. It also became part of a discipling process for that man or men. The exception was when once in the very early days when there was no male staff available.

The nation of Brazil was one of those nations; a very strategic one for the extension of God's Kingdom, both then and in later years.

I have found Brazilians to be among the warmest, friendliest, people groups in the world, and among the most openly responsive to the truths we shared from the Bible. I also loved their exuberance in worshiping and praising the Lord.

During this time, we were speaking at a spiritual leadership conference in a prominent city in Brazil. As was our custom, we met together in the morning before the service to share what the Holy Spirit was directing each of us to speak on for that day, and then to seek God for His order for their delivery.

On one particular morning we found that both of us had been separately sovereignly directed by the Holy Spirit to address the subject of immorality. Neither of us had any prepared notes on that subject.

We then decided to trust God to direct us what to say, as we prayed earnestly for His purposes to be accomplished.

Throughout the three sessions, as we obeyed God, He definitely came through. Heavy conviction of sin came on numbers of pastors.

Loren shared powerfully, and I taught a lot on the fear of the Lord from Proverbs 8:13, "The fear of the Lord is to **hate** evil..." It means to have a passion for holiness in thought, word, and deed.

The fear of God started to grip their hearts, as they became aware that adultery starts in the mind, and that our thoughts sound as loud in Heaven as our words do on earth. Genuine repentance followed.

Other pastors deeply repented of acts of adultery. It became apparent that they had been influenced by the culture around them which accepted this lifestyle as normal… evidenced by their lack of the fear of the Lord.

It was truly an historic day, as the fire of God burned out the dross from those leaders' lives. We concluded by thanking and praising God that His mercy is always extended to a truly repentant heart. We emphasized Isaiah 66:2"To this man will I look, even he who has a humble and contrite spirit and trembles at My Word."

My First Spiritual Leadership Conference In The U.S.A.

In 1973 the Holy Spirit gave me the vision of having a spiritual leadership conference in Southern California, based upon the same principles of the Massey Conference in New Zealand in 1961.

I approached Loren Cunningham and Campbell McAlpine who both confirmed it, along with the understanding that we three would be responsible to bring the messages.

I was then directed by God to ask Pastor Gerald Fry from San Jose to be the chairman, which he accepted. Pastor Wilbur Wacker was also part of the committee.

This group then met for times of protracted prayer in preparation for the conference which was in 1974. It was held at the Mt. Hermon Conference Center.

We started on a Monday night, and went through to the Friday night, with three sessions per day. We had no planned agenda. Every morning, the speakers would meet to seek God for His agenda.

It was an intense and demanding time spiritually, but undoubtedly a life changing and greatly rewarding experience for the many who came for it all. God definitely showed up at all the sessions.

When it was all over, Jim and Loren and Campbell and I went to a restaurant to relax. To unwind, the men told hilarious jokes, and I laughed so much that at one time I fell off my seat and landed on the floor. We were in no hurry to leave this wonderful therapy of laughter, which the Bible says, "Does good like medicine." I could do with a good dose right now!

This conference was very strategic from God's perspective, as it was the first of 35 more, in 12 nations, that would follow it, operating on the same principles and with the same team of speakers.

The ministry giftings were:

- Loren, as an apostolic teacher/visionary from the US,
- Campbell as a prophetic/teacher – from Scotland,
- Joy as a prophet teacher/visionary from New Zealand.

Ephesians 2:20 says the foundations are laid by the apostles and prophets.

The Saga At The London Airport

In August of 1974 Jim and I were returning to the U.S.A. from ministry assignments in England with Y.W.A.M.

We were at the London airport in time to board our T.W.A. flight at 11:45 a.m. en route to New Jersey, when I discovered I had omitted to bring my passport. (This was totally contrary to how I operate and has never happened again.)

This neglect was absolutely crucial, as I was booked to be speaking at a church in Vineland, New Jersey at 7 p.m. the following night, plus three more nights.

I shared my dilemma with the T.W.A. flight attendant. She said there was absolutely no way time wise to get a letter from the American Embassy, permitting me to enter without a visa, in order to get the 11:45 a.m. flight out the next day.

As Jim and I stood by all our luggage (I never travel light), I said out loud to God in full faith, "Then if You want to give me the same supernatural, miraculous transport that you gave Philip the evangelist, described in Acts 8:39,40, then I'm absolutely ready. I stood on my tip toes in anticipation of "taking off." I then added, "I'll need my luggage to go with me."

I sure hoped God would include Jim, who was silently processing all this and living a moment at a time! Finally, when it didn't happen, we left the airport and took a taxi to a nearby hotel, where we worked on getting the instructions needed to get to the embassy first thing in the morning.

In my Bible reading for that day, I was arrested by 1 Samuel 11:9 "By the time the sun is hot you will have your deliverance."

I believed God to somehow fulfill that promise to us.

The next morning we were up with the birds, with all our luggage, out on the street. We signaled down a taxi driver and told him to take us to the American Embassy as fast as he possibly could. He wove through the traffic at top speed and landed us at the entry way.

By the time we finally were able to find out where we were supposed to go, while pushing and carrying all our luggage around, we found a long line of people ahead of us. I jumped the line and went straight to the assistant and reported my case. She sensed the urgency, and thankfully for us, went through all the necessary protocol. Finally she handed me my visa.

Jim and I then flagged down another taxi instructing him not to waste a minute as we headed for the airport. On our way back to the airport, I rolled down my window from the back seat and saw it was 11 a.m. **and the sun had just started to shine!** .... exactly fulfilling the word of the Lord to me! I will not easily forget that awesome moment!

Having already phoned the pastor explaining that I would be a bit late, but I would still be on time to preach, he greeted us warmly and at ease when we arrived.

I gave the word of the Lord to his congregation, marveling again at the power and faithfulness of our friend, God.

"To the only wise God our Savior, be glory and majesty, dominion and power, both now and forever more. Amen." Jude 24 and 25.

Jesus The Winner

In the early seventies Y.W.A.M. had an international staff conference in Japan, where the Holy Spirit did an unusually deep cleansing work amongst us. It was historic, and life changing for many.

When it was over and everybody had left Osaka, I was left there to spend a week teaching at our Y.W.A.M. Discipleship Training School and ministering to a group of missionaries a train ride away up in the north.

The only person I knew in Osaka was Kalafi Moala, the leader of the DTS. The tiny hotel room I stayed in was so small, I had to go outside to change my mind!

The first day, I was all alone and confined to this dingy little bit of space, when it happened.

Suddenly my mind was bombarded with strong, subtle evil suggestions that could only have come from one source. Satan or strong principalities! The attack was vicious and relentless, like nothing I had experienced, nor have ever since!

My immediate response was to quote out loud and in total faith, the numbers of verses I had memorized from the Scriptures of our authority over the enemy of our souls and in total faith. The warfare was intense and longer than I would ever have thought, but I knew someone was going to lose, **and it wasn't going to be me**, because "the weapons of our warfare are mighty through God to the pulling down of strongholds."

Finally the enemy got the message and left me and I've never been attacked in that way again. Hallelujah.

I wanted to make satanic forces suffer, so I started worshipping Jesus as intimately as I knew how. And out of that, this song with a melody flowed effortlessly.

My lover God,
You're more to me
Than any other
One could be.

My lover God,
You're love for me
Surpasses any
Love I see.

Complete fulfillment
Is union with You.
My spirit with Your Spirit,
The fusion of two.

My lover God,
You're more to me
Than any other
One could be.

I believe that we should never talk about satanic attacks upon us, unless we have an accompanying account of how they were completely defeated.

If we don't, we become the biggest advertisers of Satan's power--- and unfortunately many Christians are. Food for thought.

The four basic weapons are: the Name of the Lord Jesus, the shed blood of the Lord Jesus, the Word of God, and in the power of the Holy Spirit.

One day I was out in my garden, and I had stepped over the border of my rose garden for some purpose. The border consists of a variety of large bricks, some of which are very sharp and pointed.

Suddenly I was being overpowered by an unseen force which was heading me toward the sharp objects.

Immediately I recognized that force as demonic and screamed at the top of my strong voice, "JESUS!!!"

Instantly I was delivered and back to normal. Praise God for the power that is in that wonderful name.

Calcutta, India

In May of 1975 I was in Calcutta India to teach the Word of God at the invitation of Mark Buntain. He was a legendary American missionary who had founded a church, a Bible School, and had a large daily feeding program for the poor and needy.

Calcutta is teeming with homeless people who lived and slept out on the city streets every night. I could see some of them from the balcony of the hotel I stayed in. I was appalled!

I asked God to speak to me from His Word, as to His purposes for sending me to India at this time. He answered by speaking to me "Mark 16:15." "Go into all the world and preach the gospel to every creature," and then directing me to 1 Chronicles 4:10; the prayer where Jabez asks for his borders to be enlarged. (Which I had prayed many times.)

It was inspiring to walk with Mark through the new hospital that was being completed, as part of his and his wife Huldah's missionary endeavors. I prayed for many of the sick, as the Holy Spirit directed me...going from one bed to another.

The temperatures were at an all time high of 115 degrees Fahrenheit with 89% humidity. Even the Indians were sweltering! I walked the streets and saw their misery on days when the temperatures were bearable enough to make it possible.

In order to combat the oppression that is part of the filth, abject poverty and suffering of Calcutta, strong vocal praise to God as a way of life is the key. I soon found that out. There is no substitute for it! And Mark modeled it all the time.

In my bedroom the air conditioners never worked for 2 days and 2 nights. Then for all of the night, before I was to speak at the church several times the next day, my fan broke down. This was when the heat was at its worst.

It was impossible to do anything but lie on my back with zero movement; and sweat it out. Sleep was out of the question!

I had to drink four large glasses of cold water during the hour I spoke the next morning to keep from dehydrating. I only had one fan in the church.

I was supernaturally sustained by the Holy Spirit as I maintained praise to God and prayer for others.

My diary records that at a later time of teaching in their Bible College on a day when there was no breeze, and thick smog hung all over the city, I taught with sweat pouring off my body.

Praising God helped to give me the right perspective at all times.

As I went around the filthy back streets on my prayer walks, I noticed the darkness on the peoples' faces, and that no one smiled. The air smelt thick with pollution.

I reminded myself that my wonderful, all powerful God had a plan to change all this, through not only His selfless servants like the Buntains and Mother Teresa… but every disciple in Calcutta willing to obey the Great Commission, but also through a great spiritual awakening, that He would send in answer to prevailing prayer.

Having Fun

On January 3rd, 1976, John Bills and our daughter Jill had a lovely wedding at the Osborne Neighborhood Church, followed by a meaningful enjoyable reception.

The spontaneous worship times before and during the ceremony were unique and powerful. John and Jill and Jim and I loved it.

After all the responsibilities were over, and the couple left for their honeymoon, I needed to let off some steam; so I went to the nearest trampoline place and bounced around, vocally venting praises to the Lord.

The owner wondered if I was OK? Obviously, I was not one of his normal customers!!

A Challenging Missionary Assignment

In my wild adventure of following Jesus, I found that the price is high, the rewards are higher, and the privileges are the highest, because of who Jesus is: --- the indescribably awesome. "I AM" who leads us, and works through us for His glory alone.

My next story illustrates this truth.

I am purposefully avoiding naming the nation involved, as the last thing I want to do is to cause an offence. The circumstances could be duplicated, and increased in intensity in many parts of the world today. So here we go.

In 1976, Loren and I were on a plane heading towards arriving in the main city of this nation, to teach a sizable group of young university students about knowing God in order to make Him known, for two weeks.

In Loren's typical style, he casually mentioned to me that this nation doesn't supply toilet paper! No explanations. No solutions.

I could have swallowed my tonsils with shock, before asking the obvious, "Then what on earth am I going to do??"

At that point he pulled out of his travel bag **half** a roll of toilet paper, and said, "We'll share this." I immediately wondered how on earth this would work, as of course we would somehow be housed separately. I was left silently wondering?

As it turned out, the directors of the school, who were an older married couple, along with all the students, and both of us, were housed together in a really old, well used institutional building.

Typically of how Loren operated, he chose to sleep in the full dormitory along with the male students. I admired him for that. I asked to have some space of my own, and they gave me a room with just 2 bunk beds and bare floors, for which I was deeply grateful. It was near the men's dormitory, so the ½ toilet roll worked its purpose!

The biggest challenge for me was negotiating my way through the human excrement that poured out of the women's toilets and across the floor. Obviously the drains were badly blocked, and for some unknown reason nothing was seemingly being done about it. If it was, we were not informed! Only God's grace can help us pass these tests.

In the classroom, those precious students absorbed everything we were pouring into them every morning and evening, by the hour. It was a privilege and pleasure to minister to such open hearts to the truths from God's Word.

In the first week, I developed severe back pain from some virus, and when teaching, the only way I could get relief was to completely bend over between sentences, as the interpreter did his thing, and then straighten out and teach again, and repeat the pattern until the end of the message.

When those wonderful students later prayed for me, I was completely healed. Praise God.

In the second week Loren developed severe back pain and had to stay in bed for some time before he could walk. By God's grace and much prayer, he came through that trial.

The water was contaminated, so the only safe way to get liquid was to consume a lot of watermelon daily, which we did. I've never wanted to eat watermelon since!!

We were aware that we were in a pioneering situation, which gave us such a sense of purpose, which proved to be true. Many of those students went on different overseas evangelistic outreaches around the world; while some became missionaries… all were marked for life.

In later life, some of them would come up to me in church in Los Angeles and testify to what God did in their lives in those historic days.

What a reward and great privilege to be sent from Headquarters Heaven --- anywhere, at any time, under any conditions.

A Warning

Because my dad was my hero, and I was raised with four brothers, each of whom I had a warm relationship with, it has always been easy for me to relate to the large number of male spiritual leaders I've been submitted to, and the many I've been teamed with over my long lifetime. I thank God for that.

Having a natural gift of teaching comes from it being part of my family's D.N.A. My Dad was an excellent Bible teacher and communicator, and three of my brothers made school teaching their profession. Wilbur and Stuart became very proficient music specialists and were teachers of teachers.

Both my children have teaching gifts, as well as four of my adult grandchildren. It's very important to add here, that the stronger the natural gift of communication a person has, the more he or she will have to purposefully guard against relying on the gift, instead of on the person of the Holy Spirit, when sharing God's truths.

Anyone with a gift of communication can preach with liberty. They can make people laugh and cry and quote scripture and stimulate the intellect, but have no authority. It happens all too frequently.

To speak with authority, which marked Jesus' ministry, we have to know the truth from God's Word and live the truth as a way of life. We also need to have God's clear directions as to whether or not we are to accept any invitation to speak, including the right timing. We also need to make sure that we are empowered by the Holy Spirit, and operating in the fear of the Lord which releases us from the fear of man.

As a spiritual refresher course, I read my book, "Jesus the model," published by Charisma House. It's potent.

My Brothers

I think this would be a good place to share the following:

I had four brothers. The eldest was Wilbur who was only eighteen months older than myself. We were good friends as children, and became closer friends as teenagers.

As adults we shared a good relationship. Wilbur was a music specialist, who taught the teachers. He was also a very gifted pianist and organist from an early age, which gave me a lot of pleasure. He died suddenly in his late sixties, which was a sorrowful shock and a real loss to me.

My next brother Howard, was three years younger than I was. It was a great grief to me to watch him suffer severely from leukemia when only 19 years old. He died in a hospital three months later. I didn't recover easily from the shock and emotional pain. I was just married at 22 years old at the time, and it hit me hard.

My third brother, Stuart and I have had a very unique bonding all of our lives and still do. We have no memory of ever having a "sticky" moment. He is now 87 years old.

When he was 7 years old and I was 13, one Saturday morning we spontaneously used the furniture oil I was using to help dust the woodwork around our home, for another purpose.

We "anointed" each other's heads with it, and pronounced each other with new names. I was called "Bubble" and he was called "Squeak." ("Bubble and Squeak" was some sort of potato and cabbage combination that was popular at the time.)

I love it, that although Stuart lives far away in New Zealand, and I live in America, he's still "squeaking" with purpose and I'm still "bubbling" with it, and we still recall with joy the unique original of it!

Stuart was also a music specialist, who taught the teachers. He authored a lot of illustrated music books for children which sold well. He loves to debate Theologically and has a sharp mind, along with a caring, loving heart.

My fourth brother was Wesley. I was twelve years old when he was born and I loved "mothering" him; he was like "my baby." I spent a lot of time with him during his early childhood.

I had the immense joy of leading him to the Lord much later in his life when he was a single parent raising two young boys. He had a genuine conversion experience and was instrumental in bringing others to Christ.

This eventuated in him and his boys coming to Los Angeles, where Wesley went through a Y.W.A.M. Discipleship Training School; and then the three of them went on a two month missionary outreach overseas. Wesley had a ministry gift of teaching.

All this brought me great joy. However about five years later he died of cancer, which was very sad and without understanding.

Maybe God foresaw my genuine loss of 3 very dear brothers and so decided to give me another one, but of a different kind.

From the first time that Loren Cunningham came and stayed for a month in our home in New Zealand in 1967, I had only one name for him. It was "BRO" …and that's what I've been exclusively calling him ever since. I am 10 years older than he is, but I always think of him as my big brother. He's big and tall and I've always been small.

It is very significant to me that Loren is the one God chose to not only release my ministry to the world initially, but the one who continued to do so, more than any other person.

We have a lifetime joke between us. I'm going to let you in on it. It was 1967 in New Zealand and I was about to drive Loren in my car to somewhere that was important to him. The car had been running perfectly, but this time I couldn't get it to start up.

So I said emphatically to Loren, "There's only two powers involved in this situation; It's either God's power or the devil's. I then resisted demonic forces, quoting in faith, James 4:7 "Submit yourselves therefore to God. Resist the devil and he will flee from you."

1 John 3:8 "The reason the Son of God appeared was to destroy the works of the devil."

And 1 John 4:4 "He who is in you is greater than he who is in the world."

Then I again said in full faith, "Lord if you want to drive this car without any natural explanation, that's perfectly OK with me. We'll just sit and watch you do it." I meant every word and waited for the outcome.

In the meantime Loren, who also has childlike faith, was assessing the situation. He certainly didn't want to miss out on seeing God's supernatural power at work in driving the car without human instrumentality, so initially he was silent. He also didn't want to hinder my strength of convictions.

However, when nothing eventuated, he finally told me that it was possible that the problem could be coming from a short circuit in the wiring system and that it could be adjusted. He then went to work on it and the car started up perfectly.

I was immediately on a huge learning curve!!! My naiveness and lack of mechanical clues were on full display!

Loren never let me forget it. To this day he quotes me by saying, "There's only two powers, Loren." I have always been thankful that 1 Samuel 16:7 says "…the Lord looks on the heart." ☺

Montreal Olympics

Jim was my favorite person to do personal one on one evangelism with. We had many opportunities to have powerful times of witnessing to non-believers at Olympic Games events in Munich Germany, Montreal Canada, and Los Angeles.

Y.W.A.M. always has a week of training prior to the Olympics for the many Y.W.A.M.ers who come to infiltrate all spheres of the Games with a powerful witness of the gospel.

I was in a little trailer with Loren and Darlene Cunningham in Montreal, Canada. We were fervently praying for the Y.W.A.M. week of training for the Montreal Olympic Games Outreach.

It was the night before, and I was scheduled to speak the next morning. Suddenly the Holy Spirit revealed to me that I had lost the cutting edge of the burden for lost souls that I used to have.

I saw that I had unconsciously allowed the weight of the responsibilities related to the Bible teaching ministry God had given me, to crowd out my zeal to witness to lost souls. I was absolutely undone, as I wept my heart out to God in deep repentance. I claimed 1 John 1:9 as the basis for receiving His forgiveness.

The next morning when I spoke, I acknowledged all this to over a thousand Y.W.A.M.ers and said I'd rather die than go on living without this God given burden for the lost. God was faithful and moved in power among us that day. God was also faithful to not only restore to me what I had lost, but He gave me so much more. What a God!!

Having Fun

In July of 1976, Loren and Brother Andrew and I were together again in Montreal, speaking at the training sessions Y.W.A.M. was having for those witnessing at the Montreal Olympic Games in Canada.

As usual, it was an intensive time of ministry. On the last day, Andrew and I were in the airport area when we saw what had to be by far the longest and tallest escalator on the planet at that time!

Without missing a beat, Andrew saw that the escalator was coming down toward us, and immediately challenged me to jump on and walk on it going upwards in the opposite direction.

I unhesitatingly took the challenge and did just that!

I had enough ability to match his dare, and enough sense to know when to turn around and get back to the ground.

A Significant Day

There were many vital and spiritually rewarding times when we would all come together doing the games.

One such day was Friday July 30th, 1976. I started at 9 a.m. by giving a message titled, "Preparations for the end times." It related to warning against traitors and betrayers, plus the conditions to be able to endure.

Loren followed by preaching the second half of the same message. I loved it!

From 12 noon until 4:25 p.m., Loren and I lead everyone in a deep move of God's Spirit. The majority humbled themselves before God and each other, as they repented of their sins. This was an awesome time in God's holy presence.

We all met again at 6:30 p.m., when I spoke on "Suffering, grace, and glory."

In large capital letters right across my diary I had written, "TREMENDOUS DAY. HIGHLIGHT OF MONTREAL OUTREACH. All glory to Jesus."

P.S. Obviously a lot more must have taken place, but I have written only what my diary recorded.

Unique Witnessing Opportunity

One of my favorite times of witnessing with my precious partner Jim, was in the living room of a multi-millionaire's home in Beverly Hills, Hollywood. The owner was a strong Believer who wanted her doctor friend to come to Christ. He was the leading neurosurgeon in Los Angeles at that time. Famous people would fly in from other countries to have him operate on them.

Our friend had invited him and his wife, and Jim and me to dinner in her mansion.

As this highly educated, medically acclaimed, non Christian man would ask hard questions of us in rapid fire, I was intrigued at how the Holy Spirit worked through us without fail.

Because I was introduced to the Doctor as an international Bible teacher and author, and he knew nothing about the Bible, he **assumed** that I was a "specialist in my field." This meant he would aim most of his questioning at me.

Most of the time the answers from God came quickly through. But right when I didn't know what to say, Jim would automatically come through with a truth that was right on and impactful.

Jim had a considerably greater general knowledge than I had, for which I was always very thankful. He had the freedom from me to correct me anytime I was speaking, if I had my facts or figures wrong in some illustration I'd be giving. I would always thank him publicly and tell him I always knew I needed him!

We truly were a team!

Significant Times With Little David

At fifty years of age I became a grandparent to John and Julie's first child, David. I was totally captivated by this little guy from the start. He was strikingly good looking, with a strong outgoing personality, and I loved him like crazy.

Consequently he and I developed a strong bonding together, in the times I managed to spend time with him.

One time, Jim and I, along with John and Julie and baby David, were in the car together going to the Los Angeles International Airport. I was heading for a ministry trip away somewhere.

David was sitting on my knee in the front seat, and nowhere near being able to talk, when I suddenly said, "David, what are you going to call me?" Immediately he replied, with total clarity, "Nan." I said, "O.K. that's it!!" I then said to the other three adults, "Did you hear what David just said?" Each one responded, "Yes I did!" David then returned to his baby chatter. And that's been my family name for three generations.

When David was two years of age, the Holy Spirit convicted me of the sin of idolatry. I had expended more heartfelt devotion on my grandson than on the Lord. I deeply repented, and then received God's forgiveness. I love it that God is a jealous lover of our souls.

Now let's fast forward to when David was four years and four months. While I was reading my Bible, David was sitting beside me on a chair. Suddenly, he picked up my small daily devotional, called The Daily Light, which has nothing but Scriptures for the morning reading, surrounding a particular theme, and then correspondently for the evening reading. He called it his Bible.

To my amazement and total delight David spontaneously "took off" preaching his first sermon. Instantly I knew I had to write it down, word for word, and managed to do so with the Lord's enabling.

Here it is:

> *"Jesus is not a person, He's the Boss. He's the Son of God. He's the Lord Christ. When God punished me He still loves me. When Nan punished me, she had to and she still loves me, these two persons.*

When I was crying because my Daddy was still on an airplane and I was having my birthday party, the teacher said, 'Don't worry the angels are looking after you and Jesus will be your Daddy.'

You can't see Him, but He's there.
And the poor refugees, you bless them down Lord. And punish the guys that are shooting the refugees. The place that they come from is called hunger where all the poor people are.

*I'm not talking to you Nan, I'm talking to the Bible (*meaning from the Bible*). The refugees forgot to say that Jesus died on the cross. You can't see Him, but He's here. He lives up in the mountains. Jesus doesn't live on the dirt, He lives on a big huge cloud high above the sky.*

Moses was Jesus' friend, and Noah, His two friends. They were as tall as Jesus. Those two guys. They went on to Bethlehem too and they found the cute little baby. There were no cars there, or super-sonics to fly on, just camels and ponies. They ate turkey, beef, and ham.
One day there was a big star, and do you know what was in the big star? A big angel. That star was a miracle one.
Jesus had to go to Bethlehem because He loved the people and Jesus died on the cross. Jesus had a Bible too. He has real words in the Bible. Jesus was a boy like me. He had strong bones.

One day Jesus and Mary were making a snowman in Bethlehem and playing with it. They found out it was a miracle snowman because it was a real one. It had a real man inside, and that's all I want to say."

I was fascinated with the mixture of this four year old's imagination, and some real theology.

The National Prayer Committee

In our early days of living in America, Vonnette Bright, of Campus Crusade for Christ, invited us to join the National Prayer Committee, for which she was the chairman.

The N.P.C. was made up of prayer leaders in the USA representing denominations, missionary organizations, and prayer movements.

There were ten of us, who met together several times a year for two or three days, in a Central City to strategise and pray for National and International Prayer Conferences that we would convene. Many of the events were in Washington D.C.

This was an enormous privilege and responsibility, as some of us would always speak at them, of which I was one.

An Unexpected Visitor

In 1976 a very historic international prayer conference was held in a large hotel in Manila, Philippines. Over 2000 prayer participants came from all over the world for 10 days. The speakers were renowned prayer leaders.

Jim and I both spoke at the training classes on intercession, and were part of taking shifts at a nonstop daily prayer meeting that met behind the scenes all throughout the conference. The unity was as strong as the fervent prayers. I also spoke at the session for all the women.

On the first morning of the conference Jim and I were out on our early morning prayer walk, when we saw a Filipino boy in front of us. We stopped and asked him his name. We told him we were out prayer walking and explained about the conference being held in the large hotel nearby. We invited him to come and have breakfast with us, just as he was. His response was an immediate, "Yes."

He had lunch and dinner with us and we learned he was 14 years old and lived on the streets. We became bonded with him to the point that we invited him to stay with us the entire 10 days. The hotel gave us a floor mattress for him, which we put down beside our bed. He was content and so were we!

The next day we took him to a Christian Filipino dentist who treated him for a badly abscessed tooth. Then we had great joy in outfitting him in sporty clothes and shoes and buying him a Bible, a guitar, and a basketball. He loved everything and said he'd longed for these things all his life.

He had been exposed to the gospel as a child and responded positively, despite the fact he had rebelliously left home against his mother's pleadings. We encouraged him to return, but he wasn't interested. However he gladly attended most of the conference sessions with us.

He particularly enjoyed interacting with the team in the prayer room, who totally received him.

He loved bouncing his basketball around our good sized bedroom, and learning to play his guitar. He was sharp, with an outgoing personality and was enjoying our genuine love.

Eleven days later, it was very hard for him and for us, when we had to say goodbye at the airport. We had arranged for him to stay with our Y.W.A.M. team at the Manila Base. They had graciously agreed to take him in, despite knowing that he had stolen as a way of life while living on the streets.

Jim and I believed that God had a wonderful plan for this teenager's future life, and those ten days were a big part of helping to bring it about. In Heaven we'll hear how and what!

Even More Fun

Here are some more of the lighter side of things, which are just as real a part of who God created me to be.

Back in the forties, ever since I rode a good long distance on the back of Jim's motorbike before we were married, I've been hooked on motorbikes! I used to say into his ear, "Faster, go faster." He did, and overheated the engine! We had to wait until it cooled off, before Jim could start it up again.

In the seventies, I was teaching all throughout the week at a large and vital church in Northern California, in a very demanding schedule. I was at a special luncheon on the Thursday, sitting beside Paul Kauffman, the guest speaker. He was a veteran missionary statesman from Hong Kong, working among the Chinese.

During the conversation Paul shared that he was in the process of writing a book. To get some relief from the intensity of the project, he would do stunt riding on his motorbike in the middle of nowhere around this area.

Immediately, I asked him to take me on a ride. It took some convincing that I was serious, and the sooner the better. Finally, he said, "I'm going out this afternoon." I said, "Great, I'll have time before speaking again tonight."

When I got on the back of Paul's motorbike, I realized I'd have to hold on to something, so I put my thumbs in the back loops of the waist of his trousers. I feared the Lord and didn't want to do anything inappropriate. We were both married people, and, I had only just met this man of God. Paul quickly informed me I would have to hold onto him tightly in order to negotiate the stunts that were coming up.

While we were heading for the countryside, I kept saying my usual line, "Faster, faster!," to which my driver complied.

Finally we reached an area with large mounds of dirt, twists and turns, and more large mounds. These were perfect for throwing us up in the air then making us fly through the air before crashing us down again repeatedly!

I was charged with excitement, when suddenly we were both hurled off the bike onto the dirt. Paul was OK, but my right leg was bruised so that I had to limp; but that was no big deal to me. It was well worth it!

On returning back, this veteran missionary told Pastor Gerald Fry light heartedly, "She's wild!" The pastor just smiled, as he knew very well the serious side of me.

That Thursday evening, I limped onto the platform of the church smiling inside at the subject that God had already shown me to speak on. It was "The justice of God." He alone knew how appropriate the message was to the exhilarating experience He had just given me.

My Creator made me to love this kind of wild stuff and in His justice and love for me had again surprised me with an appropriate blessing. It caused me to love and thank Him more and more. I taught from His Word with enthusiastic conviction, that night and to the end of the week. **God is just.**

Return Visit

Jim and I had our return visit to New Zealand in 1976. We stayed for three weeks from November 19th to December 9th.

It was a joyous time meeting up with precious family members, and numbers of our dear friends. It was also fulfilling to speak several times at our home church, Hillsborough Baptist, and once at Valley Road Baptist church. We were always warmly received by all we contacted. Thank You Lord.

P.S. God turned on a particularly relaxing and fun time for me by spending the day sailing in my brother Stuart's yacht with his lovely wife Margaret and my dear Jim. The hospitality, weather conditions, scenery and fellowship were first class. Thank you again Lord.

Brazil

In October of 1977, it was a privilege to be teamed again with my dear friends Brother Andrew, who wrote the best seller "God's Smuggler," * and Loren Cunningham, who wrote the best seller, "Is that really you God?" ** for a 3 weeks ministry trip to Brazil. In my estimation, those two men of God, along with Dr. Bill Bright, the founder of Campus Crusade for Christ International, are the greatest world visionaries in my generation. (Only God has the final assessment on that statement!)

We spent a week each time speaking at a spiritual leadership conference in the 3 major cities throughout the nation, Saõ Paulo, Belo Horizonte, and Porto Allegre. The interpreter, George Foster, was the visionary for this trip and a missionary to Brazil... a dear man of God who did a great job.

As soon as I arrived in Belo Horizonte, I realized this was the initial fulfillment of part of what God had spoken to me at the close of the Massey Conference in New Zealand thirteen years previously.

** Brother Andrew "GOD'S SMUGGLER" ©2015 ChosenBooks.*

*** Loren Cunningham "IS THAT REALLY YOU GOD?" ©2011 by LorenCunningham.com*

Our only day off from ministering 6 days a week was a Saturday… and that was spent flying to the next city with the accompanying ramifications, which were intensive, but so rewarding. God's presence, power, and purposes were evident. The Holy Spirit was re-shaping the minds and hearts of His leaders, imparting differing aspects of world vision and the price to fulfill it, along with a deeper understanding of God's character and His ways. The unity between us as a team was very strong. We were fulfilling the conditions in Psalm 133:3 for God to be able to "command the blessing."

At the beginning of each week we spent the day in powerful times of prayer and fasting.

On the first day of the conference in Saõ Paulo, I noted that after Loren had introduced me to speak, I was spontaneously given a message on my feet. It was explaining why God is a God who at times hides Himself, as described in Deuteronomy chapters four and five, Jeremiah 25, and Isaiah 45:15. (I had previously studied this subject from God's Word.)

YWAM Property In Solvang

In preparation for recording what to write in this book, I was reading through the constant references in my diaries as to where I traveled over many years and what specific message I spoke at each specific place God had directed me to go.

Only God knows the mammoth task that eventuated in understanding what to record, what to leave out, and then having wisdom to know how to share it…so that God gets all the glory.

In that context, I came across something pertinent that I had long since forgotten. It was in January of 1978. Jim and I were in Charlotte N. Carolina and I had been interviewed by Jim Baker on one of the many times he had me share truths on his daily television show. I have always appreciated his genuine burden and vision to reach lost souls, and still do.

Our Y.W.A.M. director at that time for the America's, Leland Paris, was also there. Consequently we spent time seeking the Lord together about whether Y.W.A.M. was to purchase a former resort hotel for the rich and famous that was for sale in Solvang, Central California. It would make another ideal training base. It had additional houses on the property.

After thirty minutes of listening for the Holy Spirit's directions, both Leland and I had received nothing. Jim said God had been impressing upon him that any work that really counts for God in a big way, has intercession as its main emphasis!! He then named some of them. After pondering that, we all sought God again but there was still no answer.

Finally Leland acknowledged out loud to God that he received what Jim had shared, and this was God's voice speaking to him. He also acknowledged that a staff member had told him the same thing. He then declared that if God wanted Y.W.A.M. to own this choice property with the unique hotel, that he would communicate to whoever God would choose to lead the ministry from it, that intercession was to be the main ministry focus.

Immediately the Holy Spirit said to me, "Now I can answer. It is 'Yes'. Now I can give you this property." Scriptural confirmation was given to Leland to commit to buying it by faith, while Jim received even greater understanding that the priority of intercession should be given to every ministry that would be used by God to significantly advance God's kingdom. After steps of obedience and faith, by many that were involved, the whole property was finally owned by Y.W.A.M.

Years later, I was speaking at this same Solvang Y.W.A.M. Base, at a S.W. American staff conference. The subject God had given me was "The Fire of God," part one and part two." It was serious stuff.

At the close of the second message we were informed by the police that a serious fire had broken out in the surrounding forests and was heading in the direction of the hotel. We were ordered to pack up our belongings and be ready to leave, if needed. It was the final day and we were scheduled to leave the following morning.

The fear of the Lord came upon us, as we all realized God was underscoring the truths that had been taught from God's ways, about the many aspects of the fire of God in God's Word that related to our lives. The fires were reported in the local news that evening.

The fires came right up to the edge of the Y.W.A.M. property and then abated. God had made His statement.

Radical Witnessing

It was 1978 and Argentina was the nation where the World Cup Soccer Games were being held. God had directed us in Y.W.A.M. to have an aggressive evangelistic outreach in each of the main cities throughout the nation during this time.

The Holy Spirit had previously revealed to me from 1 Kings 20:14 that the younger leaders of Y.W.A.M. would spearhead the evangelistic thrusts in each of these cities. "But who will do this?" asked Ahab. The prophet replied, "This is what the Lord says: 'The junior officers under the provincial commanders will do it.'"

That was wonderfully fulfilled!!

Our son John was one of those leaders, who later reported on the highly significant impact the sharing of the gospel had on the city of Cordoba. I have taken the following report on it from John's book, "Taking Our Cities for God."*

"We were frustrated. The international Youth With A Mission team had been on the streets all day, and we were not getting anywhere. All two hundred of us met the next day for prayer in a rented monastery on the edge of town. We cried out to God for answers.

The crowds were there. Thousands of Argentines from all over the country had come to the finals of the world soccer play-offs, but our witnessing lacked power. Nobody was coming to Christ.

During that day of prayer and fasting, the Holy Spirit began to reveal the nature of the unseen realm over Cordoba. We realized that our timidity and weakness in proclaiming the gospel were partly due to the work of satanic forces manifesting themselves in the culture of the city.

Cordoba is a proud and beautiful city with proud and beautiful people. The population is largely of German and Italian descent, and much importance is given to position, possessions and appearance. In the midst of this fashion-conscious culture, we felt very out of place. We were Christians from over twenty nations, simply dressed, struggling with Spanish and carrying gospel literature.

The Lord responded and gave us a plan. As we prayed in small groups, the Holy Spirit revealed the same strategy to many minds. There is only one way to overcome a spirit of pride. It is through the humility of Jesus, through Jesus' life lived out in acts of obedience by His people. We were discerning a principality attempting to rule the city in the pride of life, so we had to confront it in an opposite spirit with a strategy of personal humility.

** John Dawson "TAKING OUR CITIES FOR GOD" How To Break Spiritual Strongholds. ©2001 Charisma House.*

Here is what we did. We went downtown the next day-all two hundred of us-and formed into small groups of about thirty. We positioned ourselves all through the fashionable malls and streets for pedestrians of the downtown area. Then we did it. We knelt down right there in the midst of the fashion parade, surrounded by expensive bistros, outdoor cafes and boutiques. With our foreheads to the cobblestones, we prayed for a revelation of Jesus to come to the city.

Breakthrough was immediate-breakthrough in us and breakthrough in the city. Large crowds of curious people gathered around each group.

I remember vividly how Christ strengthened me when I set aside my dignity and knelt in the street. The intimidation of the enemy was broken along with our pride. As the crowd became larger, I stood and explained through an interpreter why we had come to the city. As I lifted my voice to communicate to the people at the edge of the crowd, the boldness and compassion of the Lord filled me, and I began to preach.

All over downtown Cordoba, Youth With A Mission workers preached to attentive audiences, and a harvest of souls began. The people were so receptive that they would wait patiently in line for us to autograph personally our gospel tracts. They insisted on this unusual way of honoring us and constantly expressed gratitude for these small gospel portions. These large street meetings went on for several weeks until our departure. Large numbers came forward publicly to indicate that they had turned to Christ.

When at first we were greeted with chilling indifference, we could hear the enemy's accusation: 'You are not cool enough.' He followed with this temptation: 'Don't demean yourself. Don't lose your dignity.' He was appealing to our pride. Our response was to humble ourselves publicly.

I will never forget one evening when I was preaching in the plaza of San Martin to a large crowd and the scythe of God went through the audience. People dropped to their knees in public repentance. One woman stumbled forward weeping and, kneeling down, grasped my knees. 'Can I receive Jesus right here?' she said. 'Do I have to come to a church?' I assured her that she could find Christ anywhere.

Now tell me. How could a city so resistant to the gospel suddenly become such a place of harvest? The enemy holds the nations in deception and accusation. When we minister in a given city, we too are hindered by the spirits oppressing the people, until we discern the nature of the enemy's deception and "bind the strong man" by acting in the opposite spirit.

To overcome the enemy we must resist temptation ourselves and then continue in united, travailing prayer until we sense that we have gained authority and that God has broken through."

During this time, Jim and I had a thrilling time evangelizing every evening in the heart of downtown Buenos Aires. The Argentine people love to spend their summer evenings walking around the main shopping areas and talking animatedly to one another.

Jim and I took advantage of this culture trait. We would stand outside one of the shops and start talking very enthusiastically with up raised voices to each other in English. This immediately caught the attention of the extraverted Argentines, who would immediately flock around us to listen in. It always worked!

To our sheer delight, we would then start sharing in a conversational way the good news of the gospel, without an interpreter. We noticed that whenever we would use a word that they couldn't understand, (most of them had learned English) someone in the crowd would immediately speak out the word in their language! It was awesome!

At times the crowd grew so big, Jim had to move away so that half of them would then gravitate around him. At one time I vividly remember losing sight of him altogether. All I could see was the mob listening to him attentively.

I continued doing what I so love to do: talking about the most awesome Being in the Universe, JESUS, and His plan to redeem us.... especially where He did most of His evangelizing....out where the people were! This was pure joy. I fully expect to see some of those people in Heaven. Some of the highlights of my life were doing radical witnessing sessions with Jim.

Glimpses Into The Unseen World

For months I had been fervently asking God in faith to "blot me out" while I was speaking, so that all the attention would be on the message, not the messenger.

One of my many spiritual leader friends heard me praying that prayer, and gently let me know it was an unrealistic one. I just kept on praying, anyway! I knew God could do it.

Many months later, in September of 1978, I was in Toronto, Canada, speaking at the Odeon theatre on a Saturday morning and afternoon, to a small audience of only 30 women from different denominations and walks of life. In the morning session I spoke on "Making History through Intercession."

At the close of the meeting, an intelligent woman who was a leader in the Women's Aglow Fellowship, approached me and shared that as I spoke, she saw the glory of God like a gold mist that started above my head and then covered my head and upper body and face. It finally tapered off at the sides of my body.

I sincerely thanked her for sharing this with me and gave God the glory, and said no more. On my own, I thanked God for encouraging me and giving me the desires of my heart.

In the afternoon I spoke on "How to pray for the lost."

Another time I was speaking at a regional Women's Aglow conference in America, near the Niagara Falls. At the close of one of my messages, a woman came up to me and said that when I was speaking, she saw a huge angel, about 10 feet tall hovering over me.

She concluded that this was a normal occurrence for me and that I would be well aware of it. She then said very seriously, "I've seen your angel! I wouldn't want to mess with you!!" ---whatever that meant??

Anyway, I explained that I wasn't aware of any angelic visitations surrounding me, but thanked her for encouraging me. I pondered on God's goodness to let her see into the realm of the Spirit and then share it with me.

Sydney, Australia

On January 1st, 1979, having come from being back on a short trip to New Zealand, I arrived in Sydney, Australia for three weeks of varied ministry purposes. The first two weeks I was teamed up with Campbell McAlpine and Loren Cunningham speaking at spiritual leadership conferences. There were three sessions per day.

On the Thursday evening of the first week I gave a message on "God the great Deliverer." I then invited anyone who needed counseling related to some form of healing or deliverance, related to mind, body, soul or spirit, to stand to their feet.

The whole audience stood!

We were able to counsel about 75% of them individually but had to stop at 12:15 a.m. for sheer exhaustion on our part. The next morning we continued counseling about 50 more people, from 9:45 a.m. until 2 p.m. There was a great need for people to receive healing of their wounded memories, among other needs.

Jesus said in John 8:32 "You shall know the truth and the truth shall set you free."

Many were set free, as we obeyed the Holy Spirit's promptings while seeking Him on behalf of these precious people. All glory to Jesus.

These Aussies really worked us hard! On Saturday, on our only day off, Campbell and I were assigned to travel in temperatures over 100 F, plus high humidity, in a non air-conditioned car for three hours to Newcastle. This was in preparation for our speaking in churches the next day.

I spoke morning and evening in two different churches, with perspiration pouring down my whole body all the time I was preaching. My diary also recalls that dear Campbell spoke four times that Sunday in those conditions.

In 2 Timothy 4:2 we're instructed to "preach the Word; be prepared in season and out of season"….so we did that. It also says that "when we've done all that we're supposed to do, we're unprofitable servants…" so I acknowledge that we were.

We flew back to Sydney the next morning, and met with Loren who had been ministering to Y.W.A.M.ers. We spent the rest of the day in prayer and fasting for the coming week's next leadership conference.

We prevailed in serious intercession for God to reveal some of His strategies for reaching Australia with the gospel. This resulted in hearing the Holy Spirit say, "Neighborhood Evangelism." We enquired, "Which method?"

He then gave us the understanding of His people going door to door in pairs and asking the people if they had any prayer requests they would like them to pray about. If so, then the Believers would assure them they would pray earnestly for those needs to be met and return in a week's time and check on the answers.

I recalled hearing, about two different churches on the East Coast of America, from the same city, uniting together with this same unique vision. It resulted in marvelous answers to prayer, with many people then being exposed to the gospel and subsequently being converted and joining churches. We prayed believing all this for Australia.

It was significant at the end of that week that God directed Campbell and me to prepare new messages related to the ministry of a prophet. Campbell worked on "The preparation of a prophet" and I worked on "The function of a prophet's ministry and the price."

The Holy Spirit gave us confirmation from Hosea 12:10 "I have also spoken by the prophets, and I have multiplied visions, and used similitudes, by the ministry of the prophets." It came out of protracted times of intercession for the U.S.A. and Australia.

The third week was very different. Allan Langstaff, an Australian pastor, who was a visionary for what God was doing at this historic time, spoke an anointed message on the Sunday at the Sydney Opera House to 9,000 people. His subject was "It's a new day." Hallelujah!

My diary records that I spoke at "The Uniting Church" and a Baptist church, as well as to a Y.W.A.M. conference, and then at a Women's Aglow conference.

In the middle of that lineup, I spoke at the Royal Randwick Racecourse to a crowd of between nine to ten thousand people on "God's innovative ways in Evangelism" Loren also spoke at the same session.

The Holy Spirit directed me to which messages to give and then anointed me to give each one. God's Kingdom was definitely powerfully extended; so of course all the glory goes to the Lord Jesus.

As always, my favorite ministry assignment was to be out on the streets witnessing to lost souls. Where better than at downtown

Kings Cross, Sydney in the evening with Loren and a bunch of Y.W.A.M.ers?

My good friend, Noel Gibson, who was the director for Open Air Campaigners in Wellington, New Zealand, was faithfully preaching the gospel right there that evening. The motley crowd standing around was very diverse.

It was a tough scene. A brawl was in progress and hecklers were yelling out. But God was at work. Loren had a very meaningful time of witnessing to a man who had a lot of serious questions about God that Loren was well equipped to answer!

I was very burdened in prayer for a young man lying on the ground who personified someone right out of hell. I had never seen anyone in the shape he was in, nor have I ever since! His face was covered in blood, and his appearance was grossly distorted. He was under the influence of alcohol and/or drugs. One of his eyes was completely closed and the other eye only half open. He looked very grotesque!

After continuing for some time in intense intercession for his lost soul, I went close enough to him for him to hear me clearly. I then bent over and said loudly, with a deep sense of Divine purpose and agape love, "Jesus loves you, and God's power is far greater than the power of the devil." I repeated it twice!

I sensed the power of the Holy Spirit at work as I released faith in the following:

- Light overcomes darkness.
- Truth is greater than error.
- Love heals the deepest wounds.

I believe the Holy Spirit miraculously made it register into his spirit, and I believe God answered my anguished cries for his lost soul…in His way and time. I believe to see him in heaven! God is able to save to the uttermost…and the guttermost.

The next day I was interviewed for one and a half hours by a representative of Vision Magazine and then went straight on to teach at a conference on "Knowing God."

That evening Frances McNutt, a Roman Catholic priest with a powerful healing ministry, gave an anointed message to a crowd of about 12,000 people, probably at the opera house.

On the final day, a film team interviewed me on the subject of "Interceding for righteous leaders to be put into places of authority and influence throughout a nation." This was followed by a filmed interview on "The Neighborhood Evangelism Vision," and another interview with Vision Magazine.

Upon returning home to Los Angeles, it was great to meet up with Jim who was just returning home from a vital ministry trip to Tonga and Samoa.

Thrilling Witnessing Opportunities

It was February, 1979 and I was in Nagoya, Japan on a grueling schedule, teaching the Word of God.

I then took a plane to Kumamoto. On the journey I witnessed all the way to a Japanese teenager who spoke English, using a Japanese / English New Testament. He had never heard the gospel.

He owned a Bible given him by a teacher, so I urged him to read the gospel of John. I also gave him one of my cards explaining how he could commit his life to Christ. I also put him in touch with the pastor who met me at the airport.

I was given by God a new prophetic message God had for Japan from 2 Kings chapter seven. I gave this to a receptive, warm, group of pastors and their wives who had come to this pastor's church.

I then travelled by train to Hiroshima, where I had a marvelous opportunity of witnessing to three Japanese school boys, who were placed in seats facing mine. I had the help of my interpreter, and a Japanese / English New Testament. I was able to give two of these boys a copy of them to keep.

They knew nothing about the implications of the gospel, but had heard about the Lord Jesus six years ago through a Japanese / English speaking teacher.

They had never seen a Bible. As always, it was thrilling for me to carefully and simply explain how they could give their lives to Christ, and make Him the Lord of their lives.

The boys were very thoughtful as they were processing all this new truth while the Holy Spirit was making it clear to them.

I followed up this contact with fervent prayers for their salvations.

Having Fun

I am reminded of a time around the late seventies, when Jim and I were in England with Loren and some of the European leaders of Y.W.A.M.

We were inspecting through a very large house that was for sale, with the possibility of purchasing it for a Y.W.A.M. Base and training school.

When we were in one of the bathrooms we came to a big bath tub. I decided to jump in and measure it by lying down stretched out.

Immediately Loren turned on the cold tap and I was soaking wet, before I could jump out.

So as not to give him any satisfaction for playing this joke on me, I acted as though nothing had happened for the rest of the afternoon – despite the wet clothing.

The Refugees

In August of 1979, Jim and I were in Osaka, Japan at a weeklong strategic International Y.W.A.M. conference.

One day, the Holy Spirit spoke clearly to me that I was to go and visit the refugees at the end of the conference. I immediately shared this with Jim. After seeking God, he shared that he was not to go, but to return home, at that time.

I shared it with Loren, who sought God immediately. He said that the Lord had spoken to him that he was to go, and that he was to ask Don Stephens in Switzerland, to partner with us.

Loren then contacted Mike Carroll, the World Vision leader, who was over the refugees camps in Hong Kong and Thailand. He gave us permission to go.

Jim and I had no money for my airfare to Hong Kong and Thailand, or the hotel expenses needed, and only God knew about it.

At one time, while Loren and I were praying for God to move mightily to meet the desperate need of the refugees, a single woman in Y.W.A.M. could hear us from where she was, through the wall. Some of us in leadership were living in the same Y.W.A.M. house during that week. The Holy Spirit then spoke to her to give me $1,000 which she did. It covered everything. Hallelujah!

A few nights later I had a powerful time all evening witnessing in Y.W.A.M.'s coffee shop to three Japanese men. One of them named Hiroshi Hashimoto, was very keen to read right through an English – Japanese New Testament.

The next night I was seeking God until very late for the message I was to give on Sunday morning. It was to be at our Y.W.A.M. leader's home church. His name was Topi.

Finally directions came to prepare a new message on "The place of the Word of God in the nation of Japan-<u>now</u>." I was still working on the message while travelling to the church, and prior to standing up to preach!!

The next day when I was alone seeking God for the timing of going to the refugees, I had an impression of September 10th. This was then later confirmed when seeking God with Loren and Jim.

Loren was directed to Daniel 10:12,13. Verse 13 speaks of 21 days from the time Daniel first started seeking God. We then calculated that it would be exactly 21 days from the time we first started seeking God about the timing to leave. Jim had perfect peace about this, plus directions that he was to return home at that time.

The next day we all went as a team to a park to witness and to preach the gospel. I gave out gospel tracts for a long time with an interpreter, as I communicated with the people. Later, I preached the gospel with a loud speaker with Jon Benedict interpreting for me. As usual it was thrilling for me to preach the gospel in the outdoors.

In the middle of this, hundreds of Japanese high school students lined up right in front of us. They were on a tour, and were getting their photos taken in groups right beside us. They were forced by their circumstances to listen to the gospel message for about fifteen minutes. Our Y.W.A.M. leader for Osaka, Topu, was able to pray with several of them later to personally receive Christ as their Savior.

On the next day in the early afternoon, after a protracted time of intercession, I met up with a Japanese student for 1 ½ hours, as I presented him with the gospel. To my intense joy, he fully responded and gave his life to Christ.

Straight after that, I was taken on a long journey by car, where I spoke at a church with an interpreter, on "The place of the Word of God in the life of a Christian."

The next day, at an evening meeting in a home, I was able to share about the reality of how God miraculously supplies the needs of those who put their trust in Him. I also shared about the Japanese student's conversion experience from yesterday, and then led the people through my card, "What it means to commit your life to

Christ." Mr. Fukushima, a Japanese businessman interested in Christianity, attended that meeting!

Later on Jim and I had a vital time at the coffee house witnessing to Hiroshi and Hitoshi, who were two Japanese men who spoke English. They were very interested as we shared the gospel.

Jim and I then sought God if we were to leave the Y.W.A.M. house that we'd been staying in, and have a couple of nights in the city near to the coffee house. God spoke clearly from His Word to both of us confirming that this was right.

We packed up and found that the cheapest good hotel that had previously been booked out, had just received a cancellation. So we moved right in, thanking God.

We stayed for two nights at $34 per night. My diary records that I shampooed and set my hair, and enjoyed the luxury of a bath instead of a bucket and a hose of cold water in our Y.W.A.M. housing.

When Jim and I went by car through to Nagoya, I spoke in two different churches on a Sunday on the "Greatness of God." At the end of the messages I emphasized that God was grieved with the unbelief in the Christians hearts about God's ability to move in mighty power across Japan.

This was evident by the many times I've heard it said, "Japan is a hard nation to reach with the gospel." My response was and still is, "Hard for whom? It's not difficult for God----only unbelieving Christians."

The Holy Spirit broke through that Sunday bringing deep conviction of the sin of unbelief among His people which led to genuine repentance.

The next day we returned by train to the Y.W.A.M. house in Osaka. I then had such a sense of fulfillment, as I contacted the young Japanese man whom I'd led to the Lord last week. This time I was able to lead him into receiving the infilling of the Holy Spirit, as well as teaching him how to read his new Bible.

The next day Jim and I went on subway trains to huge department stores, shopping amongst the masses who were everywhere. I kept praying in faith for God's Spirit to be poured out on these multitudes of Japanese people in unprecedented ways, for the extension of His Kingdom.

In the process of getting my airline tickets re-routed to Hong Kong and Thailand at the Pan Am office, we had an opportunity to witness our faith in Christ for hours in the afternoon to an attractive young Japanese woman and two young Japanese men (one whose family were Christians). They spoke English. While there was no evident breakthrough, they listened very attentively, as we lovingly shared the realities of Heaven and Hell, and the way of salvation.

They gladly received the literature in Japanese that we gave them. We left them with much to think about.

Once again, I thought that our vital time together could be the result of the faithful prayers of Christian family members.

I had previously asked God in faith that day, to give me someone that I could lead to Christ. That prayer was answered when we went back to the YWAM house and met a young Japanese man. He was brought there by a staff member who had contacted him at the bookstore where she worked.

I spent the evening with him, and had the great joy of sharing the gospel with him, to which he fully responded. I then prayed for him to be filled with the Holy Spirit, as in Ephesians 5:18. One of our staff leaders was a great help in interpreting all this. At the end of that full day, I was very tired but very fulfilled.

The next day I spoke on the subject of "The Implications Related to Giving" at a Women's Aglow Conference in Osaka. The following day I spoke at a meeting for missionaries on the subject of "What to do when things go wrong." It is an enlightening message.

Later, Loren and Joe Harbison, our YWAM staff leader, met with Jim and me for prolonged intercession for the ministry trip to the refugees. God then showed Loren he was to contact the World Vision leader in Bangkok for permission to get into the refugee camps. This was granted.

At the close of the conference, we received God's final directions and flew to Hong Kong where we visited a refugee camp full of Vietnamese, who had fled the Communist Regime.

While we were walking slowly through it, I stopped beside two little boys who were about 7 and 5 years old. I was very drawn to them. One of the camp directors who was accompanying us explained to me that they were brothers. Both of their parents were recently killed and they were now orphaned.

Immediately I reached out and put my arms gently around them, trying to impart some genuine love and affection. To my shock, there wasn't the slightest response. They were like zombies!

I started to understand that the horrors and grief they had just lived through, had now paralyzed all normal emotions and reactions.

I just made it to a walled fence outside, which I leaned on before sobbing my heart out to God for some time. I would never be the same! A burden to pray for refugees ongoingly was birthed!

We then flew to Bangkok and met up with two of our Y.W.A.M. leaders. After seeking God, Loren contacted World Vision again. They sent two of their missionaries who came and shared the whole refugee situation with us, which was very enlightening. We then had a time of powerful intercession together. This greatly fueled my vision and prayer burden for the starving Cambodians facing famine and the refugees.

Sharing the gospel with two refugee families.

The next day we ministered in three transit camps in Bangkok during the day, and then went back to the biggest one at night. It was a very impacting experience to say the least.

There were 22,000 refugees in great need. The camps were filled with Cambodian families who had escaped the horrors perpetuated by the Khmer Rouge with only their lives. They existed by living in very small spaces, crammed together in huge tents with only a grass mat to sit or lie on day and night.

I would go and sit on the floor with a little family and lovingly share the gospel message with them. I only spoke English, but God always had someone among them to fill in with the right word, if there was something they didn't understand – which never ceased to enthrall me! I always trusted God to do this, as I never had translators.

I would move from one family to another, in high degrees of heat and humidity for many hours, reveling in this awesome privilege with intense joy, and then go back the next day to do the same thing.

There was one particular family which included the father and mother, their two daughters, and a son, who all gave their lives to Christ after I had shared the gospel with them.

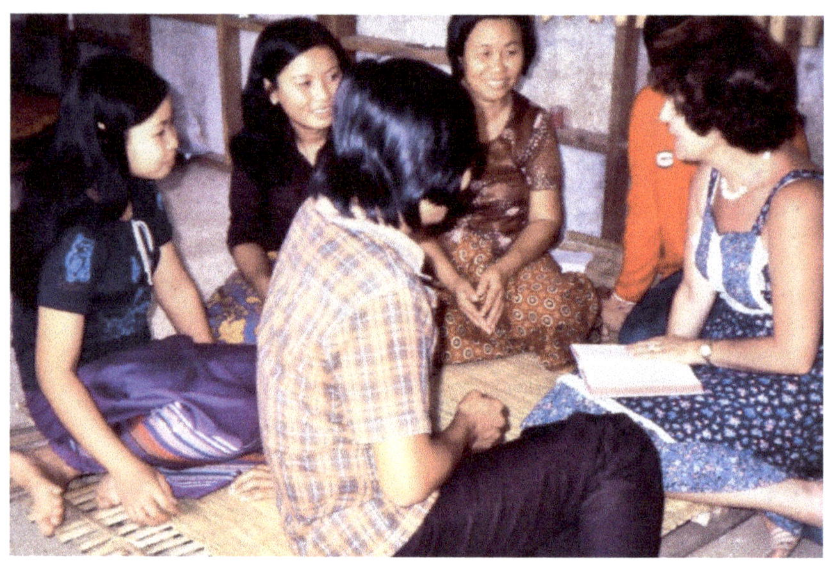

This family of five all received the Lord Jesus as their personal Savior that day.

We were up before the birds the next morning to catch a plane to Loei. The plane had some mechanical problems, and we were considerably delayed out in the middle of nowhere! Finally, on arrival we were met by World Vision staff who drove us to their missions house, where we met their director, Mike Carrol. He then drove us the two hours to the large refugee camp at Baan Vinai, where we saw the hospital cases of children dying of malnutrition.

My heart was broken, and I wept deeply. Then I took many individuals in my arms and prayed for each one. When I went outside the hospital clinic, I preached the gospel with my Y.W.A.M. leader, Joe Harbison, interpreting for me. People were always lining up there.

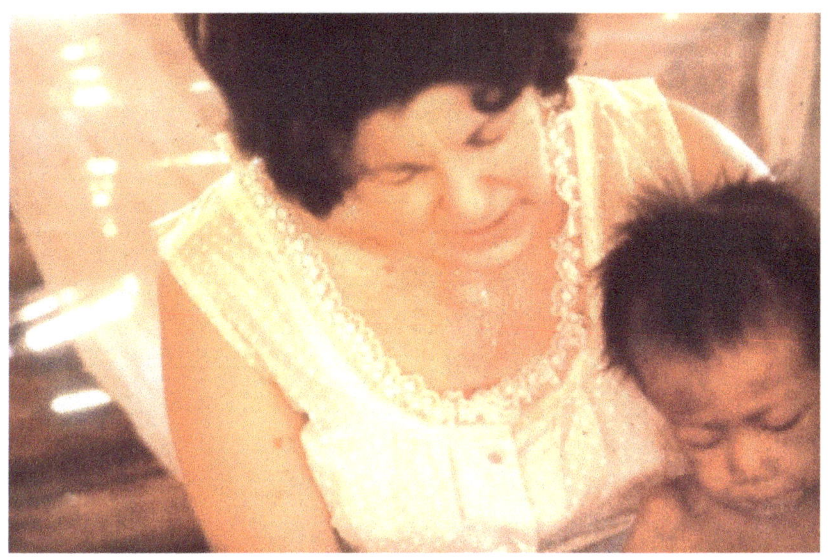

Weeping and praying over suffering children.

We then travelled for two hours back by taxi to the World Vision house. After that we were taken on a truck drive for four hours, to a train station. We boarded a train at 12:30 midnight, and I headed up for a top bunk in a section for six people.

I hadn't eaten anything all day, since a light breakfast on the early plane flight into Loei. I marveled at the grace of God upon my body as He mercifully took away all desire to eat, while supernaturally sustaining me through a rigorously long day. Thank you Jesus.

We arrived from Chiang Mai, Thailand, at 8:15 the next morning. Loren and Don and I had numerous times alone and together, seeking God about matters related to the purposes of the Anastasis Ship ministry in Y.W.A.M. This included how it related to our involvement with the Refugees situation…presently and ongoingly. As always, a lot of intercession was involved.

As Loren, Don, and I, and a Thai taxi driver drove through to Chonburi, we were praying much for the desperately needy Boat people refugees we would visit that day.

Don spoke to them on the subject of forgiveness to everyone who had caused their suffering. I followed by sharing on "What it means to commit your life to the Lord Jesus Christ." I emphasized the "narrow" way and the price of discipleship, and quoted Romans 10:9 "If you will confess with your mouth that Jesus is Lord and believe in your heart that God has raised Him from the dead, you shall be saved." I then invited those who really wanted to follow Jesus to come forward and openly declare it, by slowly repeating a prayer after me, which included "I make Jesus Christ the Lord of my life." To the glory of God, eleven men came forward and followed through.

Doug, a Baptist missionary, then led them into receiving the fullness of the Holy Spirit.

Joy and Dave Boyd sharing Jesus' love with refugee children.

The next two days Loren and Don and I spent in seeking God again about the numbers of imminent challenging situations related to the Anastasis Ship Ministry. Just one example was that half a million dollars was needed in the next two weeks for payments on this big ocean liner. It cost $20,000 just to get into the docking yard in Germany. And it cost $12,000 every month for fuel.

We were directed by God from 2 Kings 20:8-11 to "strike the arrows" in faith for the financial miracles needed. We did just that, and our faithful God met us by varied ways and means.

God directed Loren to a very significant verse of Scripture at this time of seeking God. It was 2 Chronicles 28:15 "And they did not turn aside from what the King had commanded the priests and the Levites concerning any matter and concerning the treasuries."

After flying out from Bangkok to Hong Kong and Tokyo, I changed to a Pan America flight to Los Angeles. On that same plane were three families, of 19 people who were refugees from Laos, who had never been on a plane before and were unaccustomed to modern facilities.

Before we boarded the plane I had developed a warm relationship with the father and mother of one of those families. Their names were Somsak and Somchan Sengsouvong. They had three children. Somsak spoke English.

I had a great time helping the family of five to navigate the wonders of toilets that flushed after you sat on the seats and pushed a lever. You quickly get bonded at times like these!!! I kept in touch with them during the long flight to L.A.

On arrival I introduced them to Jim and we exchanged phone numbers and addresses. They were being sponsored by a family member living in the U.S.A.

It wasn't long before we had led Somsak to receiving the Lord Jesus, and then Somchan followed later. They had to forsake their former religion to become followers of Jesus. It was serious business.

It was our joy to help Somsak get a job and be able to help them furnish their apartment.

They later settled in Atlanta and soon joined a Baptist church, along with their three children, who all became Christians. They kept in touch with us on a regular basis for many years, to our great delight.

I had only been home for 2 days and was experiencing severe jet lag, little sleep, and trying to cope with nearly 7 weeks back-log of correspondence, when I had to prepare for going away on another ministry assignment.

Jim drove me up to Twin Peaks in the San Bernadino Mountains to speak at the Calvary Chapel Women's Retreat. They were women hungry to know more of God and His ways. In addition, they had generously contributed towards the costs of the expenses related to my extended recent ministry time in South East Asia

.

On the Friday night I had no prepared message, but God had spoken to me to read **Luke 9:51-57**, **Matthew 20:15**, and **Matthew 24:12-14**, and to trust Him to speak through me as I read them out. Once again I was out on a limb, with the Holy Spirit's enabling power alone.

That eventuated in my sharing about the need to give up all our rights, that the unreached millions may have the right to experience the freedom of knowing and following the Lord Jesus.

I challenged them to ask God to create a plan in their lives that would lead them to be used of God to reach the maximum number of lost souls for the extension of His Kingdom.

I shared about our responsibility to be involved with the refugee crisis.... starting with intercession on their behalf. God was enlarging their vision and testing their depth of commitment to His Lordship in their lives.

The leadership team was wonderful to work with. Knowing I was so weary from so little sleep, they interceded fervently for God to supernaturally break through on my behalf.

I spent the rest of the weekend teaching on the fear of the Lord.

The leader of this vital ministry was precious, Godly, Kay Smith, the wife of Pastor Chuck Smith.

I had just been in 9 weeks of extensive travel and numerous intensive ministry assignments and was greatly in need of a break, and serious rest.

Because my Heavenly Father is "Just in all His ways and kind in all His doings" Psalm 147:5, and is "full of compassion," He had already made a provision for me.

God had previously given Jim and me clear directions to have a little place up in the mountains in Wrightwood, California.

In this place I prepared many new messages that the Holy Spirit was giving me; sought God for specific directions related to the numbers of invitations to speak, and started working on the writing of the first of my eight books. There were also many prayer walks, while absorbing the beauty of God's handiwork among the big mountain trees. It was also therapeutic to be away from all the inevitable demands of city life, at this time.

After four days, I was back home, in preparation for teaching all the next day at the Melodyland School of Theology in Southern California. Pastor Don Wilkerson was the leader.

Right up until ten minutes before I was due to teach at the first class, I really thought I was supposed to speak on "Knowing God." The leadership had asked me to speak on "The character and ways of God" and I had thought God had confirmed that to me, along with that subject.

When I asked God for specific confirmation in the last few minutes, it didn't come. As soon as I switched questions, and asked

God if I was to teach on "The Fear of the Lord," He immediately clearly confirmed to me that this was "the word of the Lord" for both sessions---5hrs altogether.

In a couple of minutes I was on my feet, having just swapped my teaching notes. That was a close call!

The 1980s

Colossians 1:18 …that in everything

He might be pre-eminent.

Time For Expansion

In 1980, it had become apparent to us that we needed to enlarge the home we owned which was in the northern mountainous area of Los Angeles. God spoke to us from **Isaiah 54:2-3** to strongly confirm this. At the same time He clearly gave us the exact plan of how we were to "lengthen our cords and strengthen our stakes," as we "spread abroad to the right and to the left."

Also, God remarkably spoke to us from the book of Ezra. Three times in chapter five there are references like verse eleven, "We are the servants of the God of Heaven and earth, and we are rebuilding the house that was built many years ago." Chapter six verse seven says, "Let… the elders… rebuild the house of God on its sight."

We then shared our plans and confirming Scriptures with an architect friend from our church. We told him we would pay him for doing the builder's blueprint as soon as we had the money. He trusted us and went ahead. God came through again, on time… for us and for him.

Later, when the Christian builder had completed all the structural work, **Jim did all the finishing work inside**. This was a very lengthy time consuming job. He did it after hours, as he was full time operating in his pastoral and administrative ministries.

J.B. and Jill had been four years as missionaries in Thailand, ministering to the Cambodian refugees and were now returning home for Jill to give birth to their first child. She was beautiful Jenny Marie.

Our enlarged home now made it possible for them to come and have their own space, plus the baby's. They were with us for 6 months until they could rent an apartment. We so enjoyed having them.

Cause For Rejoicing

I rejoice that both of our children have a heart for the world. After serving the Mission since he was nineteen years old, John became president of Y.W.A.M. International from 2002 to 2011.

When John was just a young leader in Y.W.A.M. Los Angeles, Pastor Dan Sneed privately gave him a prophetic word. It was that one day he would be the President of Y.W.A.M.

Wisely, John shared it only with Jim and me. We in turn kept it totally to ourselves, and like Jesus', mother Mary, "we pondered it in our hearts", but never discussed it!

Many years later in 2002, John phoned us, and reported the news that was surprising to him and to us, that he had just been elected as the new president of Y.W.A.M. We then recalled the prophecy.

John's Inauguration Ceremony followed on August 22nd, 2003 as he was inaugurated as President of Y.W.A.M.

I sought God to speak to me from His Word concerning this significant appointment. He directed me to Ezra 10:4 "Arise, for it is your task , and we are with you; be strong and do it."

Also, 2 Kings 3:11 "And Jehosphat said, 'The word of the Lord is with him.'" (describing the prophet Elisha) John has a prophetic ministry!

And, Nehemiah 7:2 "I gave my brother Hana'ni and Hanani'ah the governor of the castle charge over Jerusalem, for he was a more faithful and God-fearing man than many."

John is also the founder of the International Reconciliation Coalition, known as I.R.C. It was founded in 1990.

This powerful ministry exists to uncover ancient and modern wounds of injustice, pride, and prejudice and to heal them in a Biblical way. That means without self-righteous accusation or dishonest cover up.

John has written a number of vital books.

Jill had a passion for missions from her childhood and she and her husband John Bills have both served as teachers in Y.W.A.M. International for many years. J.B. still does.

As I add to this manuscript in 2019, I can say that all of our six adult grandchildren have been through a Y.W.A.M. Discipleship Training School, and are going on for God.

One has been a pastor in Brazil for 16 years, another is a pastor in Canada, and another is in leadership and teaching in Y.W.A.M. New Zealand. And one is a teacher, and a children's pastor in New Zealand. There are also fifteen great great grandchildren being influenced by their parents to know God and make Him known.

God has promised me from Isaiah 59:21 that this fruitfulness will continue in my extended lifetime and after. "As for Me," says the Lord, "this is My covenant with them: My Spirit who is upon you, and My words which I have put in your mouth, shall not depart from your mouth, nor from the mouth of your descendants, nor from the mouth of your descendants' descendants," says the Lord, "from this time and forever more."

Psalm 102:28 is an additional promise. "But our families will continue; generation after generation will be preserved by your protection." From The Living Bible translation.

God has also given me Isaiah 8:18 "Behold, I and the children whom the Lord has given me are signs and symbols in Israel from the Lord of hosts, who dwells on Mount Zion."

All the glory goes to our merciful and amazing God! Amen!

Wonderful Counselor

As I've been looking through some of the more than sixty years of journaling, there's a consistent pattern.

I've recorded exactly where I was reading in the Bible, on a daily basis. I've also recorded the questions I asked the Lord, for which I needed answers in the present, as well as the days, or months ahead. Then I wrote down His answers, and the methods the Holy Spirit used to speak to me. This included every time I received an invitation to speak anywhere. There is a predominance of His speaking to both Jim and me through His Word.

There are also a significant amount of times when God tested us individually, or together, where we had to keep waiting and trusting and persisting until the answers came from headquarters Heaven.

Waiting on God, related to matters small and great became part of our spiritual D.N.A.

It's the only way we could be sure we were the right person, at the right place, at the right time, in the right condition of hearts in order to get the right results.

Also, whenever I have had the need for answers to my life's questions and there have been many, I have always inquired of the "Wonderful Counselor," as described in Isaiah 9:6.

I can then say with the Psalmist, in Psalm 73:24 "…the Lord has always been my Counselor" I can then believe the promise in Proverbs 19:21 "The Lord's counsel will stand."

A One Time Only Test

Since 1971, when Jim received his final pay check, Jim and I have lived entirely by faith financially, without sharing our needs with anyone, except for one occasion only.

It was in October 1980 and Campbell McAlpine and I were the speakers at a Spiritual Leadership Conference in Pasadena, Los Angeles. Our son John was the leader of the conference.

At that time I was very involved, along with Loren Cunningham and Don Stephens, in seeking God about the difficulties related to launching the Y.W.A.M. ship, the Anastasis. It was docked in Athens, Greece for some length of time.

God had just made it clear that Loren was to fly to the ship from Hawaii and I was to fly from Los Angeles to meet with him and Don, who was on the ship…immediately following the conference, and we both committed to go.

We had already been in touch with each other for days by phone over urgent matters.

For the first time, Jim and I shared with John that we had absolutely no money for my airfares to Greece and back. John said he felt directed by God to share this urgent need at the conference, which he did. This resulted in my airfares being released. Praise God!

The Apostle Paul instructed Titus to do exactly what John did for us on this occasion. Titus 3:13-14 "Send Zenas the lawyer, and Apollos on their journey with haste, that they may lack nothing. And let our people maintain good works, to also learn to meet urgent needs, that they may not be unfruitful."

I have often wondered why this isolated experience during our lifetimes, of sharing our financial need took place.

I have concluded that God was testing us in relation to pride. It was very humbling for both of us to have to disclose our financial need. The test was passed by God's grace and I'm thankful I've never had to go through that again.

I came home exhausted; from daily speaking at the conference, and had to pack and prepare to leave again the next day on an overseas flight. My diary records, "I can't believe the pace I'm living at, and the pressures I'm living under."

Worth Waiting For

For nine l-o-n-g years I was traveling and speaking internationally without having a secretary. People would ask why I didn't hire someone when they saw the real need. My answer was always that, "I was waiting for my 'Isaac.'"

I believed that God had someone specially hand picked for me, and I was waiting for Him to bring that one to me. I didn't want to have a substitute like Abraham did, when he chose Ishmael.

One afternoon while in my office, a young woman who had recently been through a Y.W.A.M. Discipleship Training School walked in and very simply announced that she could help me with secretarial work. Instantly I thanked her and sensing that God had sent her, I said, "You can start now." She did. I discovered that her name was Janet Izett; which is about as close to Isaac as it gets in pronunciation!!

This precious, godly girl could not have suited me more perfectly in every way. What a gift from God….and so worth waiting for! She later married Sean Lambert, another Y.W.A.M.er and some years later was having her third child. She continued helping me right up until she was due for its delivery!! Janet will always have a special place in my heart. We've kept in touch for all these years. Sean and Janet lead one of Y.W.A.M.'s most effective bases today in Ensenada, Baja, Mexico.

Arnie Abraham

Back in May of 1973, I was speaking at a church in California during its Missions Convention. While there, I had the privilege of meeting one of God's choice disciples, Arnie Abrahamson. At the time, Arnie was a Wycliffe missionary from the jungles of Brazil on furlough in the United States. I listened to the gripping story of this man's burden for three unreached tribes up the Amazon River. And his many lone attempts to reach them with the gospel. Arnie shared about the numerous times he'd faced death through lack of food, illness, and murder attempts by the natives. Two things became vividly clear to me:

1. I was to become an intercessor for this man and his vision.
2. I was to encourage others to do the same.

The following week I was teaching in Switzerland at a YWAM school of evangelism. I told Paul Hawkins, one of the leaders, that I had brought with me a tape of Arnie's story, and I shared with him some of the facts. Paul didn't try to hide his excitement and amazement, as he in turn recounted what had taken place in his intercession-for-the-nations group the week before. As the young people had diligently applied the ten principles for effective intercession, which were on a card, God, as usual had given them remarkable revelation.

To one was given the impression of the nation of Brazil. Another was impressed to intercede for a missionary working alone in the jungles of Brazil. Another said, "I believe God is showing me that the man is working with the Wycliffe Bible translators." For some time the Holy Spirit burdened this group with the needs of a man who they didn't know existed, and for the souls of the tribes the missionary was seeking to reach with the gospel.

The next morning, another staff member, who had not been able to attend the intercession group the previous morning and had heard nothing of what was prayed for, led the group in prayer. God did it again—He gave the woman detailed revelation of Arnie and his needs without any prior knowledge on her part of who he was. This was an undeniable confirmation that the group had been hearing from God. Imagine the encouragement when they heard Arnie's story on my tape verifying everything in detail!

The greatest encouragement was kept for Arnie himself. I returned to California and told him how God had uniquely singled him out and made him the focus of intercession through a group of young people on the other side of the world who had taken time to pray for the nations. I also shared my call from God to pray for him.

In November of 1980 I arrived in the city of Manaus, Brazil where our missionary friend and interpreter George Foster had set up an itinerary for Loren and myself to speak at weeklong spiritual leadership conferences in the three main cities of Manaus, Belo Horizonte, and Porto Alegre.

It is significant that just prior to this trip, the Holy Spirit had directed me to make a Biblical study on what it means "To Endure." This resulted in my getting an insightful message on that subject. It deeply ministered to me then, and has done since. It was also a much needed message for those attending these conferences, for the circumstances they were in.

It was deeply meaningful to me to meet up with my precious missionary friends, the Abrahamson's in Manaus. Arnie and Joyce and their two sons Steve and Stan, were at the conference. God had enabled me to keep my commitment to intercede fervently for Arnie and his vital ministry, for the last seven years.

The first time I saw them was when I got up to speak. Immediately the Holy Spirit directed me to share with the audience about Arnie and his call from God to reach the Indians up the Amazon River with the gospel and how difficult it had been.

I shared about how one day God told Arnie to build an air strip. This was a bit like God telling Noah to build an ark. Arnie had zero experience, and didn't understand why.

I then stopped and listened to the Holy Spirit, who directed me to ask the audience to seek God to show them anytime they had quit, after He had directed them to do something difficult; or had waited until others could join them before proceeding in obedience. If this applied, I invited them to repent and receive God's forgiveness, on the basis of 1 John 1:9.

The audience took the challenge and followed through. I then lead them into groups of three, to intercede fervently for the 165 Indian tribes up the Amazon; particularly the Juma tribe who Arnie had targeted. I encouraged them to release their faith and believe.

While the audience was co-operating in unity of purpose, I asked the Lord to speak to me from His Word about what was happening. He answered me from Luke 11 "Keep on asking and you will receive."

While Loren and I were having lunch with the Abrahamson family, they shared their disappointment and grief over the unbelief among those who were meant to be giving them the greatest encouragement for this project.

The Holy Spirit directed me to say, "You are a Joshua and or a Caleb, and you will lead a younger generation of Believers into reaching these tribes with the gospel." This prophetic word was confirmed by the Holy Spirit speaking directly to me: "Turn to page 220 in your Bible." And there it was as clear as delight!

It was Deuteronomy 31:23 "And the Lord commissioned Joshua the son of Nun and said, 'Be strong and of good courage; for you will bring the children of Israel into the land which I swore to give to them; I will be with you.'"

My next message on "To Endure" fitted right in here and brought strong encouragement, as I tied it in to having faith and patience to see the fulfillment of the vision to reach the Indians, with real joy. We finished with strong praises to the Lord.

On the last day in Manaus, Loren and I met again with the Abrahamson family as we prayed through every prayer request Arnie and Joyce had given us related to their God given mission.

My diary records, "The Holy Spirit moved upon me as I prayed a desperate prayer of faith in God's character, with weeping, for Him to move today for the Indians to be reached by a new thing God would do – a big thing that would bring a big advancement to this cause." I then asked God to answer me back by speaking to me through His Word, the Bible.

He directed me to 2 Chronicles 9:12 "And King Solomon gave to the Queen of Sheba all that she desired, whatever she asked…" This was accompanied with the Holy Spirit directing me to Isaiah 55:5 "Behold, you shall call nations that you know not, and nations that knew you not shall run to you, because of the Lord your God, and of the Holy One of Israel…" I then had the assurance my prayers had prevailed and the answers were on the way.

God confirmed this again by speaking to Loren from Acts 10. (I didn't record the verse.)

When Steve and Stan shared about their difficulties in obtaining the permanent visas to come and work with their parents, I did strong spiritual warfare against the powers of darkness in Jesus all powerful name, and with the Word of God.

Stan was given a prophecy stating that "God had heard our cries and would answer our united prayers of faith, but it would still cost us much (as a family.)"

It may well be that you, the reader, may be wondering why I have spent so much time sharing about this particular vision to reach lost souls.

I can understand that reaction. I believe it's possibly because you could be part of the answer to the fulfillment of it.

Why don't you stop and enquire of the Lord if that is so. I know I've been meant to share it all, for God's glory alone.

Enjoyable And Fulfilling

Before and after the 1981 era Jim drove me down to the Trinity Broadcasting Network (T.B.N.) studios in Anaheim, California on numerous occasions.

I would bring the Holy Spirit directed messages from God's Word on the "Praise The Lord" programs regularly. Christians and non-believers lives were irrevocably changed by these truths.

This led to being interviewed on almost every Christian T.V. Broadcasting Station around the nation. I was also interviewed a number of times on the "100 Huntley St" T.V. program in Toronto, Canada. And I was interviewed on the Winnipeg Christian T.V. programs as I did series of teachings.

In both places I had excellent T.V. hosts, whom I enjoyed. God had opened these doors of ministry so I could teach about God's character and ways.

I always felt very fulfilled. All glory to Jesus.

Harpenden, England

In obedience to Gods clear direction I am now going to divert from some of the previous ways of referring to teaching assignments, by sharing the highlights of how God moved both before and during the course of a week's ministry overseas.

In 1981, at the directions from God's Word, we had accepted an invitation given to us by Trent, Tre and Tori Sheppard and Mark and Krista Harris, who were on Y.W.A.M. staff at Harpenden, England, near London.

They were leading a radical discipleship course for young people for six weeks during the summer. It was called "PREPARE". They wanted me to teach for a week.

In July, two weeks before we were due to leave, the pain levels in my lower back, plus acute insomnia, were so severe, that we inquired of the Lord if there were any changes in His directions regarding this overseas assignment.

My diary records confirming Scriptures given to both of us that we were to go.

One week later, the intensity of my physical suffering was to a degree that I wrote in my diary, *"In the natural way of thinking, it seems insane to go on this ministry trip to England."*

During the waking night hours we both sought God again. The Holy Spirit spoke to me, "Isaiah 46:10-11" and then I opened my Bible to Psalm 118. Jim was directed to Isaiah 43. The witness in both of our spirits was to proceed…. regardless of the status quo! So that settled it.

On July 25th Trent phoned and reported on a remarkable time of intercession they had for me! I need to report here that a few of them on the leadership team had cashed in their airline mileage points that they'd been saving, so that they could pay for us to fly first class both ways, because of my physical condition. That melted me to the floor boards, and still does, as I record it for this publication.

The next day, our son in law, J.B., along with our 17 year old granddaughter Jenny, took us to the LA airport. While there, I suddenly had a burst of revelation. I asked Jenny if she would seek

God about coming to England with us, getting the first available flight out. We would cover all expenses for her to come and remain for the final three weeks of the event. God speedily confirmed to Jenny and her dad that this was from the Lord. In three days she was right there with us. My granddaughter didn't mess around! God was obviously up to something. From the time I arrived in England, it was obvious that God's tests were passed, by His grace alone! I was so much better physically!

My first message to these hungry-for-the-truth young people, was part one of "What it means to live for the glory of God." This is a weighty subject and I wanted them to understand it with clarity.

I threw it open for their meaningful questions during the teaching, and then gave them the Biblical answers. God's presence was very evident. All glory to Jesus alone!

The next day I completed teaching this vital subject, while the students absorbed the contents into their spiritual blood streams. Then they wrote down their answers to the penetrating questions I had given them.

I taught the next morning on "The character of God in relation to being single or married." The room was predominantly full of single young people of both sexes.

I made it clear that many of God's children will be directed by God to have a life partner of the opposite sex. But there will also be those whom God will call to remain single, for the purposes of extending His Kingdom in significant ways that only a single person can.

Only total surrender to God and then obedience to His revealed will, will bring the ultimate fulfillment to every child of God. Period!

All through the comprehensive teaching that followed I majored on God's absolute justice and faithfulness, with significant illustrations from some of those whose lives had proved the truths I was sharing.

One of the points I emphasized, was that all women have the opportunity of either being a stepping stone to provoke men to holiness of life, or they are a stumbling block, provoking men to unholiness in many ways.

At the close of the message there was an immediate response to my invitation to do whatever they sensed the Holy Spirit was directing them to do.

Some of the girls went immediately to some of the guys and privately asked their forgiveness for not being provokers to them of holiness at different times, and told them they had repented of this sin.

Most of the guys humbled themselves openly in a very revealing way. They confessed and repented of the sin of how they related to girls generally.

They apologized for the selfishness of dating a girl,_**frequently**, because of loneliness, or boredom, or just to have fun with, without any sexual connotations, BUT NO SERIOUS THOUGHTS about their future together.

They now understood for the first time how hard emotionally and mentally this was on the girl, specially if she had serious thoughts about him.

The Holy Spirit revealed to them that casual dating outside the revealed will of God, having earnestly sought Him, was OUT!

They shared that they'd been using the girls as a personal convenience, and conviction of this sin was deep, as was their repentance.

The next message I gave was titled, "Our Greatest Need". It was all related to having a revelation of the sin of pride in our hearts. The application time was spent checking the points on the papers I handed out.

On the left side was a list of many characteristics of humility. Opposite them, was the corresponding list of how pride operates.

The leadership team then called everyone to an extended time of silence, as they invited the Holy Spirit to speak to them individually.

His presence was riveting…doing a deep work.

Later, the leaders spent hours together in humbling themselves before God and each other, until 3 a.m. The next morning they continued seeking God, with such diligence and desperation for a revelation of their hearts, that in prayer Mark actually broke his hand while he was pounding it on a hard surface, and had to have it in a plaster cast!!

These leaders spent the whole of the next morning together as God continued to answer their fervent cries…And they've never been the same!

When the students saw that there was no leadership that morning, some of them lay on the floor seeking God's face, desperately praying for His glory to be revealed. Some remained in their chairs; until one girl went to the microphone and said, "Everyone should be lying on the floor seeking God," ….and so they all did.

After that, one by one they called out the names of different nations. Then they all cried out to God for an outpouring of His Spirit to come to each one and for the lost to be saved. God powerfully met with all of them!

At a later time, the students shared with everyone what had taken place that memorable morning.

One morning I taught indirectly by opening up the session to let the students ask me anything related to difficult circumstances they go through, and or things related to God's character that they don't understand.

The students freely responded and I enjoyed sharing God's wisdom.

The next day I taught extensively on what it means from a Biblical perspective to be "Walking in the light of the Lord".

Then I opened it up for anyone to share what the Holy Spirit was speaking to them. One by one, most of them came forward with deep and meaningful confessions.

Then one girl started to weep under conviction of the sin of pride. She then fell to the floor sobbing, then wailing and screaming, "I'm so sorry God."

This triggered off others crying out desperately for a revelation of their hearts as only God knows them; according to 2 Chronicles 6:30. God answered and screams came forth from them that can only come in a cloud burst of genuine revival.

They were lying on their faces on the floor uncontrollably sobbing their hearts out, like I'd never seen before.

It was a sustained, deep awesome move of the Holy Spirit, of which my granddaughter, Jenny, was totally involved. She later told me that she not only saw her own sinful heart as God sees it, but had seen that all sin, as God sees it and hates it, **breaks His heart**. She said she had a totally life changing experience and was so grateful that we had made it possible for her to come.

We couldn't have felt more fulfilled.

Jenny went into missionary training in Y.W.A.M. and has been powerfully used of God in unique ways to extend His Kingdom…and continues to be! It delighted my heart to recently hear her give an anointed message at a Sunday morning church service in Los Angeles. She is a multi-tasked staff person, and the children's pastor at her home church in Tauranga, New Zealand. Jenny is also a very good wife, and mother of 3 school age boys.

I am convinced that one of the reasons God moved so powerfully at that time among some of the students, was because the leaders of the group were prepared to get desperate before God for life changing encounters with Him first.

Please ponder this before the Lord!

Great Contrasts

On one of the many times I sought the Lord as to which diary I was to write from for this book, He clearly stated, "August 1982." I had no idea what that contained. What now follows is in obedience to that mandate.

The preparations and pressures related to going on a four week ministry trip into Asia with Y.W.A.M. in July of 1982, were particularly challenging.

Jim and I had experienced unusual and lengthy harassment related to working with a travel agency during the past month over the intricacies involved with this itinerary. At the same time we were working on my itinerary and airline schedules for my trip to South Africa, which was to follow. All the ministry preparations needed were an inevitably intensive priority. We were maxed out.

I asked the Lord to give me something personal from His Word related specifically to the ramifications of this mission's trip. He answered me by opening my Bible at

Hosea 14:8 "It is I who answer and look after you. I am like an evergreen Cyprus; from Me comes your fruit."

I thanked Him for such a meaningful, precious word of encouragement.

The pressures continued as I needed to prepare and pack for the inevitable unusual and unexpected circumstances that would emerge on this kind of trip. I was also working at my office desk right up to the last minute before leaving for the airport and then still sorting out work all the way there. Jim and I were operating like zombies with exhaustion, when we checked in at Pan America's Clipper Club room. That's when I received an important phone call from a senior leader in Y.W.A.M. reporting on a crisis occurring in another part of the world and asking me to seek the Lord for an answer, along with Loren Cunningham!!

Then, when upon enquiry I was told that all the seats with room to stretch out your legs were taken, God sure had mercy on me! He moved upon a kind and understanding flight attendant, after I told him I was a frequent flyer on Pam Am....and he allocated me to the first seat, on my own in FIRST CLASS.

Only God knew how depleted I was and how I badly needed the quiet, plus the comfort of being able to get my head down and my feet up. I was so thankful to my magnificent Master.

At the end of the flight, I had to take another plane into Sapporo, Japan. Then I was taken on a **long** car ride, where I waited the **longest** time outside a church for our Y.W.A.M. director to carry out his responsibilities there, before driving me on to my destination. It was to crash on a mattress on the floor in a small and bare room of a Japanese home, **totally exhausted**.

The next morning I spoke to a church that was held in that home, on "What it means to be filled with the Holy Spirit." This was followed by my ministering to each one individually as they all responded to the Holy Spirit's invitation. His presence was very evident. All glory to Jesus.

Over lunch that day with three of our Y.W.A.M. leaders, I shared the need for them to have humor with our Y.W.A.M. staff, as a means of unity, healing, and pleasure. In Proverbs 17:22 the Bible says, "Laughter does good like medicine."

I illustrated this truth by sharing that when my son-in-law J.B. and my daughter Jill were Y.W.A.M. missionaries in Thailand for four years, they and their team discovered a unique way of carrying it out.

Many evenings were spent standing together in front of the oven door in the kitchen of the place where they were housed. They would then pretend it was a television screen, and start making up hilarious skits, which they would all act out, while **roaring** with laughter.

To this day, that fabulous memory is re-called to the delight of anyone who hears it.... particularly to me! I think the therapy to those missionaries who had no access to T.V., were **far** greater than if they had had it.

The next day, in the convenience of a hotel room, I spent quality time working on a new message under the Holy Spirit's direction. It was titled, "I am the light of the world." After earnest prayer, I then went and delivered the message in an outdoor amphitheater.... not to as many non Christians as I had hoped, but to mostly Japanese church people. I believed God used it for His eternal purposes, as He alone knows the hearts of everyone.

Lastly, I spent quality time with my special, godly cousin Richard Goodall and his lovely wife Connie (both originally from New Zealand.) They had been pioneering missionaries to Japan for many years, along with their four children, a wonderful family! This was a special treat for me.

The next day I travelled by bus and then by plane to the city of Nagoya with my very dear friend Kalafi Moala, the Y.W.A.M. director for Japan, at that time. We had quality time in prayer concerning needs in Y.W.A.M. Japan that needed adjusting, which Kalafi then took care of.

I went by Taxi to a big department store, where I landed up in the large shoe department witnessing to the manager about Christianity. He spoke perfect English and was receptive; and then very helpful in getting me a quality pair of shoes at a discount price. I thanked him and promised to pray for him in return.

After three days of being in very intensive Y.W.A.M. business related to Japan, I was ready for a change of ministry....so at the release of the Holy Spirit I took off to the same large department store and the same shoe department.

This time I found my new friend the manager was on a 15 minute coffee break; so I directly asked if I could further explain to him about Christianity. He readily agreed that it could be tomorrow, and that we would have lunch together. I had already explained that I was an international Bible teacher, doing missionary work in Japan.

The next day was a Sunday and I spoke in a Japanese pastor's church at the 9:30 a.m. service which was for English speaking people. I spoke from Ephesians 5:18 with emphasis on **obedience**, illustrated by stories out of my life. God moved by His Spirit. All glory to God!

After packing up in preparation for leaving on two train rides to Osaka later that day, I kept my lunch appointment, as arranged.

God's Spirit was very evident as I shared with great freedom the full implications of the gospel message. I left this fine, intelligent man with a Japanese New Testament and three gospel tracts in Japanese. Of course I had him on one of my prayer lists for many years. I expect to see him in Heaven.

Interspersed with the days I spent with key Y.W.A.M. leaders, as we sought God over many crucial Kingdom matters, there were times I ministered to the leaders one on one. These many hours behind the scenes were an intrinsic part of why God had us together at this time.

I received a very welcome letter from my beloved Jim, and wrote two long letters back to him.

After receiving by phone my proposed itinerary for the rest of my time in Japan, I sought God diligently about each event. Some He affirmed and others He didn't. He also added a new one and gave me the exact message for it, "The Holy Spirit is my ultimate Adviser."

The next day was spent driving and arriving in steaming hot temperatures at a campsite in the mountains, where I would speak for two days to a youth group from a local Japanese church. The pastor, his wife, and their staff were present, along with an Australian singing group (Christian rock style). Two Australian girls were also there. One of them had a prophetic word spoken over her that she would hear teaching on this trip that would change her life.

It was a challenging assignment. The Japanese girl interpreter had limited understanding of English, which made each teaching session considerably harder and much longer.

My first message spoken in intense humidity on "Healing through forgiveness" was used of God to bring a number of people to face the truth about their bitterness to people who had hurt them and repent of it before the Lord and then release His forgiveness. I then prayed for the healing of those hurts in everyone.

The next morning I called everyone to serious prayer. After asking several of them to state what they wanted God to do that day, I emphasized that God only moves in response to faith filled prayers.

I then taught on "How to hear God's voice." Under those conditions, that session took 2 hours.

In the closing session, I taught the older age group "Reasons why God delays answers, and what it means to wait for God to answer."

All the sessions were taped. I was wiped out after each session, but it was worthwhile for the extension of God's Kingdom.

The next day I was involved for hours in more intense ministry involvement with Y.W.A.M. I also spoke at an Army base, and later in a city park, where I spoke on "Jesus came to show us the truth." I delighted in these two vital ministry opportunities. This terminated my time in Japan.

In extreme heat and humidity I then went on to take a plane to Fukuoka and another plane to Seoul, Korea. To my great delight, I was met at the airport by my precious daughter Jillian and dearly loved J.B. They had come from Thailand to attend the Y.W.A.M. Leadership Seminar, being held in Seoul, which was open to all spiritual leaders.

At God's directions they were en route to America, terminating their four years in Thailand. They were expecting their first child after waiting for seven years.

We went straight to the spacious Chosen Hotel for the night, and ended up in the Lotte Hotel for dinner. We then moved to their lounge and had very interesting times of sharing, interspersed with lots of laughter.

In the background a fabulous orchestra was playing, with the sight and sound of two large waterfalls that came from a nearby wall.

This was a special treat God turned on for the three of us, for which we were very grateful.

The next afternoon we were moved on to the World Missions Center Hotel next to Pastor Yongi Cho's enormous church.

This time I was speaking daily at a Y.W.A.M. Leadership Seminar, interspersed with a lot of time spent over important Y.W.A.M. matters. This Conference was also open to all spiritual leaders and they came from different denominations.

I spoke the next morning on "Jesus the leader in ministry." It's a challenging, powerful message.

In the midst of all this, the Holy Spirit released the birthing of what would become a powerful series of messages on "Idolatry in the life of a Believer." My first message was "Idolatry mixed with righteous leadership," illustrated by men of God in the Bible.

God wants to purify our motives by revealing any subtle forms of idolatry. To consciously or unconsciously deflect any glory away from God is to be participating in some form of idolatry. It's what we're impressed with, that we'll exalt and give primary emphasis to.

At the end of the message, the Holy Spirit directed me to ask the leaders who had been convicted by the Holy Spirit to come forward to the microphone and acknowledge idolatry in their leadership.

They came from the Baptists, the Presbyterians, youth leaders from Yongi Cho's huge church, Y.W.A.M. D.T.S. leadership, plus a University lecturer and Bible teacher. To help make their repentance real, I instructed them to make movements with their hands that symbolized "grinding the idols to dust."

I then encouraged everyone to give God all the praise and worship for what He had just done. This eventuated in people taking off dancing with joy all over the building. Hallelujah.

I concluded that week's teaching on two of my favorite themes. Message one is "What we owe to God for what we are today," and message two, is "What we owe to others for what we are today."

At the close of these messages, it was evident that significant new revelation had been released to the audiences. They responded with weeping as they repented before the Lord, and then outbursts of joy as they received God's forgiveness. This was followed by lying prostrate before the Lord seeking Him for further revelation on what is meant by "The transcendent power belongs to God" as it relates to human vessels.

What an awesome day that was!

The whole of the final week was spent in another location, in the center of the city of Seoul, with a complete change of ministry responsibilities.

It included having quality time with my good friend Mr. Choi, who was the owner of an impressive, **enormous** 63 story building in the process of being completed in the city.

We were praying that the government would grant him permission to own his own Television stations, to be placed on the four top floors. God confirmed to me that this was right from Nehemiah 1. It definitely came to pass; as I would see on a later ministry trip to Korea.

I continued on teaching to spiritual leaders. One of the messages was "Satan's challenge to The Church related to the unreached nations of the World." That always stirs up some dust in the heavenly realms. This time was no exception.

This was interspersed with a number of vital social encounters with very key spiritual leaders in the city. Some had powerful international ministries.

Behind the scenes I was involved with counseling at length very needy people high up in the social scene. It took its tolle on my strength. Thank God they came to freedom! I was then able to call on "God who is my strength" for replenishment.

Finally it came time to board my long flight back home. I had to go to Seattle first, and my wonderful Father God, did it again! I was given a superb front seat in the upstairs lounge, with only 2 others in it. Only He knew how much I needed it. Then I got a flight out of Seattle that went to Burbank, California to "Home Sweet Home."

The very next day Jim and I went down to the San Pedro seaport, in South Los Angeles for the welcoming ceremony of Y.W.A.M.'s large ship, the Anastasis. It was coming in from Greece where it had been docked for a considerable time, due to lack of finances.

Loren announced that Don Stephens was now the director of this ministry as he welcomed him and the crew. My part was to pray the prayer of dedication over them. The Holy Spirit had directed me to: Zechariah 14:20 "And on that day there shall be inscribed on the bells of the horses, "Holy to the Lord." And 2 Kings 17:28 "So one of the priests whom they had carried away from Samaria came and dwelt in Bethel, and taught them how they should fear the Lord." I interceded for the fear of the Lord and holiness to be the basis for everything that is done through this ship's ministries to the nations.

I taught on the Anastasis for varied reasons many times. Sometime later, Don and Deyon Stephens felt directed by the Lord to leave Y.W.A.M. and concentrate making the Anastasis predominately a training center and a mercy ministry center. This included having a fully equipped hospital with highly trained doctors and nurses in residence.

Years later they purchased another big liner named The African Mercy.

Whenever these mercy ships arrive in a port, the needy people come standing in long lines, in the hopes of having their medical needs met free of charge. Babies with cleft palates are a specialty need that is met on a regular basis, through surgery. We praise God that His love is demonstrated so openly and freely to so many desperately needy people.

Now to report on Y.W.A.M.'s ship equipped ministry network. To date there are 26 ships of varying sizes being used in Evangelism, Training, and Mercy Ministries for the extension of God's Kingdom internationally.

These include large relocatable hospitals where local people are trained in the medical arts as they serve their fellow citizens' medical needs.

In some countries, such as Papua New Guinea, the Y.W.A.M. volunteers are helping to build out the national health service in collaboration with the National and provincial governments. Y.W.A.M.'s University of the Nations collaborates in a similar way through helping build National education systems.

Some Wild Fun!!

My most exhilarating, hilarious, fun adventure was on a Saturday in between Bible teaching assignments in Northern California.

A 19 year old guy who had been listening to me teach, asked me if I'd like to go up with him in a hot air balloon that he owned.

Would I ever! --- and how soon? Again I explained I had no fear.

We went out into an open field and took off. He explained the basics as he went into action: Keep pumping on a cord to keep us up in the air and floating around. Maneuver another cord when we wanted to go down. Simple. After a while that got relatively boring; so after asking my new friend if I could take over, he said, "Sure."

As we floated towards dangerous objects like telephone poles and tall trees, I would get close enough for it to be exciting and then quickly drop to the ground. Sometimes we would land in someone's back yard, sometimes in a field.

Quickly I would pump us up to float again, only to repeat the scenario. My 19 year old buddy was totally relaxed!

Then we saw a police car, and two other official vehicles below, and heard an officer calling out loudly, "Do you need help? What's going on?" I cheerfully yelled back, "We're perfectly OK, thank you!"

I saw the humor in all this and continued having fun, but then decided not to give "the powers that be" any more undue concerns and time. To me the whole thing was just another adventure, which I loved, and thanked my Creator for! ☺

At the same time I would highly recommend that no one else follow such a potentially dangerous pursuit the way I did. I think my two guardian angels were on special alert that day. Seriously.

Bondage Breaking

In my diaries I have recorded significant things the Holy Spirit was revealing to me where I needed to change, in order to match the standard of the Word of God.

• A milestone occurred the day I realized I didn't have to prove that I was right, whenever Jim and I had a disagreement over small things. What a relief that was!! So much easier to say, "Let's drop that one" and move on cheerfully as a way of life.

• Another thing that needed to go was my need to stop at every garage sale and check it out. It had become a real bondage. When I acknowledged this and deeply repented, I was completely set free. Hallelujah!

• In 1984 Jim and I faced the facts that we were both addicted to drinking coffee and tea. To me there was only one way to be free from that bondage. Quit drinking them! So I did it completely, in one day. And I've only had non caffeine tea since.

Jim did the same and found that a stomach problem he had, cleared up immediately.

Ministry Trips To China

When I arrived for the first time in a nation in which I had invested a significant amount of time over the years in intercession, it was always extra special to me.

This was how I felt when Jim and I arrived in the city of Beijing, China in June 1984. Our trip was planned around meeting with Believers in the Underground Church.

While checking out the International Friendship Store in the first afternoon, we met up with a Chinese lady and her son who spoke fluent English. He was a student from the University of California, Los Angeles.

They were returning to the same hotel as us, and invited us to go in their taxi with them. That gave us the opportunity of having a meaningful time of witnessing with the young man about the Lord, which was so fulfilling.

In circumstances like that, God shows us that we must never underestimate the plans and purposes of the Holy Spirit to answer our prayers for lost souls in the most extraordinary ways and places. He was from Los Angeles and so were we; but it took for the both of us to be in Beijing, China at the same place and time for him to have exposure to the gospel. I sensed someone's prayers for him were being answered.

That evening we went to an obscure little place where we had the joy of meeting up with five dear Chinese women Believers. They taped the message, as I spoke on "The Greatness of God," as it relates to interceding for the nations of the world. What a privilege!

The next day we took a taxi to the Internationally famous GREAT WALL OF CHINA. We were struck with the incredible feat of human endurance and costly achievement by the vast numbers of Chinese lives that were sacrificed to build it.

The steps up to the highest point are **very** high and **very** steep. Not many make it to the top. To my delight the Lord enabled me to do so. To the amusement of the Chinese, I found it easier to walk down backwards – slowly. Jim almost made it to the top, which was great.

On the long way up, we sang many praise songs to the Lord, interspersed with strong prayers for revival to come to the church in China and for a great spiritual awakening to come to the lost. We also prayed for the conversion of our Chinese taxi driver, to whom we had witnessed.

The following day we flew to the city of Shanghai.

By arrangement we were escorted from our hotel around all sorts of back alleys until we arrived at the humble apartment of a former medical doctor, now consigned to some menial job under Communism.

He and his wife graciously gave us a lavish Chinese meal. I wept when he told us he spent 23 years in prison for his faith in Christ; and then he shared some of his experiences.

At one time he was so hungry that he rationed out and shared his leather belt to eat with other prisoners. After that, he existed solely on some very poor flour and grass!!

I then shared the vision God had given me for China and the way it had been discharged in fervent intercession over many years, which greatly encouraged him. This precious man of God then asked us to return the next day, which we did.

This time we had another beautiful meal followed by an extended time of powerful intercession together for China.

A former pastor then came who could also speak English. I wept again as he shared he had been in prison for 5 years because of his faith in Christ, followed by 20 years of hard labor. Now he couldn't get a job at all. The price these men have paid to follow Jesus is beyond our comprehension.

Praying for a mighty move of the Holy Spirit to keep moving across China, and praying for God's grace, wisdom, courage, and strength to be upon His people, in their times of great trial, should be a regular part of our lives.

I also recorded in my diary that to be able to urinate we had to go to a small bedroom outside and use a potty (or chamber), then empty the contents into a drain outside. We washed our hands from an outside tap, where the potty was rinsed out. There were no carpets on the floors, and we used toilet paper to clean our hands. It sat on the dining table.

My reaction to all this was great compassion and admiration that their faith was so strong, and gratitude for the enormous privilege God had given us to be with these tried and proven mighty saints of God. We then prayed for healing for the Doctor's wife who had a broken leg.

The next morning to our delight, the Holy Spirit directed us to bless our hosts financially; and Jim was able to help the doctor and his daughter with the ramifications of obtaining a visa for America for her.

On our last day in Shanghai after having our usual time in the Word of God and intercession, we took some time to see around the city in a taxi. We came across a giant-sized Russian woman basketball player – approximately 7 feet tall, who looked like a man! We marveled at this phenomenon. There's a surprise per minute on this journey with Jesus!

I was praying fervently for God to lead me to someone to whom I could share the gospel. The answer came in the evening.

We were having dinner on the 23rd floor of the Shanghai hotel. At our next table an interesting looking man was sitting alone, so we asked him to join us. We learned he was a Chinese businessman from Hong Kong. Conversation flowed easily as he shared his story with us. After learning that we belonged to an International Missionary Organization, it wasn't long before we were able to ease into a meaningful time of sharing with him what the Lord Jesus meant to us personally.

He had a Roman Catholic background from childhood and was very receptive, as we shared the claims of the gospel with this delightful man. I was able to leave him with a copy of my brochure "What it means to commit your life to the Lord Jesus Christ." Later that evening we interceded in faith for his soul to be saved. I expect to see him in heaven.

The next day we were 2 hours in the Shanghai airport in high humidity before boarding our flight to Tokyo. As I stepped on the aircraft, knowing we were on the first half of our long journey home, I said a hearty "Hallelujah" to the air hostess.

Later we found, to our delight, Daddy God surprised us with upgraded seats in our continued long journey of 9 hours from Tokyo to Los Angeles. We were assigned to front row seats in the exclusive upstairs section of Clipper Class on Pan Am Airlines. Hallelujah!

Friday August 10th 1984

The 1984 Los Angeles Olympic Games proved to be a pivotal time for a significant advancement of God's Kingdom.

I was heavily involved in teaching at the numbers of training sessions related to the Olympic outreaches. They were packed out at The Church On The Way, where I spoke on "The place of prayer, before evangelism, during evangelism, and after evangelism." The same thing occurred when I spoke on "How to have a burdened heart for lost souls" at Melodyland Christian Center in Anaheim.

Another 1,000 Y.W.A.M.ers showed up at the Bethany Baptist Church in Long Beach, where my subject was, "Making the Lord

Jesus Christ the center of this outreach." My diary records.... "This is the most wonderful message on Evangelism and witnessing I've ever been given."

Finally I spoke at Angeles Temple, in downtown Los Angeles, on what is involved when Jesus said, "Follow Me," followed by "Making the Lord Jesus the center of this outreach."

The Holy Spirit's presence and power were evident throughout, in response to much preparation, prayer, and the peoples hunger for truth.

At the start of the Olympics, Jim and I drove down to the Coliseum to witness to people outside the entrance. There were 96,000 inside. Every inch of parking had been taken, with $20 and $10 signs up to prove it!

We drove right to the nearest street of the Coliseum, thanking God in faith for a parking place. Right then a guy came running towards us. Upon recognizing me, he said that he lived in this street, and that we could share his parking place, by putting his car in behind us for $5. It was a cul-de-sac street!

We took it, and in less than two minutes' walk were outside the walls giving out the Olympic Christian paper and New Testaments to people from different nations who gladly received them! Hallelujah.

The atmosphere leading up to, and during the Olympic Games, was charged with expectancy of the best kind. Little wonder!! It had become the focus of so much faith filled intercession for God to move in unprecedented ways, from people near and far.

Just one example is that Jim and I had the privilege of attending a vital monthly morning prayer meeting held in downtown Los Angeles related to the coming Olympic Games Outreaches, attended by mainly pastors, and spiritual leaders. The unity was very strong, causing God to "command the blessing" as He promised in Psalm 133:3. Our son John was the leader. He has written a remarkable best seller, titled, "Taking Our Cities for God"* in which he amplifies the events surrounding the Olympics.

It was the last day of Y.W.A.M.'s outreach teams who had been witnessing daily at the 1984 Olympic Games in Los Angeles.

Loren Cunningham had called them all to congregate at the Hansen Dam, a large city park in Los Angeles. They would be reporting on what God had done, so that He would be glorified.

A young married couple from the Los Angeles area, with reputable characters, who were known to have given 100% accurate prophetic warnings about coming disasters, which then took place in different parts of the world, had announced that God had revealed to them

that on Friday, August 10th, 1984, at 4 p.m. there would be a sizeable natural disaster in Southern California.

John Dawson was the South West leader of Y.W.A.M. U.S.A., which included the Los Angeles area, and he knew the couple, along with others of us, who took the warning very seriously.

John had shared his heavy burden in much intercession for the City of Los Angeles with Loren. They agreed to turn the gathering of 3,200 Y.W.A.M.ers who had come from many nations, into a serious prayer meeting.

After Loren had shared a brief message from God's Word, he invited me to lead the large group into intercession related to the intense situation we faced that day.

** John Dawson "TAKING OUR CITIES FOR GOD" How To Break Spiritual Strongholds. ©1989 Creation House.*

I will quote from my diary.

"I lead out the intercession time for Southern California by first sharing the impending crisis of the hour that we faced. I then explained that the Holy Spirit had shown me that the far bigger thing on God's heart at this hour was to pray **in full faith** for genuine revival among God's people, and a spiritual awakening among the lost, to come to Southern California regardless of the cost. And that this was a privilege and an opportunity given us by God! I totally believed it. I told God if part of the price was being convicted of sin and repenting and making restitution then bring it on!

I prayed desperate prayers of intense longing, mixed with full faith, that the unleashing of the Holy Spirit would be unprecedented, and that shock waves from it would affect every nation."

While the timing for this was unknown to me, I declared my belief that God had told me this will happen in His time and that somehow this Olympic Outreach is part of that vision.

I went on to say that our role in intercession today was similar to Queen Esther's in the book of Esther chapter 4. She was desperate and a lot of people were at stake.

I then shared that first thing this morning God had given me Joel 1:13,14 for this day, "Gird on sackcloth and lament, O priests, wail, O ministers of the altar. Go in, pass the night in sackcloth, O ministers of my God! Because cereal offering and drink offering are withheld from the house of your God. Sanctify a fast, call a solemn assembly. Gather the elders and all the inhabitants of the land to the house of the Lord your God; and cry to the LORD."

I asked the prayer groups to pray through Daniel, Chapter 9, identifying with Daniel's humility, and desperate prayers for God's mercy and forgiveness along with repenting, wherever the Holy Spirit brought personal conviction.

This went on all over the groups, with a great hush and sense of solemnity.

John and I had an intense and effective mighty time of intercession together, with weeping, and crying out to God for genuine revival and spiritual awakening for Southern California. We prayed in full faith.

Among those to whom we were able to witness at this time, Jim and I had the opportunity of spending a significant amount of time with three younger men who were obviously from the Middle East.

They wanted to share their religious beliefs, and did so freely. They also wanted to hear ours....and listened respectfully.

I noticed that they were more interested in interacting with Jim than with me; so I went with the flow and played a supportive roll to him.... who had "right on" answers of truth, every time they had a question.

While they didn't surrender their lives to Christ at that time, we left them with a whole lot to think about. I was confident that the genuine love of God that they experienced that day, as we peacefully shared about our deep love for the Lord Jesus Christ, as the Son of God, would never leave them.

Witnessing teams reported that more than a thousand people each day were giving their lives to Christ during the games Outreaches!

The effect on the city of Los Angeles from the buildup of genuine, powerful spiritual activity in 1983 and 1984 surrounding the Olympic Games Outreach was profound.

For an example, a coroner reported that normally the morgue received 78 bodies per day, but during the two weeks of the Olympic Games there were **no murders**. Truly amazing!

On the final day of the Olympics' outreach, John became ill from total exhaustion. He had coughed up blood and had pain in his chest, so his wife Julie, took him to a Doctor. John was so weak he passed out in the Doctor's office. The Doctor said that he had severe bronchitis and was bordering on pneumonia.

When he got home and was lying down, John saw the Lord in a vision standing over him; and He said, "I have My champions." Then He put a gold medal around John's neck.

Can you imagine what comfort and encouragement that brought?

Diverse Ministry Assignments

On September 29th, 1984, I packed for three weeks away ministering in Norfolk, West Virginia; New Orleans; and then Holland.... with big differences in temperatures.

In West Virginia I spoke to the women of the Christian Broadcasting Network, known as C.B.N. The following day I addressed the 9:30 a.m. chapel service which included a large audience, comprising the faculty, the staff, and many students.

The subject the Holy Spirit directed me to speak on was, "Inconsistency, phoneyism, and hypocrisy." God granted me real authority; and the majority stood in response to the appeal I made. They indicated that they were determining to repent and make the needed changes in their lives. All glory to God.

This was a **very influential** group.

I need to make it very clear that <u>every</u> time I have given this penetrating message, there is always considerable conviction.... regardless of the people group.

In New Orleans, Jim and I had quality time with the National Prayer Committee. Following that, I spoke at a "Concert of Prayer" event on "How to pray for the Body of Christ in every nation." I then put the people in pairs, and asked them to seek God to direct them to two nations they'd never prayed for before; and then pray for those Believers, as I'd directed them from the Bible. People were also praying in thirty minute segments throughout the day.

David Bryant headed up the "Concerts of Prayer" movement and was on the N.P.C., with us. He was also a very dear and close friend of both Jim's and mine.... and still is!

The next day I spoke at the Victory Assembly on "The ways of God in testing," followed by more serious intercession. I also confessed to God my lack of a burden for the lost souls of New Orleans, and asked Him to give that to me before I left this city.

As soon as I came out of the hotel the next day, and was stepping into my friend Fred Market's car, en route to the airport, I saw an emaciated tall man staggering past our hotel. He was drunk and looked like walking death.

I knew immediately God was answering my prayer to give me a burden for the lost souls in this city. I asked Fred to drive me past the man so I could communicate with him. When I called out to him that Jesus loved him, he came over to the side of the car.

He was the second worst human being I had ever seen riddled with the evidences of sin, and the inevitable consequences of despair.... matched only by the man at Kings Cross Sydney, for whom I had prayed desperately at an earlier time.

Repeatedly I told this man Jesus could forgive him, cleanse away his sin, deliver him, and heal him. I urged the man to turn to God and ask for His help. I finally asked him if he had ever asked Jesus to come and live within his heart? That's when he opened up.

He said, "I've been all the way lady....16 times!" Then he said that his nephew was killed. That was it.

I then asked him if he needed money for a meal? And he said, "No, I've got money." I said, "I'm going to pray fervently for you;" and then I asked him his name. He mumbled incoherently, "Everett.... something."

I was reminded by Jim or Fred that we needed to leave for the airport, so we drove off. That's when I cried out to God for his lost soul and wept and fervently asked God to keep on pursuing Him and have mercy on him and answer his mother's prayers. I told God I believed His shed blood, His mercy, and the power of the Holy Spirit and His grace were all greater than the power of sin and Satan that bound him. I stood against the enemy and went into warfare, binding the powers of darkness and loosing the man from the grip of the enemy. I finally praised God for the man's salvation. Jim and Fred interceded with me. Fred asked God to bring the Y.W.A.M.ers in touch with him again.

We flew on to Amsterdam, Holland and arrived there at 7:15 a.m. the next day. We were immediately taken on a 2 ½ hour drive out to a Conference Center, where Y.W.A.M. was having a leaders conference.

Loren was scheduled to speak first. As soon as the meeting started God burdened my heart to intercede fervently for him. I was then directed to pray, that through the oncoming of the Holy Spirit, history would be made today in Loren's teaching ministry and that he would be given a fresh impartation of the wisdom of God

Loren then gave a powerfully anointed **new** message on "How to discern and then deal with false prophets and cults." It was enlightening. He said that if we would receive and live this message as a Mission, it would help to outsmart the enemy who is attacking us.

Also, that as we as a group would do spiritual warfare together against the powers of darkness, history would be made in this conference and in our mission. Everyone co-operated.

On the morning of the last day, Floyd McClung had us all intercede for Africa. Following that, he had every white leader wash the feet of an African, publicly. Then he had the same process reversed. A deep move of God's Spirit followed these sincere acts of humility and love.

At the final meeting that night, I spoke on "Are you prepared for revival?" Again Floyd led the people in responding; which manifest in a lot of genuine repentance with weeping before the Lord. All glory to God.

Back in the Amsterdam vicinity, I had four free days off, before speaking at the next conference. Interspersed with our regular vital times in the Word of God, and interceding for needy people; we spent considerable time seeking God related to the many ramifications of being in South Africa again the next year for ministry.

In line with God's character as our Master and Lord, it's important to share that He delights to give us treats along the journey. On two of the number of occasions when Jim and I were together in Amsterdam Holland, related to ministry with Y.W.A.M., we had some of our best treats.

In the afternoons, between my teaching assignments, Y.W.A.M. staff would loan us their bikes and jackets and we'd take off biking around the uniquely quaint little villages. The air was clean, the countryside scenery was superb, and the weather matched it.

We would go around a corner and discover an elderly couple sitting on the porch of their little home, right up against ones that were similar. They were fully decked out in their Dutch attire, hats and all. We would then exchange warm greetings with them.

The biking was delightful enough, but I also loved poking around the numbers of little shops and finding unique useful things. For example, I found white lace curtains that were exactly the style and size I needed for a floor to ceiling window in my home. And then, the cutest and prettiest cups and saucers ever, were just waiting to be bought.

After that, we would go to a little restaurant and have a Swiss fondue meal. As we slowly wended our bike ride back, we would be anticipating how soon we could repeat the treat. I realize none of this may appeal to some of you, but it was exactly what I needed!

My experiences in Amsterdam, Holland were in great contrast to each other, although both in God's perfect plan, and therefore equally fulfilling.

In October of 1984 I was teaching in Amsterdam at Y.W.A.M.'s leadership training schools, mornings and evenings, a week at a time. In the afternoons I was out where the people were.

Floyd McClung was the director of Y.W.A.M. Holland during that time and a very dear friend… and still is! One day we went on a prayer walk together, right into the heart of the "red light" district. The young women prostitutes were blatantly on display; sitting behind the fronts of their "shop's" glass windows!

I cringed then, and I do so again as I write this. But Jesus cared about their lost souls and their horrible lifestyles. Consequently, we were there to compassionately, quietly intercede for them, that they would find Jesus and make Him their Lord.

I expect to see at least some of them in Heaven, because no prayer that's in the will of God, and prayed in love and faith is ever wasted. Hallelujah!

Another afternoon, a young woman on staff in Y.W.A.M. Amsterdam and I were walking through the densely crowded streets, in the center of Amsterdam, when we noticed a young man sitting down in the middle of all this, leaning his back against a wall. He looked dejected.

As we got down beside him and gently asked if we could help, he started to open up. We then took him to a restaurant and gave him a good meal. He was not at all resistant to our sharing about the Lord. In fact he accepted our invitation for him to go back to our

Y.W.A.M. Base with my mature Y.W.A.M. friend. They accepted him, and it wasn't long before he gave his life to Christ. Hallelujah.

A year later we returned to Amsterdam for vital ministry purposes. Because of Jim's and my lifelong love for bicycling in attractive places, we were able to further explore the beauties surrounding the quaint little villages, of Edam and Volendam.

The next afternoon we cycled to Monnickendam and Marken and again saw the cutest, quaintest, prettiest villages.

On the last day we cycled back to Volendam and had lunch at a very good restaurant overlooking the fishing village and surrounding water. Again I was able to get things for Jill's and our homes that I couldn't get anywhere else in the world, in the quaint little shops.

You may well wonder why I'm recounting all of this, when I've previously written up about our earlier biking adventures outside Amsterdam.

The simple reason is that this is by far the most relaxing, enjoyable thing I could do between all the myriads of ministry assignments globally. And I want to accentuate it!

I realize to most other people, there would be scores of ways that would be far more enjoyable. But this is my story.

Our Greatest Need

One of the most powerful messages God has given me is called, "Our Greatest Need." This is to see our pride as God reveals it in His Word.

One of the most prevalent forms of pride is manifest in the sin of presumption – through the lack of seeking God.

David, as a leader cried out in Psalm19:13 "Keep back Your servant from presumptions sins: let them not have dominion over me. Then I will be free from great transgression."

Jesus in His humility, mentored the total absence of this sin by "Only saying and doing what He saw and heard the Father say or do first." John 5:30 & John 12:49. Jesus spent a lot of time listening to and waiting on the Father.

God has been tolerating men's private and public agendas in the lives of spiritual leaders and followers for a long time. I believe we're entering a time where He'll increasingly manifest His disapproval of this form of pride.

He may well embarrass us publicly in His love for us, to bring us to repentance. He did with Jonah and Baalam. I used to say "God is a perfect gentleman. He'll never embarrass you." WRONG.

Here's an illustration. A young leader in Y.W.A.M. with strong leadership gifting, was asked to speak to a group of Christians in another organization that he deeply respected.

Without seeking God, he accepted the invitation, and went with a message he chose. When it was announced that he would speak, God brought him under such deep conviction of the sin of presumption, all he could do was stand to his feet and tell them that he was never sent by God, and God showed him therefore that he had nothing to say.

The leader of the group asked him if he would at least pray, and when the young leader tried, God paralyzed his tongue, and he couldn't utter a single word, only nod his head negatively.

The young leader had been taught at length and in depth, in his training years, to wait on God before accepting any ministry assignment, and to wait on God for the exact word of the Lord in every situation, if God confirmed that he was to speak.

God knew the many thousands of people who would be influenced by his life and teaching in future days, and wanted to guard against the pride of presumption being perpetuated through his ministry.

John 3:34 "He who God has <u>sent</u> utters the words of God."

Humbling ourselves before God and men is not difficult. If we are committed to truth. Are you committed to truth?

I am now going to quote from my book, "Forever Ruined For The Ordinary." *

"Jesus makes it clear that He never spoke anything other than what the Father told Him to say. And John 7:16–17 explains that when anyone speaks on his own authority he does so to bring honor to himself, not God. When God sends us to a person or situation, He may well test us in regard to what we are to say and when we are to say it.

I was teaching at a conference in Cyprus to a number of different missionary organizations that had come together from the Middle East. I had spoken in the morning and was scheduled to speak in the evening of the same day. I spent the afternoon seeking God for the message, but received nothing. About 4.30 P.M. I asked the leader of the conference to join me in inquiring if God had another agenda. God strongly confirmed to us both from the Scriptures that I was to speak. I remained in my room seeking God.

The meeting started with worship at 7:00 P.M. and at 7:30 P.M. the leader announced that I would bring the word of the Lord. I still had no direction whatsoever, and explained that until I did, I had nothing to say.

Jesus was, and is, my mentor. He said, 'For I have not spoken on My own authority; but the Father who sent Me gave Me a command, what I should say and what I should speak' (John 12:49). He also said, 'He who speaks from himself seeks his own glory; but He who seeks the glory of the One who sent Him is true, and no unrighteousness is in Him' (John 7:18).

I continued seeking God. The leader asked the conferees to pray for the release of the message. They did. God was still silent. When you've chosen to be nothing so that He may become everything, you don't sweat it.

**Joy Dawson "FOREVER RUINED FOR THE ORDINARY" ©2001 Thomas Nelson Publishers.*

Exercising the rest of faith as taught in Hebrews chapters 3 and 4, I waited in silent expectancy. Forty minutes later, the Holy Spirit quickened two verses of Scripture to me related to waiting on God. Understanding came that I was not to give my teaching on that subject, but to share two stories out of my life of other severe testings and results from waiting on God for His agenda, in His timing, His way. I obeyed.

When the fear of the Lord is on us, we will choose His way every time. Through humility, faith, and obedience we'll experience that 'the government will be upon His shoulders' (Isaiah 9:6)—not ours.

God can also test us by delaying an answer to see whether we will understand the immense privilege of waiting on Him because of Who He is, or whether we will be impatient or resentful.

I had been seeking God on numerous occasions to know how to respond to an invitation to speak at a spiritual leadership conference, without receiving any answer. One day, the phone rang and the sponsors said they had to have my answer on that particular day in order to meet their publicity brochure deadline. I was desperate.

I had a full day of other ministry-related responsibilities planned. At 10:00 A.M. I knelt down by a chair in my bedroom and asked God to speak to me for the sake of the sponsors, and believed that in His faithfulness and infinite understanding He would come through. Five hours later, at 3:00 P.M., I was still there, having heard nothing.

I then said, 'Thank You for the great privilege of waiting before Your blazing throne as You are seated there in Your dazzling beauty and magnificent splendor. Because of Who You are, impatience and resentment from me would be an insult to You. I will gladly continue to wait in Your Majestic Presence.'

Very quietly but clearly, He then spoke one word into my spirit. 'Yes.' I had an answer. The test was passed because of the knowledge of God's character. This is where Psalm 69:13 and Micah 7:7, as quoted previously, are invaluable faith builders." I was then able to convey my answer to the sponsors.

Multi And Diverse Ministries

It was April 1985. After teaching over the Easter weekend on Y.W.A.M.'s ship the Anastasis, I then flew to Hawaii and spoke at a Women's Aglow Fellowship Conference.

From there I flew to Hong Kong and on Sunday morning spoke in a Chinese church, and in the evening spoke at a Y.W.A.M. sponsored event in a high school auditorium.

The next day I went to the Trans World Radio Station and taped six radio programs. Each were ten minutes long, with a Chinese / English speaking interpreter.

Next, I flew into Shanghai, China with a Y.W.A.M. leader and our Chinese interpreter. I shared vision with a group of pastors, and then led a meaningful Bible Study from Jeremiah 31 in the home of one of the Believers. I flew back to Hong Kong at night, exhausted from lack of sleep, but fulfilled that the mission was accomplished. All glory to Jesus.

The following day was very significant for me, as I got to go into the Walled City, and attend a Bible study that Jackie Pullenger was leading among a bunch of drug addicts.

The next day at lunch with Jackie, I shared how God had given me a significant burden in much intercession for her and all the inmates of the Walled City. We were both encouraged.

The same day I spoke at length to a significant group of people, on "How to have a burdened heart for lost souls." There were pastors, and people from the Women's Aglow Fellowship, the Lydia Fellowship, and Y.W.A.M.

I recorded eleven more radio programs for Trans World Radio, and then spoke at the Full Gospel Business Men's Fellowship on "How to pray for the Church in every nation." I concluded this diverse ministry trip by speaking on "The peace of God."

I flew from Hong Kong to Honolulu where I met up with Jim who had been visiting all the Y.W.A.M. bases in Hawaii. Obviously

God supernaturally sustained me to minister, as I had so much insomnia. All glory to Jesus

Randers, Denmark

I was in the city of Randers, Denmark, in July of 1985 when Y.W.A.M. was having one of their many international "GO FESTIVALS."

At one of the plenary sessions, I spoke on "The character of God as it relates to The Great Commission."

Matthew 28:19 "Go therefore and make disciples of all nations, baptizing them in the name of the Father and of the Son and of the Holy Spirit."

After I had taught about His infinite knowledge and understanding of us; and how limitless He is in power, I realized I had only given a portion of the whole message when the Holy Spirit directed me stop. He then directed me to lead the people into speaking out their love responses to our Commander in Chief, which they freely did. I led them to clap their hands solely on the basis of WHO GOD IS.

Sustained clapping went on for the longest time, and suddenly everyone spontaneously clapped in unison. This was followed by an outburst of shouted praises and worship, with more extended clapping. **The Holy Spirit had broken through.**

As we were clapping our praises to God, I had a vision of a great throng of people from all over the world, marching toward the light. As we continued to clap, more and more people joined the marching crowd. It was an endless sea of heads.

Those at the back were still in the shadows, but as they marched on towards the light, they were enlightened as the light fell on them. It was an incredible sight. It was as if with every expression of genuine praise we offered to God for who He IS, another soul would join them.

Thank God I had recorded this in my diary. While God sovereignly led me to lead the people in expressing their praises to God mainly by clapping their hands at that time and place, I do not believe it is necessarily the highest expression of our praises to God for Who He is.

In the Bible, we're only commanded to clap our hands before the Lord twice; whereas we are told to shout before the Lord forty eight times; and to dance before the Lord twenty four times. Think about that!

The next day, I spoke to another large audience on "Having a burdened heart for lost souls." This was followed by meaningful contacts I had with some significant generals in God's army.

I was able to encourage Louis Pallau, an internationally known evangelist from Argentina, who was having outdoor meetings in Randers City over the next two nights. We prayed for him to have the greatest anointing he'd ever had to reach lost souls, and believed.

The next, was praying powerful, Spirit directed, faith filled prayers over Brother Andrew just before he spoke at the Go Festival.

Coming out of that meeting I met up with my long time friend, Arthur Blessitt. We stepped aside to pray for each other. He asked God that over the next six months I would see the glory of God to the point of being speechless. I thought that was awesome!

I then interceded for the greatest manifestation of the life of the Lord Jesus to come forth from him; and the greatest anointings of the Holy Spirit to come upon him, for all God's purposes to be fulfilled during his ministry time in Denmark. We both released full faith!

Significant Times During Teaching Sessions

Also, in July of 1985, Jim and I were in Johannesburg, South Africa, where Y.W.A.M. was having an important conference.

My diary records that on Wednesday 17th, "I started teaching in the afternoon seminar on "How to pray for the Church Worldwide." When I got to point 2 in my notes, which was "the need to pray for revival," I was so burdened in my spirit for revival to come to South Africa that I stopped teaching and called everyone to join me as I knelt down to intercede for it right there. The audience seriously co-operated, and individually went to serious prayer. It was a powerful time.

I was then prompted by the Holy Spirit to call up onto the platform Cedric Coates, one of the white leaders whom I knew, and another black leader who I didn't know. I asked them if they were willing to learn from **any** other black or white spiritual leader, and declare that need, and die for it if necessary, for Jesus.

Each man answered "Yes," one at a time to my question.

What I didn't know, was that some Christians in South Africa had already been killed trying to bring about that unity between the blacks and the whites.

Then the black pastor wept as he shared that the night before, God had spoken to him the following:

1. That he was to come to this conference.

2. That today someone would speak on revival.

3. He would be called up onto the platform.

4. But he didn't believe God.

5. In spite of his unbelief, God had totally fulfilled everything.

The next morning I shared with Loren and Ian Muir, Y.W.A.M.'s director over South Africa, and Jim, what had taken place in my meeting yesterday. We then asked God if He had anything to say to us, and we waited on Him.

The Holy Spirit answered by coming strongly upon me with desperate praying for revival and spiritual awakening for South Africa, as I wept and paced around the room. I continued with this intensity, praying for God to break through during this conference, and also that Y.W.A.M. would increasingly have more of God's priorities by becoming more like the Moravian missionaries on a world basis. I then released faith and thanked God for the answers.

Today Y.W.A.M. is presently operating in over 180 countries, with approximately 1100 operating locations with 18,000 full time staff members.

While these statistics are impressive, my prayers are that we as a Mission will go deeper in our understanding of God's character and ways.

If we have more breadth than depth, we'll become top heavy and less effective.

The Holy Spirit then spoke clearly to Loren confirming that there would be a fulfillment of this prophetic intercession.

God also spoke to Jim from 2 Samuel 22:7-16. The prophet David had called upon the Lord in desperation. Verse 7 "In my distress I called upon the Lord; to my God I called. From His temple He heard my voice, and my cry came to His ears." God then came through in many mighty ways as described in **verses 8-16**.

There is a strong link between having the office of a true prophet, and exercising the ministry of intercession. It is found in Jeremiah 27:18 “If they are prophets, and if the word of the Lord is with them, then let them intercede with the Lord of hosts….”

A Hilarious Crisis In Hong Kong

Our Y.W.A.M. Director in Hong Kong in 1986 was Gary Stephens, and he had invited Pastor Bob Mumford, an internationally known Bible teacher and myself, to speak at a weeklong leadership conference, held at our Y.W.A.M. base in January of that year. God had confirmed to Jim and me that this was from Him. This was the first time Bob and I had met each other.

In the middle of the week’s teaching, in the afternoon, my Y.W.A.M. friend Judy and I took off to do some shopping.

We had a hilarious experience in a small Chinese shop where I tried on a straight skirt without an opening; with only an elastic waist. I couldn’t pull it up over my hips, so I **forced** it over my shoulders and bust and then couldn’t get it off me, up or down.

I was JAMMED and the man had no fitting room. I had knee high’s on from the slacks I had taken off! I was having hysterics with laughter, mixed with panic! I had to control the laughter to have the strength to try and prize the waist over each of my bosoms and then Judy had to try and peel it off over my shoulders. Judy said, “You may have to buy the skirt.” I thought that was the least of my worries. How was I going to get back to the Y.W.A.M. base in a taxi, and then the underground train, and another taxi **LIKE THIS?**

I said, “Lord, I’ll serve you for the rest of my life in Indonesia if You will just get me out of this skirt.” I was calling on the Lord to help me, while laughing my head off and feeling utterly

TRAPPED. Judy was **SHRIEKING** with laughter. The Chinese shop owner's face was expressionless! It was only by God's mercy that he didn't come to the back of the shop to see what was going on.

It took a display of God's miracle working power to finally extricate me from my dilemma (I don't remember how).

All I know is I was able to make it back to the conference and fulfill my ministry assignments. **Such is life with Joy and Jesus ☺**

I deeply appreciated every time Bob Mumford spoke and we became good friends. At the end of the week he said to me, "I can sum up everything you teach with one word. It's **obedience**." He was right. Later, Jim and I met Bob's wife, Judith, and that eventuated into many years of close friendship.

More Lessons To Learn

God had a lot to teach me about receiving from Him to meet a genuine need in clothing, when the price was out of my normal low price range. I was a slow learner.

For example, in the first week of July 1986, I was due to be speaking at events coming up later on that required my need of some "dressier" clothing. As was my custom, I trusted God to meet my needs and got on with His business.

At this particular time I was speaking at a church in San Francisco on "The ways of God in times of testing." At the close of the meeting, I spent time with Wayne Macatarie, the associate pastor. I was given the word of the Lord from significant Scriptures that were pertinent to his life and ministry. He was very grateful.

The next day he contacted me, and shared that the Lord had directed him to take me to the Neiman Marcus Store (known to be the most expensive) and buy me a dress on his credit card. In strict obedience to God's directions he had recently opened an account there.

I immediately said that I thought it was an obedience test from God, which he had passed, and I would release him from going through with it.

He said an emphatic, "No," so I immediately suggested we go to Macy's Department Store (less expensive) to which he again stated firmly that God had spoken clearly that Neiman Marcus was the place.

My diary records, "We went and I felt **terrible.**" **WHY?** Because I had a warped understanding that it wasn't spiritual for me to have clothing that was expensive. It came from my background.

Almost any means of saving money was considered a real virtue in my upbringing. I had to battle against this concept…as though our God is short on funds. Psalm 50:12 says, "He owns it ALL." I just have to obey His specific directions. But my hereditary was deeply ingrained in me, and I hadn't learned these truths yet.

After I had checked out the sales racks and found nothing, I then followed my friend to where the normal priced dresses were, and found a lovely purple paisley one for the winter. He spotted a sharp dressy outfit in red and black and was insisting on paying for both.

My response was that we needed to have the fear of God on us, and not do anything rash!! I also said that I needed God to speak to me from His Word about all this. (I always had my Bible with me.)

God immediately opened my Bible to Romans 15:15 "But on some points I have written to you very boldly by way of reminder, because of the grace given me by God…"

Remember this man had been blessed through the Holy Spirit's ministry through me and to further confirm that all this was a God set up, the next verses topped it off from **Romans 16:1,2** "I commend to you our sister Phoebe, a deaconess of the church at Cen'chre-ae, that you may receive her in the Lord as befits the saints, and help her in whatever she may require from you, for she has been a helper of many and of myself as well."

Of course, God had my exact need met at that time costing way more than I had ever experienced.

He was teaching me that He is neither poor nor mean, as my Provider. He just wants my trust and my obedience.

Another time, while still in the learning curve of all this, I had just finished speaking at a National Womens Aglow Convention in Sydney, Australia. My dear friend, Jane Hansen was the other guest speaker.

I had flown in from there to the Sydney Airport, where I had a four hour layover, before flying back to Los Angeles.

During the last part of that time, I had dropped into a classy little boutique and was browsing through, when I soon spotted a beautiful silk jacket in exactly my size. The colors were a blend of blues and purples, which were perfect for the many times I was being interviewed and taught on numerous Christian Television stations, across America.

I loved the jacket and had a skirt that would match it, but it was way out of my price range. I simply couldn't afford it! I was torn between seeing how useful it would be and the dilemma of being a responsible steward of our financial status at that time.

So I diligently repeatedly sought the Lord for His directions. His answers spoken into my spirit were "Buy it." I finally wrote out a check and purchased it. All this had taken much more time than I had realized.

To my horror, I saw by my watch, that my plane was about to leave, and it was at the end of a long terminal.

I took off in top gear, pulling my travel cart and praying for God's mercy and overruling. I needed both, as I encountered one of the airline stewards coming towards me asking if I was Joy Dawson?

When I said "Yes," she threateningly said, "Where on earth have you been?, We've been waiting for you; everyone else is on board, and it's a full flight." I silently proceeded toward the plane. How on earth could I ever explain my inexcusable circumstances?

When I finally crashed into the only unoccupied seat on the whole plane…the implications set in. I had held up a jumbo jet of 500 passengers because I was still learning that I could trust God to direct me to purchase the **right** thing, at the right time, when I didn't know how He was going to balance the budget. I finally got it.

I wore that lovely jacket over the years more than anything else; until it became too big for me. I had shrunk. One day when my dear intercessor friend Donna Jordan and I were having lunch together; I knew that I was to give it to her. It was in perfect condition and ideal for her many Bible teaching assignments.

Teen Challenge U.S.A.

In July of 1986, I found some challenging ministry settings I had recorded, along with accompanying rewarding moves of God's spirit.

I had flown to and spoken in a church in Cleveland, Ohio, for two nights before flying to Harrisburg, on the east coast of America. After an hour's drive I was taken to the large effective Teen Challenge ministry operating there.

They were having special meetings in a huge tent with large audiences where Loren and I were speakers. It was the middle of summer and HOT and VERY HUMID!!

I spoke on "The implications of Obedience" the first night, followed by "The causes of disobedience" the next day. The Holy Spirit did a deep work.

Loren spoke powerfully that night on "The Greatness of God," followed by, "How to disciple the nations through evangelizing those in the seven categories of the greatest spheres of authority and influence." He then invited people who really wanted to be involved in this vision with their lives, to go into the counseling tent.

A large number of people responded and then Loren asked me to take over. I totally submitted to the Holy Spirit. My diary records: "He took off through me with a strong flow of authority as I instructed them first how to hear God's voice.

Then I invited them to listen in silence for the Holy Spirit to reveal to them the method, or the place, for them to be trained.

Following that, they were to enquire about the name of the country or countries God may want to send them as missionaries, for any lengths of time. When that was completed, I invited them to share, one at a time, the names of those nations. It was thrilling to hear nations from every continent that were spoken out as a result of that remarkable day – despite the heat and humidity.

The next day I spoke on "what it means to be involved with the poor and needy; with vivid illustrations of how obedience to God is always for our good." This time, the conditions were more challenging!

The next day I was assigned to a forest area, where the audience was seated under trees, in the rain, complete with umbrellas, raincoats, and towels. After my hair was soaked with water falling from the trees, someone held an umbrella over me.

With holding a microphone on one hand and my notes in the other, my notes got wet, and I couldn't use my glasses because they were full of water.

At times music was being played over the loud speakers from a stage nearby, while I was speaking as loudly as possible over my microphone to be able to be heard.

At the same time another preacher was doing his thing in another adjacent part of the forest!!! **Despite all this**, my diary continues to record that the Holy Spirit moved in power. At the close of my message, I invited the people to respond to what He was saying to them. One after another humbled themselves, and openly acknowledged their real need to repent of areas in their lives where changes needed to be made.

I was relieved to fly home to Los Angeles and be out of strong heat, humidity, rain and mud, but so thankful to have seen God powerfully at work again in extending His Kingdom purposes for His glory alone!

It also reveals the truth that when we who are called to teach God's Word, and we have made sure that our **hearts are right at all times** toward God and mankind, God will always come through in power… regardless of the circumstances.

Some Of The Price

I'm going to give everyone a glimpse into some of the price God required of me to keep saying "Yes" to Jesus. For decades I averaged only two weeks at home between traveling and ministry trips away.

Keeping up with the large amounts of correspondence I received, and the constancy of new message preparations, along with working on complex airline schedules, was challenging and often exhausting.

It was not unusual to have to pack for being in several different time zones and climates…. the really cold, the really hot, and the in between…. all on the one ministry trip, for at times five weeks and more away. The preparation was really time consuming, as I was always on platforms and often in front of T.V. cameras.

In September 1986 I found an entry in my diaries which is typical of so many like it.

Monday Sept 22nd, my diary records: - "hectically busy all day related to going away. Bone weary at night. Sept 23rd – Another incredibly busy day. Jim and I worked until 1 a.m. We pushed through mountains of office work. I then packed up for going to Ottawa, Canada.

Sept 24th – Up at 6 a.m. Headed for L.A.X. airport. Due to heavy rain and with dense traffic going at a snail's pace for most of the way, I missed my 10:00 a.m. flight to Toronto. Got another flight out at 1:00 p.m. Then I changed planes and arrived at Ottawa at 10:45 p.m. Both flights on Air Canada were packed out, and I was jammed in like a sardine.

Before I put the hotel light out after midnight….and in exhaustion, I wrote in my diary, "Hallelujah anyway! It's amazing I'm still living at this incredible pace at 60 years of age. Only by God's grace and supernatural strength, obviously. The price is high. The privileges higher."

I also found a diary record related to one year later, where I recorded the following:

On this trip of two and a half weeks, I have spoken 13 times in meetings, done 5 television interviews with teaching messages, attended 3 lengthy committee meetings with the National Prayer Committee, and traveled on 7 different planes.

I've never worked harder. The pace has been incredible. But as always, it's been a great privilege.

Gordon Conwell Theological Seminary

In September of 1986, I spoke three times at the vital Women's Aglow Conference in Ottawa, Canada. One of the highlights was being able to spend quality time with my dear friend Pastor Robert Birch, who was one of the speakers. Only eternity will reveal the impact of this legendary godly man's extensive, deep, sacrificial life of intercession for Canada and the nations. We always had "iron sharpening iron" sessions together which I loved.

From there, Jim and I went on to Boston, Massachusetts, where I spoke for five days at the Gordon Conwell Theological Seminary.

Of the times I spoke at Theological Seminaries and Bible Colleges, I often became informed of their curriculums. This then gave me a greater understanding of God's purposes in directing me to the specific messages of His choosing, each time I spoke.

I believe I am to report briefly on the messages the Holy Spirit directed me to give at that time.

The first one was given at the morning chapel service, on the first half of my "Knowing God" message. The second message was "A burdened heart for lost souls." Jim said I spoke both times with authority, under the Holy Spirit's anointing.

Jim went out to Y.W.A.M.'s New Hampshire Base and ministered to them (between sessions) and then brought some of them back to the sessions.

The next day I completed the message on "Knowing God" and majored on "How to know Him." My diary records: "I believe I had the greatest authority and anointing I have ever had in my life on this subject. I had asked God to give me an anointing to meet the NEED! Praise the Lord! I marveled while speaking, as I listened to what came through me that day."

The message on "Knowing God"* is featured in the front of the Women of Destiny Bible, published in 2000. This is a remarkable Bible – one of a kind! I contributed three more articles to it. "The release of the Spirit through brokenness" page 486, "The Spirit of wisdom and revelation" page 1442, and "Diligently seeking the Lord" page 1521.

**Joy Dawson "KNOWING GOD" ©2000. Thomas Nelson Publishers*

It is a treasure chest of godly wisdom, from many women who have been through the fires of God's testings.

"Knowing God" is my favorite of all the messages God has given me. It's also in a booklet.

The next day I spoke on "How to pray for The Church

in every nation of the world" and then on "Divine Guidance" at a lunch forum.

The final day I completed the message on "How to pray for The Church in every nation of the world." At the close I led the people into reconciliation between blacks and whites, which lasted 1 ¼ hours.

.

Both parties humbled themselves before each other, asking for forgiveness of hurts, prejudices and resentments that had divided them. It was a very powerful time.

It was a privilege and joy to be with Christy and Betty Wilson during this week, who were former missionaries for twenty-two years in Kabul, Afghanistan. I honor them.

Argentina

In 1987, Loren, Leland Paris, and another Y.W.A.M. leader and I went through the cities of Argentina where Y.W.A.M. had bases. The assignment was for 3 weeks, as Loren and I spoke to the spiritual leaders who had gathered from different denominations.

It was another pivotal ministry time. The pastors were hungry for "the word of the Lord" so that they could apply it to their lives. It was the final day of teaching and I was directed by the Holy Spirit to speak on The Fear of the Lord!

After the conference, our team had returned to the big house which Y.W.A.M. was renting in that city.

I need to backup and share that my oldest grandson, David Dawson, was at that time turning 9 years of age and I wanted to buy him something special. I decided upon an authentic bow and arrow set, made in Argentina, which I bought at the end of this 3rd week.

To reach our bedrooms we had to climb up a large winding staircase which started inside the large entryway. That's when I decided to have some fun with my new present.

I changed clothes into a long white robe, complete with my feathered headdress and started firing my arrows at closed doors randomly. Leland Paris appeared on the scene, and seeing I was undeterred by his presence, tried to find refuge behind a tall post. The trouble was, Leland is a real big guy and the post wasn't able to cover him.

I just kept on firing at that post with glee!! ....until to my horror, I saw the senior pastor who had convened the conference, walking up the curved stairway toward me with his wife!

With the speed of a jack rabbit, I shot back into my bedroom, wondering what on earth they would be thinking?? I never inquired, and still don't know. Probably just as well.

I later learned they had an appointment with our Y.W.A.M. base leaders, whose office was on the same floor.

Such is life with Joy and whoever!

On The Streets In Durban, South Africa

I was in Durban, South Africa, early in July of 1987, speaking all week at an intense but spiritually rewarding spiritual leadership conference.

Saturday was my only day off, as I was due to be speaking again, twice, at a vital church held in a large theatre in the city on Sunday morning, and then in another church in the evening.... a plane ride away.

After diligently preparing for these assignments, I chose to do myself a favor by going out in the main shopping area of the city which was teaming with intentional shoppers. Saturday morning was their favorite time to do that in Durban, as around 1:30pm everything closed down.

My sole purpose was to share the love of the Lord Jesus with anyone to whom the Holy Spirit directed me. Jesus did the majority of His personal evangelizing out where the people were, and He's my model. Besides that, this is my favorite way of serving Him.

I was walking past a large department store, when I saw a little elderly Zulu lady squatted on the ground in front, begging. Immediately, I knew to go and sit down alongside her, put my arms around her and tell her that God loved her and so did I. Her response was genuinely warm. I told her my name and she told me hers was Amina. We were bonded.

After buying her some lunch, I shared the way of salvation, clearly and simply, to which she responded with real joy. I then shared that I was speaking at a church in a theatre in the city the next morning and would arrange transport for her if she'd like to come. She would be my guest. Her wide-eyed acceptance was immediate, so we arranged to meet her at 10:00 a.m. the next morning. She said she would be sitting on some cardboard on the pavement on Leopole St by the toilet!!

When I stood up, I noticed the look of intense longing coming from the dark eyes of a boy beggar a few yards away. They said, "Please don't overlook me!" I didn't. I sat down beside him, greeted him affectionately and we shared names; his was Sceety and he was fourteen years old.

I soon discovered that he was crippled in both legs with a damaged spine. He couldn't walk, and moved his body with his hands. Upon my enquiry, he told me that when he was younger, he got into a fist fight with some older boys who beat him up so badly, that he was left in this condition--- without any medical help!!

The love of God welled up in my heart for this precious boy and I told him I deeply cared about his suffering and prayed for him. Then I gave him the invitation to be my special guest at the church service in the big theatre the next morning, with transportation provided. While it was so hard for him to comprehend, he agreed to meet me at the same time and street pavement as Amina. They were street friends. I was elated! I had less than 4 hours sleep that night.

The next morning, after I had spoken at the 8 o'clock service, on the second half of my series on "God's strategy for taking nations," I had a deacon drive me to the meeting place; only to find that a woman and her young daughter had joined the group! They were all Zulus. The deacon's car was small. Undeterred, we all piled in; putting the big lady in the front beside the driver. This meant Amina, Sceety, the girl and I were jammed together in the back seat.

The smell from the body odors was understandably strong. As I was nearest to the door, I stealthily put perfume from my purse on my top lip to try to combat it. The attempt didn't work!

When we arrived at the theatre I immediately arranged for plates of fruit, bread rolls, and fruit juices to be given to my guests, as they were being placed in seats up front and to my left, so I could readily see them.

Everything was being done in conjunction with my dear friend, Fred Roberts, the senior pastor of the church.

During my preaching at the 11am service, I noticed that my new street friends were asleep. That made sense to me. They were now sheltered, comfortably safe and not hungry, and sleep was what they needed!

When I had finished the message, I explained to the audience that I was now going down to share the gospel message with my new friends, who were seated up front. I did so with clarity and simplicity with a Zulu pastor interpreting. I then invited each one to openly respond if they were willing to fulfill the Biblical conditions to be truly born again. Each one did so deliberately, and openly. I then lead them, as they repeated after me the appropriate response.

I had already sought the Lord if He wanted to heal Sceety and He directed me to Matthew 10:1-8 and Luke 13:11-13.

I was now ready to pray for Sceety's miracle healing, and invited the pastor to join me. He authorized an elder to join us and to hold Sceety in his arms. The entire audience were watching and listening as microphones were being held in front of us.

I fervently prayed the prayer of genuine faith in the Lord, our Healer, totally expecting Sceety's legs to come alive and straighten out in front of our eyes. The men with me interceded with faith and fervency. To my amazement, there was no change!

I was then directed to pray for healing of Sceety's mind, memories, and emotions. Then I sang a lullaby song over him that was given to me by the Holy Spirit, as I held him close. I kissed him and told him he was beautiful and precious, as I wept, and then finally committed him into God's hands.

I had learned that it is entirely God's responsibility to act in His sovereignty, following my steps of obedience and faith.

Just then, church staff told me that I would have to leave **immediately** to go the airport to catch my flight to Cape Town. I was booked to be preaching at the evening service of a church in that city in a few hours. No time for lunch or dinner and no food service on the plane, but I was marveling in all that God had already done in that one week of serving Him. What a joyous privilege!

On the plane to Capetown I enquired of God again about the healing of Sceety's spine and legs, and He directed me to Luke 5:17-26; where Jesus healed the paralytic man. This greatly comforted and encouraged me that there would still be an answer to my fervent prayers of faith.

I was very tired when I had to preach that evening, but the Holy Spirit quickened me and enabled me to speak with authority on "Desperate Praying."

It was very hard to think of Sceety being left to go back to living on the streets. I prayed for him often and inquired about him by phone when I went back to Los Angeles. As I write this book I am longing for the time in Heaven when Jesus explains to me the better timing He chose to demonstrate His infinite love and healing power towards that loveable needy boy. I totally trust my Savior!

Some years later, my pastor friend Fred Roberts, told me that as a direct result of my encounter with those people living on the streets, the church leadership were directed by God to launch a whole new ministry of reaching out to the poor and needy in their city; ministering to their needs of body, soul, and spirit. That gave me further understanding of the ways of God and great encouragement!

I was in Durban, South Africa, at another time, once again speaking daily at a spiritual leadership conference, which was very vital. I was housed in a hotel overlooking the ocean which was a real treat.

Each day I would look for opportunities to witness to the hotel staff. One day when the cleaning lady was in my room, I asked her if she knew the Lord Jesus personally. Her honest reply was, "No." I then explained the way of salvation in direct simplicity as she quietly worked around my room.

The Holy Spirit worked in her heart, drawing her to the Lord. Before she left, she made a serious commitment to follow Him and I was able to give her suitable material as a follow up.

The next day as I took the hotel elevator up a number of floors, I noticed my cleaning lady got on at one of the stops with a male hotel staff worker beside her.

Instantly I felt the familiar nudge of the Holy Spirit; so right there I asked him if he knew the Lord Jesus personally. He immediately replied, "No, but I want to." As soon as they both started to get off the elevator at the floor they needed to work on, I asked if I could join them. "Sure," was their response.

I asked the maid if we could go together for privacy in the room she was going to clean? Again the response was positive. She shared that she had been telling her staff friend about her life changing conversion to Christ. I then explained the way of salvation simply and lovingly to the man, from Romans 6:23 and Romans 10:9- which include making Jesus the Lord and master of his life. He readily responded with obvious sincerity, and I believe was soundly converted. We wasted no time as they both needed to get on with their jobs in the hotel. Hallelujah!

On another day, I was chatting with one of the guards outside an impressive Official building, near my hotel. He had time on his hands, and I had a longing for him to know the Lord. A perfect setup for the Holy Spirit to work.

This man was ripe for the picking as I shared the way of salvation with him; which was the first time he'd ever heard it. Right there, he responded with obvious sincerity and faith, as he repeated after me in prayer, what it meant to commit his life to Christ. He had never owned a Bible and was so delighted when I returned the next day with one with a white leather cover.

Another day I saw the sovereignty of God working in a wonderful way. I had invited the black lady who cleaned my hotel room and the black man who cleaned my bathroom to go to lunch with me in the hotel. This is rarely done and they were amazed, but accepted my invitation.

Over the best meal that I could buy for them I shared the gospel, and found out that the black lady was a Christian who spoke excellent English as well as Zulu. She interpreted everything I said to the man who spoke mostly Zulu.

At the end of their lunch hour a manager signaled that it was time for them to go back to cleaning the hotel rooms. That was right at the time in our conversation when the black man had just said he would like to commit his life to the Lord Jesus.

I was puzzled, and wondering what to do, when the black lady said, "Oh it's alright Madam, your room is the next room that is on our list to clean today, so we're coming to your room right now anyway! It was a very large hotel and they had many rooms to clean that day!

We went into my room and the black man had a very genuine conversion experience. He was the father of five children. I got him a Zulu Bible the next day. All these precious people were so responsive to the gospel and so grateful for someone to share the Lord Jesus with them.

Witnessing is such an enormous thrill! It's simply gossiping the gospel as the Holy Spirit directs and empowers us.

You may wonder why I so frequently share about the times I witness to people about the Lord Jesus. The Bible says, "Out of the abundance of the heart the mouth speaks."

My heart towards Him is best described in my favorite song of worship:

"You are beautiful beyond description,
Too marvelous for words.
Too wonderful for comprehension,

Like nothing ever seen or heard.
Who can grasp your infinite wisdom?
Who can fathom the depths of your love?
You are beautiful beyond description,
Majesty enthroned above!
And I worship You, Oh mighty God
There is none like You."

I love to tell others about Jesus the lover of my soul, who has totally captivated my heart and the only One who can totally fulfill me….and them.

Another reason is that Jesus has commanded all His disciples to witness to all others about Him in Mathew 4:19 "Follow Me and I will make you fishers of men."

If I'm not sharing the way of salvation with others, at every given opportunity, I'm being a disobedient servant.

Finally, I have a genuine deep concern for the millions who have not yet heard of the Lord Jesus, and for the multitudes who have heard of the way of Salvation but have done nothing about acting on it.

Heaven is a very real place. Jesus said so, when He was on earth.

Hell is equally as real. Jesus said so, when He was on earth! That is a very sobering thought to me! In fact Jesus spoke a lot more about Hell than Heaven.

That's why I pray so much that everyone will have the chance to hear that "If we confess with our mouths Jesus as Lord, and believe in our hearts that God has raised Him from the dead, we will be saved," Romans 10:9.

And that's why I love to take every opportunity to tell people that **great news.**

Before Apartheid

During one of the numbers of times I ministered in Durban, South Africa, I was in a Japanese restaurant having a meal with my friend, Fred Roberts the senior pastor of the Durban Christian Center.

Suddenly, the Holy Spirit interrupted our conversation by giving me a vision into my spirit of a citywide conference, to be held in Durban. It was to be sponsored by Youth With A Mission and a united group of pastors from different denominations in the city, under the leadership of pastor Roberts.

It was to be totally interracial; related to world evangelization; and lasting ten days.

I immediately submitted this to the spiritual leader beside me, who had the respect of the other pastors. God confirmed it to him and later to them.

The huge significance was **that this was all before apartheid.** Nelson Mandela was still imprisoned. Blacks and whites and Afrikaans didn't meet together to worship God, as a way of life.

Y.W.A.M. leaders confirmed the vision, and appointed Don Price the Y.W.A.M. leader for South Africa as the leader of the event. He was very anointed by the Holy Spirit and did a remarkable job.

Every morning and evening we met together in large numbers for vibrant praise and worship to the Lord, followed by anointed international speakers who brought the word of the Lord. The afternoons were spent in varied and innovative ways of outdoor evangelism.

Following John's message on Racial Reconciliation of the sin of unrighteous judgement, the Holy Spirit revealed to me that we were to spend Friday evening washing each other's feet and praying for each other. Immediately I understood the implications!

It was radical enough that many of the ethnic rules had already been broken. But foot washing among this crowd was something else! I loved it!

I said to my practical husband, "Where are we going to get enough basins of water and towels to make this move of God work, according to John 13:14?" His immediate response was, "I'll go and buy a whole bunch of "baby wipes." That will take care of everything." Brilliant thought! He then went into action, with his "ministry of helps."

We carried out the plan God gave me, and to which I led over 1,000 people into.

Everyone was to find a person of another race or ethnic group, and ask the Holy Spirit to express the love of God to them as they sat on the floor in front of them and washed their feet. Then they were to pray the most lavish prayers of blessing over them as they listened to God's directions and release faith for the answers.

This was followed by the person who was seated, swapping places and repeating the same ministry of humility and Christ like love to the other partner.

Tears of brokenness through humility, followed; also tears of genuine love, and forgiveness and healing resonated all over the large room. It was truly historic, and could only be explained by a Holy Spirit breakthrough!

On the 10th day, the last day of this historic conference, I said to my ministry co-partner, Don Price, "I could keep on going and do another ten days," and he said, "I feel exactly the same Joy." We were so energized by the Holy Spirit, there was no depletion. Amazing!

Europe And The U.S.A.

In September of 1987 we were in England. I was speaking in cities surrounding the London area. This included teaching at different churches, having a radio interview on B.B.C., and speaking at a Women's Conference in Norwich. God showed up on every occasion.

We then flew back to the Heathrow Airport and on to Harpenden, where we stayed at the large Y.W.A.M. Base called Highfield Oval. It was where our longstanding dear friends Lynn and Marty Green were the directors for Y.W.A.M. Europe.

At that time Y.W.A.M. didn't own the property, but we spent many hours diligently seeking God together to know if we were to own it. The purpose being for it to become the European part of "The University of the Nations," headquartered in Kona, Hawaii.

We were very aware that there were a group of men involved with the sale of this very desirable property, who were strongly opposed to it coming to Y.W.A.M.

We were undeterred by this opposition and kept pressing in to God for His answers.

God spoke very clearly to each one of us from His Word that Y.W.A.M. England was to own this very choice property with houses all around a large oval area, with a lot of beautiful trees and woods in the back of it. There was a kitchen, a dining area, and a large room for meetings.

Among other scriptures that God spoke clearly to me, were Nehemiah 9:19, 24 + 25.

A shortened version of those Scriptures is that God gave them clear directions, they went in and possessed the land and God subdued their enemies. They took possession of houses, trees in abundance and delighted in God's goodness.

God gave Lynn a very encouraging scripture which we were going to need, as this battle was a long one. It was **Psalm 73:18,** referring to the opposition "Truly You have set them in slippery places, you will make them fall in ruin."

After many tests and trials, finally every Word from God was fulfilled.

We left London and flew to Munich Germany, where two women met us who were from the contingent of women from the U.S.A. Military Base in Berchtesgarden. They were from Women's Aglow International, who were having a four day Retreat.

On the first, morning, God started to give me a new message titled "The ways of God with leaders in times of crisis" which I worked on. In the afternoon we went up by bus to the Eagles Nest, where we stood under the big wooden cross that was erected. What a great triumph over such terrible evil it represented.

After I had spoken throughout the Retreat on the subjects of "Knowing God," "The Ways of God in testing," "Humbling ourselves before God," and "Jesus the master soul winner" I made this comment in my diary:

"The 200 women at this Women's Aglow European military wives Retreat were as open and responsive to the Holy Spirit and the word of the Lord, as any group **I have ever ministered to**! What a privilege and joy for me. I love you dear women.

After that, an army chaplain and his wife took us on a long car ride through to Augsburg. The next day at a city restaurant we had the opportunity of having an excellent time of meaningful witnessing about the Lord to Bernhart. He was a German engineer of a large manufacturing motor company, who had learned English at school and had been to the U.S.A. This encounter was very much a part of this man's destiny.

Teaching at European leadership conferences.

Encouraging Encounters

We were on our way to London en route to Washington D.C., U.S.A. The next day after our arrival in this city, Jim and I were typically out on a long prayer walk praying for the nations, when we stopped and talked to a Jewish woman from South Africa. This led into not only interceding for her to be saved, but for the souls of all the Jews in the Washington D.C. area.

Over the many years the Holy Spirit has given me a deep prayer burden and love for the souls of millions of uncompleted Jews worldwide.

Jim then flew home, while I remained to speak at a vital Prayer Summit in Maryland. Spiritual leaders with strong prayer ministries brought insightful messages. It was very meaningful for the advancing of God's Kingdom.

I spoke on "The reasons and the rewards for humbling ourselves before God." The people then humbled themselves before God and one another in pairs, for 30 minutes. It was powerful.

I then flew to Charleston, West Virginia to minister there. It was early in October. The first service was at a University Hall, where I spoke in the morning to a receptive audience. The main visionary for the meetings was my long-standing dear friend Ann Calvert.

Because of my itinerary and with no time to rest between services, I was very tired when it came time to speak again at night. I asked God in faith to give me His strength, and anoint me. Then I took authority over the powers of satanic forces in Jesus mighty name and quoted appropriate Scriptures.

I spoke on "Interceding for genuine revival and spiritual awakening to come to the nations of the world." Then I asked them to intercede as I'd taught them, for a nation they had seldom or never prayed for before. They all seriously cooperated. It was very powerful.

The Holy Spirit then spoke to me to share Habakkuk 3:2-5 to encourage the people. "O Lord, I have heard the report of You, and Your words, O Lord, do I fear. In the midst of the years make it known; in wrath remember mercy. God came from Teman, and the Holy One from Mount Paran. His glory covered the heavens, and the earth was full of His praise. Selah. His brightness was like the light rays flashed from His hand; and there He veiled His power. Before Him went pestilence, and plague followed close behind."

I have given this detailed report to enable the reader to understand what follows.

The next day a large number of people turned out as I spoke at a luncheon to mainly women. My message was, "The power of a woman's influence; for good or for evil…" as I emphasized the fear of the Lord. God came through with His authority.

After the luncheon, two different women reported to me that they had seen a glow of bright light all over and around my head, while I was giving the message. At times the light emanated out and formed into a figure with outstretched arms, who then took the truths to particular individuals in the audience.

The sequel to this report came at the close, when two more women spoke individually to me. Each one said that the message was very specifically designed for her. One of them shared that, as a married woman, she was planning to commit adultery with a spiritual leader, but had just deeply repented before God and had cancelled all plans. Hallelujah!

A group of precious, caring women from the Vineyard chain of ministries, ministered very powerfully to me after all this. I will be forever grateful to them and to the Holy Spirit for directing them.

One went into deep travail in intercession that God would give me increased physical stamina and strength to endure, as well as an increased revelation of truth from God's Word. Another one drew a picture of what she saw in the Spirit realm **the night before**, at my meeting. It was very significant!

She said she saw a large evil figure standing behind me about to crush me when I went to the podium. As I prayed for God's Spirit to move in power, and then took authority over all the power of satanic forces, quoting the Word of God, suddenly a shield came between me and the menacing figure and then bars went up to totally protect me. Then she saw a basket of flowers besides the podium and smelt a beautiful perfume coming from them. She then saw God's big hand to the right and to the front of me, with rays of power coming out of them toward me. They remained in that position. Then she saw an angel to the left side of me, listening to my teaching.

A significance of this report is that verse four in Habakkuk 3:1-5, exactly describes what the women saw in her vision.

I thanked the women from sincere gratitude, and received everything by faith. I was greatly encouraged and strengthened. To God be all the glory.

This was at the end of being away for four and a half weeks of ministering, nonstop. It is a privilege to serve such a magnificent master.

CFNI And The Murchisons

I had the privilege and joy of teaching at Christ for the Nations Institute in Dallas, Texas, for thirteen years. The students were so receptive and responsive; and ready to make the challenging messages part of their lives.

Flying from Los Angeles to Dallas became routine, as I also ministered regularly for years at Shady Grove Church in Irving, Texas. Olen and Sybil Griffing were the pastors, and became great friends of ours. During some of that time, Robert Morris was their youth pastor. He is now the senior pastor of Gateway Church in Dallas, Texas; one of the most influential churches in America today. Robert told me not long ago, that a message I gave at Shady Grove Church on "The four tests of Joseph", later became the basis of a book he wrote on Joseph's life. God must have a lot of fun networking people and ministries.

When speaking at a C.F.N.I. Conference, I met lovely Ann Murchison who shared how God had used the teaching ministry God had entrusted to me to greatly bless her life.

This was a significant contact in many ways. She was the wife of Clint Murchison, who designed and owned the unique and beautiful Texas Stadium, which had a retractable roof. He also owned the Dallas Cowboys. He was now battling an incurable disease. Clint had recently given his life to the Lord Jesus, and never missed a

Sunday service at Shady Grove Church, despite severe physical disabilities.

One day Anne phoned me and explained that Clint also owned a private island in the Bahama Islands with a large house, complete with separate guest units, permanent staff and that was very near a beach. Would we like to come and stay for a week? God had shown her they were to bless a few couples who were heavily involved in full time ministries.

After thanking her profusely I said what I always say, "Jim and I will seek the Lord, and I will get back to you with whatever He shows us." His answer was, "Yes, this is from Me."

Everything was turned on to bless and refresh us, including great Christian fellowship. I had great fun when we went deep sea fishing in the Murchison's boat and had some really good catches!

We had these lavish holiday treats from our wonderful Lord and through His generous servants, two years in a row.

On one occasion, Jim and I were Clint Murchison's guests at a significant game the Dallas Cowboys were playing at Texas Stadium. We were seated in Clint's Owner's Box with all the perks. It was a totally unique experience for me as I was pretty clueless on the ramifications of the game itself as football hasn't been something I've ever taken seriously. I identified more with the Dallas Cowboys' cheerleaders. Those girls reminded me of how enthusiastic I can get about Jesus!

We became very close in friendship with both Anne, and Clint, and always stayed in their beautiful home whenever I was teaching in the Dallas area.... right up until Clint's home call to Heaven. Although at the last, Clint lost most of his wealth; he never lost his faith in Christ.

Anne, moved on to have a powerful Bible teaching and writing ministry.... a wonderful woman of God and great friend. I honor her.

Jim's Heart Surgery

It was in January 1988, the night before Jim was scheduled to have very complicated heart surgery the next morning. After the heart specialists had examined Jim 24 hours previously, they both agreed that he should be operated on at the first available opportunity. No delays. It involved having quadruple bypass surgery, plus the replacement of his heart valve for a metal one.

I was very aware that there were major implications at stake, as I sat beside his bed in the hospital with him.

I quietly asked the Lord to speak to me from His Word. Immediately He opened my Bible to Isaiah 34, and the only verse I saw was verse 16, "Seek and read from the book of the Lord: Not one of these shall be missing, none shall be without her mate. For the mouth of the Lord has commanded, and His Spirit has gathered them," which I read audibly.

This was very comforting to me and I was going to need it, as there were two crises ahead of me.

The next morning, Jill was with me at the hospital. We were able to take alternating shifts in prayer vigils as we waited.

However, at 2 p.m. the Surgeon discovered that one of the veins they had taken from his leg, and had been put into the artery of his heart, had become twisted. It needed to be straightened out. This took considerable time, resulting in Jim being in the theatre for almost 10 hours.

We had prayed that the doctors would detect anything abnormal and correct it, while they were checking for any signs of bleeding!!

Jim was unconscious the whole day and evening. The next day was a grueling day for him. The pain was excruciating whenever they moved him.

That evening, I read the Word of God to him, prayed for him, sang comforting songs over him and shared some news.

It was very hard to see my sweetheart so weak and strung up with 12 tubes on each side of his body! Again Jim said the pain was excruciating when they moved him.

The next evening John and Julie and their 3 boys joined me at the hospital. The boys wrote Jim letters from the waiting room. I am sharing David's poignant attempt to share his heart. He was twelve at the time.

"Dear Pappa,

I'm sitting in the waiting room writing this letter. I know you're in pain and I wish I could take your pain for you. I Love you so much. It hurts to think that you are in pain. You have helped me and loved me for so long. Now I want to help you, but I don't know how. I know God will heal you, Because Nan and I and Dad need you so much.

Love,
David"

Five days after the surgery, complications occurred which again put Jim in a very critical condition. His temperature soared and he had fluid on his lungs, which produced severe coughing bouts. This was extremely painful in his chest and down one leg, which meant very little sleep.

The immediate family members kept on battling away in desperate prayer. I was besides Jim's side from early morning for ten days. I needed to give him a much needed nourishing breakfast. Hospital food is notoriously lacking in nutrition.

It was another grueling day for Jim. Every time he coughed up phlegm and was moved around, it pulled on the stitches in his chest.

It was very hard for me emotionally to see him suffer so much. I moved into a bed beside him, so I could better help to meet his various needs night and day. He was still very weak, and we were both short on sleep. They were dark days.

I continued to intercede fervently hour by hour, and day after day, for Divine intervention. I felt the weight of the responsibility, and had a better understanding of the meaning of the Apostle Paul's words to "Pray without ceasing." 1 Thessalonians 5:17.

Jim slowly recovered, and was finally able to live a normal life.

9 Historic Days

In 1988, from the 28th of April to the 6th of May, (9 days) Jim and I were involved in a number of vital spiritual leadership ministries and events in Washington D.C.

One of them was the huge gathering of 200,000 people who had come for the "Washington for Jesus" event held on the Washington Mall. Pastor John Giminez and Dr. Bill Bright were the co-visionaries, who had called for a day of prayer for our nation.

I was very privileged to be part of this historic event. (It was cold and showery weather.) On arrival, I was interviewed by camera for the 700 Club, by Pat Robertson's son, Tim. This was followed by my being on the platform and leading out in prayer for the restoration of our nation. After that I did a radio interview related to all this.

I was involved in teaching, as our National Prayer Committee lead several of the vital prayer events surrounding the National Day of Prayer on May 5th.

We started by participating in the sunrise service at Evangel Temple, as we prayed for humility, the fear of God and wisdom to be upon our Government leaders. We knelt and humbled ourselves before God first! The National Prayer Committee then went to the

Dirksen Building, inside the White House, where we spent many more hours in effective intercession, interspersed with relevant Bible teaching, as we targeted needy people groups. This day culminated at a banquet in celebrating the passing of the bill to make the first Thursday in May a day of prayer for America. Senators also shared their requests and they were then prayed for.

God really broke through among us in the N.P.C. as we spent from 9 a.m. – 7 p.m. at the National Christian Center for prayer. It was truly historic, with openness and brokenness amongst us, followed by clear directions for further ministry assignments and vital prayers.

At the same time, the Lydia Fellowship was having a conference in Washington D.C., at which I attended.

One afternoon we all went on prayer walks around strategic buildings. I landed up on the steps of the Supreme Court and had appropriate strong intercession.

Following that, I witnessed to 36-year-old, Danny, an African American man who was begging in the street. After about 30 minutes of explaining to him the way of Salvation, he willingly repented of his sin, and committed his life to Christ. I then gave him some money.

The next day when Jim and I were out on our prayer walk, we met Danny again and took him to lunch and gave him some more money. I loved all this!!

On Sunday afternoon, May 1st, I spoke at the Dedication and Commissioning of the National Christian Center in Washington D.C. God gave me a brand new message for this momentous occasion from 1 Chronicles 29:10-20.

If we major on the project: the property, needed possessions, personnel, and money for payments, instead of the Provider God.... we are in idolatry. He owns it all. He's not short of money! Think about it.

The next day, Jim and I attended the Lord of the Nations Conference; a new group to us.

I was spontaneously called upon to speak. It witnessed in my spirit that I was to co-operate. My diary records that as I walked towards the pulpit, I was aware that I had no idea what to share; but I was totally relying on and believing for the life of the Lord to come forth through me. He did!

I spoke for 15-20 minutes on the effects of using my card "Ten Principles for Effective Intercession," followed by sharing the amazing story at the start of my book, "Intercession, Thrilling and Fulfilling." *

The following day, our National Prayer Committee conducted a "Prayer Conference" for all the international delegates of "The Lord of the Nations Conference."

In the afternoon, I spoke on "The Battle for the Nations." The message was taped, and the leadership sent a copy of it to every one of the delegates.

Many nations were represented from the approximately 200 who attended.

All the speakers were anointed and it was a powerful and spiritually rewarding day for the extension of God's Kingdom internationally. All glory to The King.

God's Faithfulness

For quite some time I had been earnestly asking God to make us debt free from the mortgage on our home. I believed it was His will, and I trusted Him to make a way, when I could see no way.

**Joy Dawson "INTERCESSION, THRILLING AND FULLFILLING" ©1997 by Y.W.A.M. Publishing.*

I determined not to give up asking in faith. I didn't share my faith project with anyone else but Jim.

After Jim had recovered from his surgery, we were participating in an international Y.W.A.M. conference being held in the Southern Hemisphere, in Manilla in the Philippines. On the last evening, both of us were seated on the platform when it happened!

Out of the blue, one of the International Council members, Leland Paris, came forward and publicly announced that he was handing us a check for $24,000. He explained that God had directed him to contact numbers of Y.W.A.M. leaders internationally, since Jim's major surgery, and ask them to help him raise a sizeable offering to help us financially at this time. We were both in complete shock, as we hadn't uttered a word to anyone about any of our needs, period!

Immediately I knew this was God answering my many prayers, and spontaneously exclaimed, **"Thank God; we're now out of debt!!"**

That was another milestone in our adventure of closely following and obeying the most magnificent Master--- Jesus. Jim always said that He paid far better wages than the business world ever paid him!!

Also, we have always been deeply grateful to our dear friend Leland for doing what he did, out of his great big generous heart.

Korea Olympics

From September 17th to October 2nd the 1988 Summer Olympic Games were held in Seoul, Korea.

A large Women's Missions Conference was convened during that time. Vonette Bright and I were the speakers. It was held in a beautiful big Presbyterian church.

I spoke on "The Biblical pattern for the battle for the nations" to this cross section denominationally, of women who were genuinely hungry for truth. I considered it a joyous privilege.

Another speaking engagement of significance was addressing 1500 Y.W.A.Mers who had come from around the world to witness at The Games. I gave them a new message on “The faithfulness of God” with updated radical illustrations.

It was very encouraging to find that our Y.W.A.M. leader for Korea, Jong Pyo Im, was one of those 4 Korean students I had taught when I first went to Korea, under very difficult circumstances.

God treated me with getting me a ticket into the new Olympic Stadium and I saw the athletics. It intrigued me that the Holy Spirit gave me the understanding who was going to win the women’s marathon. She was a skinny little woman from Portugal. I knew nothing about her.

Outside the huge Presbyterian Church in Seoul Korea during a women' s conference.

I told the friend, Craig Snow, who had brought me, that she would come right out from the pack and take over.

About 6-8 minutes later she did just that, and won hands down! Praise the Lord. Never a dull moment when surrendered to Him.

I have a most remarkable photo of part of the huge contingency of the Christians involved in ministry around the time of these Olympics. It is in the form of a large scroll, 17" wide and 8" deep, taken outside seven large porticoes of the largest Presbyterian church in all of Korea. Vonette Bright and I are the only non-Koreans in the photo. There are people 10 rows deep and 50 people across = 500. It is more than impressive.

On one of my many other ministry trips to Korea, I was standing in the Pastor's office of the Presbyterian church that I was about to speak in. It was just before the 11 a.m. service on a Sunday morning.

I hadn't been there more than about seven minutes when the pastor told me that he was under conviction of sin. I had never met this spiritual leader before and had no idea what had prompted his remark, so I remained silent.

He then explained that he had closely observed my Bible… how very worn it was…. through obviously much use. It was heavily marked throughout, and it conveyed to him that it was an intrinsic part of my life.

Then he said, "My Bible is not a bit like that; and I need to do something about it."

Again, silence was wisdom; so after a brief prayer we went into the service.

I was silently in awe that unquestionably my most prized earthly possession: God's precious love letter to me, was powerfully at work before I ever brought the message God had directed me to speak from it that morning.

Vonnette Bright and Joy are to the

participating in

right of the center of the Koreans

the 1988 Olympics.

My Mother's Suffering

In December of 1988, my New Zealand brothers, Howard and Stuart informed me that our elderly mother of 86 was feeling the effects of having cancer in her intestines and suggested that I come to New Zealand for a visit to be with her.

When Jim and I sought the Lord, He not only showed us that this was right, but gave us specific directions from His Word that I was to arrive on Monday, January 9th, and depart on Sunday, January 15th. I was then to go and teach at a Y.W.A.M. leadership training school in Kona, Hawaii, on route to the way home.

I followed this plan, along with accepting Dale and David Garratt's very kind offer to stay with them. Each day, Dale had arranged for someone to take me to Edenvale Home to be with mother as long as needed, and then to return me to their home. To say that dear Dale has a remarkable gift of hospitality is still an understatement. I was so blessed and so grateful to God and to her.

These were precious times together with mother as I would share encouraging Scriptures and pray with her, along with sharing things of interest. I would automatically do what she always loved and that was to stroke her arm throughout the time together. It obviously brought her some needed comfort. She preferred to listen rather than talk at 86, while feeling the effects of the malignant disease.

I then started on the job of going through her clothes; sorting them into categories for distribution, and throwing out unneeded stuff. This was a long process that only a daughter could do, and I was fulfilled in doing it. When it came time to leave, I was so thankful that I hadn't broken down and wept in her presence.

In March of 1989 I received word from my brothers in New Zealand that my dear mother was in a lot of pain. This was very hard for me to hear. I wrote her a loving letter, sharing a number of Scripture verses on the subject of grace, and suggested that she could apply them to the best of her ability to her difficult circumstances. I then assured her I was praying for God to minister His great grace to her in her distress.

Six days later, Stuart phoned to say mother was very ill and dying. How I longed to be beside her! And the next phone call said she had gone to be with Jesus.

All my life, Mother had talked a lot about how wonderful Heaven is and how she looked forward to going there, ever since she gave her life to Him as a teenager. Now she was experiencing it.

Months before her death, I had prepared, and sent her a copy of what I wanted to be read out at her funeral service, from me, which was a few days later. It was so very easy to honor her.

White House Visits

For twenty five years we were greatly privileged to be part of the National Prayer Committee, which included being guests at the Whitehouse on three occasions.

At one time the American President was George Bush Senior, who couldn't have been more honoring or more co-operative toward all that we represented and were doing.

Subsequently, our National Prayer Committee received an invitation to come to a breakfast at the White House. The purpose was to honor us and some other prayer leaders from across the nation, for our vital contribution to the country. It was the policy of government then, to deliberately give the invitations at very short notice.

George Bush Senior, along with his wife Barbara were our hosts. The President went to each person sitting at the round tables and personally thanked us for coming and shook our hands. He couldn't have been warmer or more sincere.

When the breakfast ceremony was over, he saw a small group of us standing together and said, "Would you like to see our Labrador puppies?"

I enthusiastically said, "I'd **love** to!" I'd heard that they had a litter of about ten of them.

He took us outside, and there they were, all bunched together in a sizeable pen asleep; with their paws overlapping each other. Some had their heads on other puppies' bodies. They were the picture of contentment, and so TOGETHER.

President Bush said with warm enthusiasm, "That's the perfect picture of family to me." I knew exactly what he meant, and admired him for the open, natural way he expressed his values from his heart. He was a strong family man.

As we were leaving the White House, he shook hands again with every one of us. I have a framed photo of the President doing this with Jim and me, while I warmly thanked him for the vital role he was playing at this time.

On another occasion, the N.P.C. was invited to the White House. We were responsible for finally getting a bill pushed through government, with President Ronald Regan signing it into law. It was to make the first Thursday in May a permanent National Day of Prayer. This still continues!!

I have another framed photo of George Bush, Sr. and his wife Barbara, standing in front of a large fireplace in the White House, closely surrounded by those of us on the N.P.C., along with a Jewish Rabbi and a few other venerable gentlemen. Vonette Bright as chairperson for our committee is holding a framed copy of this law. Dr. Bill Bright is standing behind her.

I know there was a third time that our N.P.C. was invited to the White House, but I haven't yet been able to find where I have recorded it in one of my many diaries,

They were wonderful years! Thank you, Lord.

President George Bush, Sr., thanking us for our contribution,

while I then thanked him for his great tribute to our nation.

Vonette Bright is holding a copy of law that was passed to make the first Thursday in May a National Day of Prayer. She is surrounded by the National Prayer Committee.

The Power Of Unity

In 1989, from March 6th-9th at the Mt Hermon Conference City in Northern California, I was part of a spiritual leadership conference with a very very diverse number of anointed and interesting speakers. They were:

- Pastor Robert Birch, a veteran intercessor from Toronto, Canada
- Dr. Sam Hines; an African American pastor from New York City
- Dr. Paul Cedar, a teacher at the Billy Graham Schools of Evangelism
- John Dawson, from Y.W.A.M. leading an urban missions network.
- Pastor Gerry Fry, from San Jose, Northern California
- And myself.

We had great spiritual unity regardless of our diversities, which caused God to "command the blessings upon us" according to Psalm 133:3. To God be the glory.

I'd be about 68 and Jim 71. We were out in our garden.

Our grandson David took the photo.

A Unique Experience

In May of 1989, Jim and I drove from Interlaken in Switzerland to a spectacular little village called Laterbrunnen, which has a one thousand foot waterfall.

Despite having had severe insomnia, I forced myself to stay awake.

We then took a train way up a steep mountain where we had spectacular views of the snow capped Alps. We arrived at Wengen village, where we were amazed at the height they were functioning in.

After checking it out, we reversed gears and returned to beautiful Interlaken.

Again, we were greatly blessed.

My Rave Review On God

The only purpose in your reading everything in this book to this point, is to make it easier for you to appropriate the truths in this section. We discern God's voice more clearly for these reasons:—that we may more fully obey Him, which in turn causes us to more thoroughly know Him, so that we are able to more accurately make Him known.

Unconditional obedience to God should be our love response to Him for His unconditional love to us. This removes all the dutiful dullness from our responses to His directions. Every influence God brings into our lives to encourage us to obey Him is so that we will do so because of Who He is.

So what is He really like? He is:

- Supreme in His authority
- Dazzling in His beauty
- Flawless in His character
- Ingenious in His creativity
- Timeless in His existence
- The most exciting Person
- Unswerving in His faithfulness
- Matchless in His grace
- Blazing in His glory
- Unparalleled in His greatness
- Awesome in His holiness
- Incomprehensible in His humility

- The Author of humor
- The ultimate in intensity
- Absolute in His justice
- Infinite in His knowledge and wisdom
- Unfathomable in His love
- The Fountain of life
- Unending in His mercy
- The Owner of everything
- Limitless in His power
- Fascinating in His personality
- Majestic in His splendor
- Indescribable in His tenderness
- Unquestionable in His sovereignty
- The personification of truth
- Unsearchable in His understanding
- Terrible in His wrath
- Mysterious in His ways
- The Ruler of an eternal, indestructible kingdom
- The reigning Monarch of the universe
- King God
- The Lover of my soul

He is the One who has totally captivated me, and the only One who can totally fulfill me.

In the light of that description, can you see that we do ourselves the greatest favor by running to obey Him?

The 1990s

1 Chronicles 6:28,29 …give to the Lord glory and strength. Give to the Lord glory due His name

REVIVAL And SPIRITUAL AWAKENINGS!

The passion for genuine revival and spiritual awakening and the inevitable unrelenting crying out to God in faith for it worldwide, has been and still is my number one intercessory prayer project. I fully believe it's soon to be unleashed in unprecedented proportions, prior to the imminent return of the Lord.

In 1990, I had a written question and answer interview with a periodical publication called Cross Point, which I'm now including in this book.

The title is, "**THE BURDEN FOR REVIVAL**".

Although it was written 30 years ago and the personal statistics are out dated, it captures the heart of the greatest intercessory prayer project I have been involved in for sixty-four years and still am, for every nation of the world.

It also conveys a lot of the heart of what is dearest to me concerning truth. It warrants repeated reading, with application where needed, for those who are serious about "not being ashamed before Him (Jesus) at His coming". 1 John 2:28.

Cross Point: Joy, you have taught the Bible all over the world for the past 20 years, can you tell our readers the nature and scope of your teaching?

Joy Dawson: I have been traveling internationally for 20 years, teaching on the character of God and the ways of God. A lot of the teaching is focused toward spiritual leaders.

CP: Where did you go?

Joy Dawson: I have gone to over 48 nations (now 53), many of them repeatedly, and to every continent.

CP: Because of the breadth of your traveling ministry, you are in a unique position to help our readers have a view of where we are headed as a Church. Would you talk about that?

Joy Dawson: On a world scale I perceive that God is preparing His people for an unprecedented outpouring of the Holy Spirit in revival power. I believe this to be one of the greatest things on God's agenda.

CP: Can you tell me what you mean by revival?

Joy Dawson: Revival is the sovereign outpouring of the Holy Spirit in God's way and time, first of all upon God's people. The revelation of God's holiness is greatly amplified, and as a result, God's viewpoint on sin is revealed. Revival is also God shaking and stirring His people from apathy, selfishness, and self-promotion, influencing them to become a humble people with a single passion for God Himself and His glory. A burden for lost souls is always intensified.

A great spiritual awakening among the lost also takes place and multitudes of hardened sinners deeply repent of their sins and commit their lives to the Lord Jesus Christ. Whole communities are inevitably affected. Many demonstrations of God's mighty power are also vividly evident. Evangelism is not revival, but evangelism is always an outcome of revival.

CP: The way you describe revival seems far distant from where we are now as a Church. Is that the way you see it?

Joy Dawson: I believe we are in God's preparation period for revival. God has stirred the hearts of many and given them a tremendous vision and burden in prayer for it. God has stirred some to teach on revival and write books on it. Prayer movements in many parts of the world have been brought into being by God, where prayer for revival is highlighted. Because of the stirring of God's Spirit in the hearts of His people, we know this is an encouraging sign that God is preparing to fulfill the many promises in His Word to bring revival. Isaiah 6:11 and Hosea 6:3 are two examples.

CP: Can you give us some examples of what you're talking about?

Joy Dawson: Being on the National Prayer Committee for the U.S.A. I have had the privilege and responsibility of being a part of some unprecedented prayer events. For example, I spoke at the International Prayer Assembly in Seoul, Korea in 1984 when prayer leaders and intercessors came together from seventy-two nations for ten days. The focus of all the messages was on prayer for revival and world evangelization, and unity in the Church. Fervent group praying followed each message. A large cross section of the Body of Christ was represented. Such a thing has never happened since Pentecost.

When we returned home, we went to the Campus Crusade International T.V. Studios where I taught two half hour programs on the subject of Trinity unity. They were then sent throughout the U.S.A. with the other International Prayer Assembly messages.

I often speak at weekend and week-long events related to how people can pray more effectively for revival. This is accompanied by earnest prayer.

Where people have given God time to break through and want Him to, I have seen Him do it in many and varied ways. Only the

Holy Spirit can stir His people to participate in these events. And it's happening all over.

CP: It seems that human beings are increasing in their sin. Evil seems to be growing greater and greater. Is that a contradiction to what you see coming in a great revival?

Joy Dawson: That's a very good question. The answer, I believe, is that as evil increases, God by His Spirit is able to intensify light and truth. Satan knows that his time is limited so he is spewing out as much as he can to influence mankind to rebel more against God. But God, who is far more powerful than the enemy, is pouring out His Spirit in an ever-increasing way to influence mankind toward holiness. Also, God's awesome power and authority will be manifest more fully in and through those who will choose holiness over evil.

CP: From what you say, the Church is the pivotal factor. What then is God calling the Church to be or to do?

Joy Dawson: God is calling His Church to be obedient to the Great Commission (Matthew 28:19,20) and to prepare for worldwide revival, accompanied by an unprecedented harvest of souls. He is also calling His people to get ready to be a part of His Bride "without spot or wrinkle" in preparation for His second coming. I see many signs of this preparation. For example, I see a whole generation of youth that only need leading into a radically real Christian lifestyle, devoid of religiosity.

I see the Church worldwide being stirred by Jesus Christ the Head of the Church, to become a strong militant force against evil, refusing to bow down to the gods of apathy, selfishness, and compromise. I see a great increase in awareness of the need to be empowered by the Holy Spirit to live a holy life; to know God and make Him known to the unreached.

CP: Is there something we as Christians need to do for revival? Is there a price to pay?

Joy Dawson: Yes. Perhaps I could answer that by talking about some of the hindrances to revival. The first thing is **ignorance**. When we see what revival is we can see what it is not. Then we can see where we need to shape up in order to help fulfill conditions which bring revival.

The second hindrance is a **lack of vision** for revival. That's why it is so important to have a definition of what revival is. For example, God does more in seconds and minutes to build His church and extend His kingdom in revival than would normally take place in years through God-inspired and God-energized Christian activity.

During the height of the revival that swept America from 1857-58, for example, when Charles Finney was being so mightily used of God, it was estimated that 50,000 conversions were occurring in a single week. And that was without the help of any radio and television. The Holy Spirit was poured out. Many times the conviction of sin was so strong—in hearts of Christians as well as non-Christians—that before Finney ever came into town the people would be smitten with conviction. In some of his meetings, he would arrive to speak and the groaning and weeping over sin would be so great, he would have to wait to be heard. Oh that God would speed the day for that to be repeated!

CP: What are some other hindrances?

Joy Dawson: **Lethargy and indifference**. Most Christians would rather remain in the comfort zone of the status quo. They don't really want the discomfort of strong conviction and humbling. They haven't embraced the message of the cross to the self-life. And when we don't want the cross to come against the self-life we don't want any change.

CP: What do you mean by the cross coming against the self-life?

Joy Dawson: I mean our agreeing with God's viewpoint on our hearts as only He can see them at any moment. It is letting ourselves be exposed to the true revelation of what we are. (2 Chronicles 6:30)

CP: And that is painful to the old self-life, is it not?

Joy Dawson: It is devastating to the flesh. But at the same time it is wonderful because it is reality. **We don't have a passion for truth until we have a passion for knowing the truth about ourselves.**

CP: What causes lethargy in us?

Joy Dawson: Lethargy and indifference come from pride which says, "I'm okay as I am." Change is often uncomfortable. We don't want to be changed to be more conformed to the likeness of Jesus Christ. Humility says, "Any change would be an improvement." If revival is going to show me my heart quicker than anything else then, "God, please bring on revival."

Lethargy and indifference can be symptoms of a lack of spiritual ambition to see the Body of Christ manifesting the life of the Lord Jesus. Openness, brokenness and true repentance always release a greater evidence of His life in us. So revival is really a manifestation of the full life of the Lord Jesus in every believer. In addition, we may not want revival because of all the involvement that inevitably comes with thousands of new converts.

Another hindrance is lack of unity. I have wondered why those who have a genuine burden for revival, and have prayed as though their lives depended on it for many many years, haven't seen the answers to their prayers. Could it be that if God poured out His Spirit in true revival power on His people universally, though they were not yet unified in understanding the ways of the Spirit, it could split the Church?

Unity is such an extremely important factor to God. It is so important that Jesus said it would convince the world that God sent Him into the world, and that He loves His disciples today as much as He loved His Son. Therefore I believe that every time we pray for revival we need to pray, "God, unite Your Body worldwide and teach us what Your character is really like. Teach us the ways of Your Spirit, so that when You come in revival power Your people will cooperate with You and not resist You." Sadly, there are times when those who pray for revival become the very ones who hinder the workings of the Holy Spirit when their prayers are answered.

CP: What other hindrances to revival do you see?

Joy Dawson: A lack of a real prayer burden. Most only pray for revival when others call them to pray. They don't have a consistent daily prayer priority program for it. We should be praying for the outpouring of God's Spirit upon the Body of Christ in every country of the world. We can do it systematically, taking one or more nations daily.

God has encouraged us to cry out to Him for spiritual awakening and to believe He will answer, by giving us the prayers of the prophets in His Word. Habakkuk 3:2-6, Isaiah 64:1-3, and Jeremiah 14:7, 20-22 are a few examples.

God waits to see whether our praying for revival will be with intensity and deep desire. Why should God send something awesome to a casual people? God's heart and hand are more likely to move when He sees a desperate people, a humble people, people with a broken and contrite spirit at prayer. We ask for revival on the basis of need, not because we deserve it.

Disobedience to revealed truth and the promptings of the Holy Spirit is another hindrance to revival. Disobedience is always a sign of the lack of the fear of the Lord and the major cause for spiritual dullness. We find that Bible obedience is instant, joyful and whole. All else is disobedience. Those who take God seriously make this their standard. Disobedience to making God's priorities our priorities on a daily basis, makes us unprepared for revival.

Another hindrance is the **unwillingness of spiritual leaders to lead** in the outpouring of God's Spirit, where the unusual is the normal. If we are only comfortable with cut and dried predictable programs, we'll be very uncomfortable in revival. Spontaneity is always a characteristic of revivals. They are never cut and dried or predictable. If the leaders are not used to being flexible and flowing with God's spontaneity now, they will hinder the moves of God's Spirit in revival.

Another hindrance is **the desire of leaders to control** programs and people, or have others control every situation when the Body of Christ gets together. It comes from an unwillingness to die to our reputations when the unusual takes place because of our fear of men, based on pride. This is the opposite of taking responsibility to release people into the moving of the Holy Spirit, or to correct them gently and firmly if they're out of order.

Then there is **unwillingness for God to move upon and through anyone whom He should choose** in revival. I don't know a more vivid illustration of humility in a spiritual leader in this regard than Duncan Campbell when in the Hebrides revival. During a communion service the atmosphere was heavy and preaching was difficult. Duncan Campbell then asked four spiritual men to pray, who on another occasion had been used of God to pray until there was a release in the Spirit. I quote from a written account of that revival:

"The elders prayed, but the spiritual bondage persisted so much that halfway through, Duncan Campbell stopped preaching. Just then he noticed a boy, 15 years of age, a young teenager who had recently been converted in the revival, and was being mightily used by God. He looked at the new convert who was visibly moved under a deep burden for souls. And he thought, "That boy is in touch with God. He is living nearer to the Savior than I am at this moment.' So he leaned over the pulpit and said, 'Donald, will you lead us in prayer?'

The lad rose to his feet and in his prayer made reference to the fourth chapter in Revelation, which he had been reading that morning. He said, 'O God, I seem to be gazing through the open door. I see the Lamb in the midst of the Throne, with the keys of death and hell at His girdle.' He began to sob; then lifting his eyes to heaven, cried out, **'O God there is power there, let it loose!'**

With the force of a hurricane, the Spirit of God swept into the building and the floodgates of Heaven opened. The church resembled a battlefield. On one side many were prostrated over the seats, weeping and sighing. On the other side, some were affected by throwing their hands in the air, in rigid posture. God had come." Duncan was a man who through humility of heart and sensitivity to the Spirit allowed God to be God. Very few spiritual leaders are ready to pass that test.

Finally, we are not willing to give God time to work. We convey to Him by our actions that we want Him to break through in our midst, but not after 12:30, thank you! (if we're meeting in the morning.) And certainly not after 10 o'clock at night. And most often God's response is, "When you're ready to have My program in My way, and wait and give Me time, I'll move."

CP: What is the solution to these hindrances?

Joy Dawson: We need to invite the Holy Spirit to convict us in our own hearts where they apply to our own lives. From our repentance we then intercede for others, particularly spiritual leaders, that they will see the need to repent where these hindrances apply.

If we have no vision or burden for revival we need to ask God to give us both. Submit to the Holy Spirit and believe Him to conceive it within our hearts. Then start praying as He directs. God will give a genuine vision and burden for revival to everyone who wants it.

The more we pray for revival the more the vision and the burden grows.

We need to study the character of God and the ways of God from His Word. We need to study past and present revivals, asking God to give us an understanding of the ways of the Holy Spirit, during these times of great spiritual awakenings. We need to frequently pray, "Prepare me for the coming days of unprecedented opportunity and awesome responsibility to know You and make You known."

A Cloudburst Of Genuine Revival

Jim and I were in Hong Kong attending a Y.W.A.M. staff conference for those from South East Asia.

One morning I was scheduled to speak at 11 a.m. for 1 hour. I spoke on "Jesus the leader in ministry." Right on 12:00 noon I concluded and sat down in the front row.

Kalafi Moala, the leader of the conference then stood behind the pulpit, when he suddenly heard the Holy Spirit say, "Move over to the side wall." Kalafi immediately obeyed!

Just as suddenly, Dean Sherman, a seasoned Y.W.A.M. Bible teacher, went straight behind the podium and said that he had been giving a message related to the importance of Y.W.A.M. parents being protective of their children.... and that the Holy Spirit had convicted him that this message was based upon unbelief. He was openly repenting. And then he sat down.

Immediately following, we heard repeated high pitched wailing coming from someone we couldn't see. I whispered to Jim, "That's exactly the sound that was prevalent throughout the Welsh Revival, when God was revealing to people their hearts as He sees them!"

The wailing continued, until finally a young woman cried out, "It's my sin of pride of being a missionary." She was lying on the floor, stretched out under peoples' chairs. When she finally stopped wailing and stood up, we saw that she was an attractive tall Norwegian.

Straight after that, an Asian male missionary came forward who was very broken before the Lord. Through his many tears he shared that as an Asian he now saw the strong prejudices he had against American or English missionaries. He thought Asians were so superior.

His weeping was so intense as he saw the horrible pride in his heart, that one of our male Y.W.A.M.ers had to take him aside and help him come to peace.

The Holy Spirit was in total control, as one by one the missionaries continued to move forward openly confessing and repenting of their sins. There was no human leadership, but perfect order.

This cloudburst of genuine revival lasted for four hours, and then stopped as suddenly as it started. Kalafi then thanked God for this awesome visitation of the Holy Spirit and quietly dismissed us. We left with a strong sense of the fear of the Lord.

I spoke to Dean Sherman's son relatively recently, who also has a Bible teaching ministry in Y.W.A.M. He said his father still talks about that awesome sovereign move of the Holy Spirit.

A Surprise Visitation

It was in June of 1990 and I was in Lausanne, Switzerland teaching at Y.W.A.M.'s "School of Worship and Intercession."

One particular day I was speaking on "Worshiping God with our lives." I came to the point on "Worshiping God when He has given us a promise for something and there's no way we can see how it can be fulfilled. That's when we exercise the praise of faith."

All the students took off in clapping and singing and dancing before the Lord, while they shouted out their statements of faith. It was spontaneous and wonderful! We truly worshipped before the releases, as Hannah did before Samuel was conceived. I was believing God for J.B. and Jill to have the money to be able to buy a home.

The next day I came to the point that "True worship follows a surrendered will to God" and illustrated if from Mary's song of praise to God after saying, "Be it unto me according to Your will."

I was then suddenly, sovereignly moved upon by the Holy Spirit to speak about Mary's youthfulness. Then immediately He directed my focus on the four teenagers in the class room – Glenn and Jackie Sheppard's three children, Tray, Christa, and Trent, and Tray's friend Torey.

I challenged them to a greater commitment of their lives to God, for the greater things He wanted to do through them, and prophesized over them. I then invited them to come forward so that we could all pray for them.

This triggered off an amazing move of God's Spirit as God then revealed that they were representing all the churched youth of the world. We washed their feet and anointed them with hand cream and kissed them. Then one person after another prayed and prophesized over them.

There was an enormous sense of God's presence and a unique purity of Spirit in everything that was shared.

All this laid the foundation of many years of a deep bonding of God's love between us, and the outworking of mighty ministry times that are later recorded in this book.

The Baltic States

In July of 1990, Jim and I teamed up with Loren Cunningham and Al Akimof (who speaks Russian) for a missions trip to Latvia, Estonia, and Russia of the Soviet Union. Al's cousin, who also speaks Russian, came as another interpreter. This was during the time of Communist rule when open displays of Christianity were often opposed.

In the strategic cities where Y.W.A.M.ers had been ministering, Loren and I would bring the Word of the Lord to hungry believers and minister to them. One day at the end of speaking to about 25 people, on "How to hear God's voice." I signed and gave away 14 Bibles to people who never owned one, and kissed each person.

They responded by thanking me profusely and giving me scarves and cards.

Jim and I and Al Akimof were ministering in Riga, Latvia. I was speaking in a Baptist church, through an interpreter, when I said that in genuine revival deep repentance is followed by great joy in the Lord. The Holy Spirit then sovereignly "took off" through me, and for the next 30 minutes I spontaneously shared about the need for the joy of the Lord in our lives and all its benefits.

It became obvious that those dear people desperately needed to be released into God's joy.

Later, I was sharing about this with my interpreter, Peter Ilyn. It was then I remembered that 7 months before, during a powerful time of intercession in Bradenton, Florida, one of the intercessors had a vision of me leading people in the U.S.S.R. into the joy of the Lord!! Oh the wonders of God's ways when we are totally yielded to him.

The following day I spoke twice in a Pentecostal tent meeting. God really showed up with healings of minds and bodies as I spoke on "God the great Deliverer."

The next afternoon we went as a team to a famous beach resort to witness. Along with an interpreter, while I handed out gospel tracts in Russian, many people gathered to get them.

I spontaneously started to preach the gospel with Fred as my interpreter. The crowd doubled and remained the whole 20 minutes or more.

After I gave an appeal, a number raised their hands, and then I led them sentence by sentence into a full commitment of their lives to the Lord Jesus Christ. A very handsome young couple from Kiev came and knelt down to pray the prayer out loud. We gave them the few New Testaments we had.

It was insufferably hot at night in the church. I was pouring with sweat as I preached to a packed out audience with many young people, on "How to hear God's voice." I was mightily released in the Spirit as I taught God's ways, and then led them into a time of listening to God.

A significant prophecy was given through me that God wanted to use them in signs and wonders, but they needed more depth for the breadth of ministry coming, and they needed to know God and His ways and wait on Him. All this was confirmed publicly by the Pastor.

From Riga, Latvia we went to Tallinn, Estonia where I spoke through an interpreter to about 125 people in Pastor Rein's church on "Are you prepared for Revival?"

Jim interceded all the way through and said there was a definite anointing of the Holy Spirit on the message. The Pastor confirmed this.

All glory to Jesus.

The next day I spoke in a large church, where Count Zindendorf used to preach. It was packed out. I was way up high in the preacher's loft, which always intrigued little me. The Holy Spirit's presence was very strong as I taught on "Knowing God" to a receptive audience.

In the evening I counseled a very needy Spiritual leader's wife for four hours. God healed her spiritually and physically.

In my daily Bible reading, I saw how appropriate John 1:16 was to my circumstances:

"From the fullness of His grace we have all received one blessing after another." That's why all glory must go to Jesus.

One afternoon, Jim and I and our interpreter went out in the streets witnessing. I stopped on a sidewalk and in a natural manner preached the gospel as people passed by. At one point, two young soldiers in uniform, stopped and voluntarily fell down on their knees in front of me. They were in serious prayer.

It arrested me then, and has permanently impacted me to this day. It could only be explained by the powerful times of prayer that Jim and I had daily on this trip, with two young women from Y.W.A.M. staff. They had come for the express purposes of being intercessors. How God would reward them!!

While Jim and I were on our prayer walk, God revealed to me that there were no meetings for the women and no women's ministries in Estonia. Subsequently I was to encourage the women to believe God to give them ministries as they obeyed tonight's message.

I was directed by God to speak on "The importance of obeying God's (5) daily priorities," plus "Praying for a number of important ways for God's Church."

It was a privilege to bring the word of the Lord to the grateful hungry hearted Believers in Estonia.

The next day I preached the gospel in the Old City Square in Tallinn, from a raised up platform.

Because it was raining lightly, I had an umbrella in one hand and a microphone in the other. A good crowd had gathered, as the Russian team had sung Christian songs.

Peter, from the Olevista Baptist church interpreted for me. Seventeen people responded with upraised hands that they wanted to commit their lives to Christ, when I gave an appeal.

I was so fulfilled...only God knows! We also gave out many Bibles and gospel tracts.

A woman and her 15 year old son came and thanked me personally afterward. The mother was weeping with gratitude. The boy came and saw me off at the train station.

We left Tallinn on a sleeper train for Leningrad, but I never slept! The next evening our team went to a theater where the U.S.-Russian singers gave a good concert. Then after Loren had preached the gospel, about one hundred people responded to the appeal – Hallelujah! All glory to Jesus.

We went with the team on a very interesting tour to Peter the Great's Summer Palace. The grounds were spectacular with many beautiful fountains and humungous palaces.

A group of Muslim Uzbek's in their national or native dress and gold filled teeth were touring. We stopped and photographed them with us. Then we sang to them and them to us.

After I danced with their elderly lady leader, I then preached the gospel with my interpreter. They listened to me respectfully. This was a significant opportunity.

I was fully aware then, as I am now, that this was probably the only time these dear Muslim people had ever heard the gospel message in their lifetime. It is possible that it became their last. They were soon returning home to their own country. I have prayed accordingly.

We then saw the Russian Orthodox Church leaders do their religious traditional ceremony outdoors.

When we were in St. Peterburg, Russia, the Y.W.A.M. team was having an effective time in singing praise songs and proclaiming the gospel. It was outside a **mammoth-sized** Cathedral that the

Communists had turned into an atheist museum. The team operated on a platform that was at the top of numerous steps outside the entrance.

A crowd of about 500 had gathered. Following a prompting of the Holy Spirit, I asked the team leader if I could speak. He agreed. Immediately I knew I was to spontaneously share that "Jesus is the way, the truth, and the life." I did this for 20 minutes. To conclude, I shouted out loudly with an amplifier, "Jesus Christ is alive" three times. The audience clapped enthusiastically. They seemed pleased that it was spoken from someone who really believed it.

While speaking, I observed 3 Communist soldiers with their rifles, standing in the crowd and listening to my interpreter attentively. Aware of the Holy Spirit's power at work, I gave an invitation for people to commit their lives to Christ, and to indicate that by raising their hands.

Immediately, many responded with hands up all across the crowd. Some people wept and some were overcome with joy. Jim photographed this whole thing for the record. I went down and spoke warmly to the three soldiers on duty. They couldn't have been more respectful, friendly, and interested… and I couldn't have been more thrilled or fulfilled.

What an incredible, historic opportunity in the most unusual circumstance and places, to openly share about the Redeemer of mankind! It was an exhilarating, exciting experience and opportunity. It met a great longing that I had.

Loren and I utilized some extended time he had the next day at the Leningrad Airport, before he flew out to Hamburg, Germany. We had vital times of intercession related to important Y.W.A.M. matters and I was able to bring him strong encouragements from God's Word.

Later, some of us went and saw Isaac's Cathedral. It was "incredibly beautiful and spectacular beyond words" according to my diary's entry. We then walked among great crowds in their main shopping street.

A Historic Event

My diary entry for August 11th 1990 is significant enough to record. It was the day before we were leaving for Indianapolis, when among other events Y.W.A.M. was having a leadership conference. This is the unedited version.

"The usual pressured day of packing and preparing to leave the house. I went to bed at 12:30 p.m. and was up at 3:13 a.m. with more preparation for leaving. Only God's grace keeps me living at this pace. But it is sufficient.

The day before I leave the house is always the most difficult time because of scores of details that have to be remembered and worked through. It's mentally and physically exhausting.

Because obedience is the sign of love to God, I whispered my love to God today, as I packed up for the thousandth time.

If the privilege wasn't higher than the price, the price wouldn't be worth it. With only a minimal amount of 2 ¾ hours sleep we were ready to leave the house at 4:45 a.m. to catch a flight out of the L.A.X. airport at 6:35 a.m."

On the second day of the Y.W.A.M. conference I spoke on "Hindrances to Revival." The next day there was a Congress on World Evangelization in the Hoosier Doom in Indianapolis, where 40,000 came together. It was Wednesday, August 15th. The purpose was to reunite many who had been greatly blessed during the charismatic renewal.

To my intense delight the opening event was "The King's Kids" singing under the direction of my friend, Dale Kaufman of Y.W.A.M. It was electric, stimulating, refreshing, and spiritually challenging, as they sang under an anointing of the Holy Spirit, Graham Kendrick's song – "Shine Jesus Shine." *©1987 by Make Way Music.*" I encourage you to listen to it online.

I had been invited to speak on the subject of "Praying for the nations," and was given 20 minutes. God clearly directed me to accept this assignment, and I spent many hours in preparation. The challenge was condensing a full hour's message that I had on "Intercession for World Evangelism" into 20 minutes.

It then took numerous times rehearsing it with a stop watch to make sure I didn't go over the allotted time.

I was then informed that Larry Lea and I were the opening speakers. Larry was also given 20 minutes and he was to precede me.

When the eventful day arrived, and I was about three quarters of the way through my message, someone handed the chairman of the Conference a note saying some problem had risen about the parking of cars.

The dear chairman (whomever he was at the time) decided to terminate my message and make an announcement about the parking right then!!

Part of my message was a strong call to be interceding for the millions of unreached Muslims; in full faith that they would become disciples of Christ.

At that time, this kind of prayer was very seldom mentioned....especially publicly. But I had been praying it for many years.

We then returned to the vital Y.W.A.M. conference where the emphasis was on reaching all the nations, and including the Muslim world.

Y.W.A.M. already had 80 teams working among Muslims at that time.

I spoke again on the priorities God gave to unity and sustained intercession before the outpouring of the Spirit in Acts 1:8 and our great need to be having the same priorities. There are no short cuts! Humility heeds and agrees. Pride says, 'Business as usual."

Latvia And England

I was attempting to write about a significant ministry trip to Latvia and England when I providentially came across the following letter, which I wrote in July 1991 to a dear pastor friend, Mike Dillman, who had kindly sent us money from his church in Modesto, California.

Dear Mike,

Warmest greetings. It seems right to give you and the church a brief report on my recent ministry trip to Latvia and England – hence this letter.

The Latvian part was a rugged pioneering experience often in primitive conditions. The demands on my whole being would have been overwhelming, but for the miraculous grace of God. I spoke fourteen times in seven days, often having to work with two interpreters at the same time – one in Latvian, the other in Russian. Two trips were included in that week.

Most of the messages God directed me to give were related to the character of God --- the others were on His ways. The people had very little understanding of either.

Spiritually hungry, open, grateful, hearts responded to the truths and as a result, the messages were life changing. The people who attended the intensive Discipleship Training Course were from 20-45 years of age. Some were potentially key leaders. All this made the privilege to go and give the truths, higher than the high price.

The Leader's Conference in England, with representation from over 100 nations, was historic to say the least and will have global effects on reaching the unevangelized peoples of the world. Barriers between races, sexes, denominations, Protestants and Roman Catholics, were broken down, and stronger-than-ever-unity was a tangible result.

When I spoke on "Praying for the world's un-evangelized", and "Prayer in relation to personal soul winning," the hundreds who came to listen on both occasions were deeply impacted by the truths and the application to them ---- many vocalizing this. Jim and I spent hours daily with a group of 38 other intercessors, praying throughout the conference.

So ---- you did not give or pray in vain. Only eternity will tell how the nations have been and will be affected in relation to the extension of God's Kingdom. I will be forever grateful for the vital role you and your church played in this.

Jim sat through the multiplied hours of teaching, conscientiously interceding for me and the people. I would hate to have done this trip without him. God knows I needed him in every way.

We continue to pray regularly for you both, and the precious people in your church.

Loving & very gratefully,

Joy

Argentina And Chile

I spoke at the Y.W.A.M. School of Missions in Argentina, the Missions Conference in Santiago, Chile, and the Pastors Conference in the city Conception.

I had the joy of having dear Nancy Neville, our seasoned Y.W.A.M. leader for Chile, as my interpreter. She said that a good number of the pastors listening to me teach God's truths from His Word with genuine authority, had never had a woman teach them before. However they all received me and the life changing truths that I shared.

- I spoke on "Jesus the master soul winner," one night in a theater to a good sized audience in Buenos Aires. It was needed and headed.
- I spoke in a Methodist Church full of pastors in the City of Conception, on the implications of "Knowing God to make Him known."
- I spoke in a Baptist church in Buenos Aires, on "The need and purpose for not neglecting the Word of God in daily living" – hundreds came to the altar in repentance.
- I spoke at our Y.W.A.M. Campus in Buenos Aires, on "God's priority in implementing vision."
- I spoke on "To know God and to make Him known" in Buenos Aires at a Pastors Conference.

My diary records, "This trip to Argentina and Chile has been an incredible marathon of giving the Word of the Lord by the hour, proceeded by hours and hours of message preparation and prayer, with only a little rest and severe insomnia.

But, when I left, I felt VERY FULFILLED that I had accomplished the task for which I was sent, by the grace of God and in the power of the Holy Spirit. Praise the Lord.

History has been made in the lives of many pastors and spiritual leaders, in Chile.

Billy Graham Retreat Center

A week's meetings for prayer leaders from a number of different nations, were convened at the Billy Graham newly appointed (at that time) Retreat Center called The Cove.

It is situated in the North Carolina hills, surrounded by beautiful native forest, which included peaceful prayer walks and resting places. It is very unique.

I was one of the speakers at that vital gathering of related international ministries. My subject was on "Spiritual Warfare".

A significant highlight was having Dr. Billy Graham come and speak to us when it had concluded. He was comparatively frail in health, being carefully guarded by his staff. But he was spiritually strong, very alert, and passionate about his God ordained mission.

The setting was relatively small and intimate and the sense of privilege was enormous, as Jim and I were seated in the front row, a few yards away from this gracious giant of the Faith. We sensed he wanted to be given more time to speak to us, than his staff had planned.

A Different Setting

The following is taken from my book, "Intercession, Thrilling And Fulfilling" *:

Somewhere around 1992, on a Saturday night, Jim and I paired off with two of our Youth With A Mission workers in Hollywood. At 2:30 a.m., the converted former prostitute I was with asked me if I wanted to go into a brothel with her to witness to some of her friends.

**Joy Dawson "INTERCESSION, THRILLING AND FULLFILLING" ©1997 by Y.W.A.M. Publishing.*

I readily accepted. Jim and his partner waited in the car and interceded for us.

As we entered the room, my attractive African-American partner simply said, "Hi, this is my friend Joy" to three young prostitutes and their pimps who were seated on beds—the girls were taking a break. Since there were no chairs, we sat on the floor. I smiled warmly, said "Hi," and focused the conversation immediately on the Lord Jesus. Most of the people in the room were comfortable talking about Him.

During the hour that I was there I learned that two of the girls and two of the pimps had formerly been exposed to the Church, and Christians. The other pimp and his prostitute wore expressions as cold and lifeless as Egyptian sphinxes—and were as uncommunicative. The rest of the group entered into a lively dialogue with us. The former prostitute's radiant face was eloquent proof of the transforming work of Christ in her life.

Two of the prostitutes were bitter about experiences they'd had with Christians. I kept bringing the focus back to Jesus, our relationship with Him being the real issue. The girls readily agreed that there is no fault with Him. They chatted freely and respectfully with us. As we left, the head pimp, concerned for my safety, warned me that it could be pretty dangerous out on those streets at this time of night. I was touched by his genuine, warm concern.

As a way of life, I put the names or a description of the people to whom I witness on a list and pray regularly and fervently for their conversions. I added the names of those people to that long list, and prayed in faith for God to draw them to Himself. Three weeks later, one of the prostitutes was converted by being confronted with the gospel while out in the streets, and went to live in one of the Y.W.A.M. houses in downtown Hollywood. I met her again several months later when she had become a student at the Los Angeles Y.W.A.M. Discipleship Training School. The transformation in her was so radical, I hardly recognized her. It was a very meaningful reunion.

Taipei

In 1992 John and I went to Taipei to be the speakers at a Chinese spiritual leadership conference. That resulted in my being invited to return in 1993 to speak at a pastor's conference to those from around the nation of Taiwan.

Half of them spoke Taiwanese; the other half spoke mandarin, so I spoke to each group separately.

As is my custom, whenever the leadership over me releases me, I lead the audience into a time of application of the message just given. It's usually in the form of pertinent questions they need to answer before the Lord. The pastors responded very seriously to this.

The leadership team who invited me, reported at the close, that it was the first time all the pastors of the Taiwanese language had ever come together, and they came with their senior leaders. One of their Bishops also came.

The messages the Holy Spirit directed me to speak on to those Chinese pastors were:

1. "Conditions for speaking with Spiritual Authority."
2. Jesus the leader in ministry.
3. Are you prepared for revival?
4. The dynamics of togetherness in taking our cities for God.

God moved by His Spirit in answer to much prayer and lives were permanently changed. Those pastors would be part of those who would help prepare the coming generations for the mighty visitations of the Holy Spirit.

South Island Of New Zealand Roadtrip

In 1992 Jim and I went with John and Julie and their 3 boys, for a road trip around the South Island of New Zealand. We loved having this special time together, in unquestionably one of the most scenically beautiful parts of the world.

It was uniquely meaningful to me. Although I had been to eight other nations for ministry purposes, I had never been to the South Island of my homeland.

From Auckland, we flew down to Wellington where we met up with John and his family; and then we all took a car ferry which took us across Cook Strait to the South Island.

We drove to Kaikoura where we watched a colony of seals in fascinating action on the rocks.

We passed towns that were situated beside beautiful beaches, and then on to lush green farmlands with contented cattle grazing. Nothing was crowded! There were only 3 ½ million people in the two Islands of New Zealand at that time.

One day I reveled in the excitement of us all going on a jet river boat ride on the Waipa River. It was Power Packed, and UNREAL! ☺ We concluded that the wild driver was:

- The most skilled.
- On the most dangerous ride.
- With the greatest responsibility.

The further down we drove, the scenery changed to include large privately owned high country sheep stations, where lots and lots of sheep were contentedly grazing, or just chilling out! They were part of the 52 million sheep in the country! In the background were large snowcapped mountains, where the snow never melts.

After staying at the Frans Joseph Glacier Resort, we travelled in pouring rain all afternoon through beautiful rain forests – very unique. We stayed at the Lakeside Motel on the Esplando with a fantastic view of the lake and mountains, looking through poplar trees.

We also passed waterfalls pouring down through the fern forests on the side of the road.

Our knockout scenic adventure was when we went to Mount Cook. John and the boys and Jim and I took a helicopter ride over mountains and then the pilot landed us on a glacier. It was a thrilling experience. Our Kiwi pilot gave us double time as we were his last customers for the day.

When we walked a short distance in the snow we discovered a large avalanche waiting to happen. That really got my attention! Little Mathew started to run in that direction and we went after him in a hurry.

In the background were huge snowcapped mountains, with Mt. Cook being the center peak. The pilot took a photo of us sitting on a big rock peak. John had it enlarged and framed and gave it to me. I have it on a wall in my home, and never tire looking at it!! I specially love what he wrote on the back of it.

"Here you are with your boys at the top of the world. You have taught us to look down on life from the safety of God's throne. We love you. Happy Mother's Day 1992."

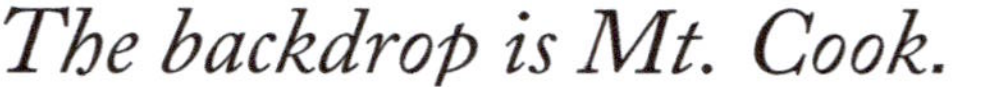

The backdrop is Mt. Cook.

Later, when in Queenstown, we took the cable cars up to a peak stop over where the breathtaking panoramic views of a mountain range named "The Remarkables" are on full display. The only appropriate response was to stand in awe of the Creator of this universe and worship Him.

It boggles my mind to think that He is at the same time my closest companion, and the lover of my soul....and I'm going to spend eternity serving His eternal purposes.... which are humongous. Hallelujah forever!

A Surprise Ending

I went to my regular doctor for a routine checkup. When he X-rayed my uterus it clearly showed a critical mass which he identified as cancer. He also let me see it for myself, as he then strongly recommended surgery.

My immediate reaction was, "How soon can you do it?" His answer was, "Early tomorrow morning." I said, "O.K. book me in."

When I returned home and shared the news with Jim, he prayed a powerful prayer for my healing, in whichever way God would choose to do it.

God then gave us an encouraging verse of Scripture from 1 Corinthians 6:14 "And God both raised up the Lord, and will also raise us up by His power."

Before we drove off to the hospital very early the next morning, I asked God to speak to us again. He did from Revelation 10:11 "And He said to me, 'You must prophecy again about many peoples, nations, tongues, and kings.'" The understanding given, was that there was still a lot more ministry years ahead for me.

I was lying on the gurney in the hospital, just before being wheeled into the operating room, when my Doctor came and said to me, "Before every surgery, doctors have to take a final X-ray before proceeding. When I did this with another surgeon, we couldn't find a sign of that cancer anywhere. We cannot explain it. You're released to go home."

I got dressed and phoned Jim, who had just arrived home. To his delight he came and got me and we marveled at the sheer mercies of the Lord with this miracle of healing. Thank You Holy Spirit.

August 1992

I have always had the deepest appreciation for Dr. Charles Stanley's ministry. He is the senior pastor of the First Baptist Church in Atlanta, Georgia, with a powerful International Television ministry.

In August, 1992, I was grateful when the Lord confirmed to me that I was to accept the invitation to be the speaker at a weekend Prayer Seminar at this vital church.

In the Saturday morning sessions I spoke on, "How to go deeper in our prayer lives." In the afternoon session I spoke on, "Praying in the most difficult circumstances, for the most difficult people, and with the most difficult kinds of prayers."

When I asked for the people in the audience to stand to their feet if they had experienced a 180 degree change in their thinking, and were now determined to follow through with their lives regardless of the cost, as it related to these truths...everyone stood!

These precious people were hungry and ready for truth. According to Jim's report, there was a very strong sense of our wonderful Lord's presence and power all day. All glory to Him alone.

That Saturday evening we met up with the precious Cambodian Sengsouvong family for dinner at the Marriot hotel and had two and a half wonderful hours together. They shared about regularly attending the local Baptist Church in their suburb, and that their son Sonpasong, and daughters, Pelina and Pelanita had been converted. We saw how real this was and that Somsak was a leader and a good father. Only God knew how much joy this brought me to see this former refugee family that I had found at an airport, now fulfilling their destinies with the Lord. Hallelujah!

At the 9a.m. and 11a.m. Sunday services the next day, I testified to the unfailing faithfulness of God to me as an unsalaried missionary, traveling internationally, to direct me and then provide for me. I shared the conditions I needed to fulfill, and then gave brief, pertinent illustrations. I had to talk fast to get it into the 7 minutes allotted me!

A Typical Ministry Day

There is no way that I can report on countless other days when away in effective ministry, but this day is a sample of many like it.

We were in Rapid City, South Dakota, after having quality time reading the Bible, Jim and I went on a long prayer walk. Then we drove out to our Y.W.A.M. Base and had quality time with the directors, David and Sheri McPherson; a great couple.

They then drove us to a commercial T.V. Station, where I had a taped interview for ten minutes. The director said he was making a whole program out of it.

We then went up to Mt. Rushmore and saw the incredible carvings out of the rocks of the heads of Presidents George Washington, Thomas Jefferson, Teddy Roosevelt, and Abraham

Lincoln. They are on the side and at the top of the mountain. The video we saw of how this was achieved is truly amazing.

We also heard David McPherson's remarkable story. The testimony of how he came from darkness to light.

We drove back to Rapid City and spent the evening as follows:

At that time our Y.W.A.M. director for Europe was Lynn Green. He and his staff, were going through a severe time of testing related to the ownership of the beautiful property they were ministering from. They believed God had directed them to own it. It was called the Highfield Oval in Harpenden, just out of London.

Lynn had asked us to seek God, and report back to him anything that God might have to say to them at this difficult time.

Jim and I sought God diligently, being very aware that satanic forces were at work through adamant people trying to hinder God's eternal purposes being extended internationally, through this very vital ministry center in Europe.

The Holy Spirit directed us to the whole of Psalm 75, which is loaded with God's promises to thwart the enemies' tactics and to establish God's plans. We then re-iterated our convictions that Y.W.A.M. would own that strategic property. I wrote this in a letter to Lynn for his encouragement. (In the fullness of time it came to pass.)

My diary records that I also wrote letters to two other people. Following that, I responded to David McPherson's request for me to seek the Lord for everything God may have to say to him.

The first thing was encouraging him to keep reaching out to the Native Americans, with an emphasis on God's justice to them, from Proverbs 29:4, 7, & 14.

There was much more encouragement and things related to his future which are personal to him. Later he confirmed it all. Praise the Lord!

I noted that the night before this full day, I had recorded in my diary, "I had broken sleep because of pain in my spine. This has become the normal for almost every night." The night after this day, I recorded, "I had very little sleep." Obviously, I was being sustained by God's amazing grace, as the next day reveals.

From my diary on Friday, October 9th and Saturday October 10th, 1992:

"We went for our prayer walk in the lovely park in Rapid City. A drunk Native American man asked us for a light for his cigarette. As soon as we told him we didn't have one because we didn't smoke, I knew God had given us the context for intercession for the Indigenous people of that area.

We immediately went into fervent prayer for God to stir the hearts of His people with confession for the wounds and injustices of these people and that the Body of Christ in the U.S.A. would reach out to them in love and acceptance. We asked God to give us some Native Americans to share His love with like we had with the Maori and the African Americans and we believed a door would open.

Right then we saw 3 Native Americans sitting at a park table and bench. We prayed for a wise approach. We asked them to tell us which State had the most Indians, and said that we loved Native Americans and thought they were a great people. They received us warmly and said, "Arizona, South Dakota, and Oklahoma." We established a warm relationship and then witnessed to them.

I explained the gospel to Chris, Chunkoo, Harley, and Chops (who joined us later). Chunkoo said he had been hearing voices lately and said someone had told him he was going to change and give his life to Christ. The Native American men said they believed the end of the world was coming.

We told them about David McPherson and gave Chunkoo his address. Chunkoo said he'd like David to contact him. We shared all this at lunch with David."

The main purpose for my being in each city was to teach from God's Word, so, on this same day I spoke at a Pastors Retreat that was held out in the Black Hills. I spoke on "What it means to exercise Spiritual Authority". The next day I spoke on "Jesus the leader in ministry." The presence of God was very strong. All glory to God.

God's Personal Announcements

I don't remember the year or the place, but Jim and I were in some city, where I was speaking at a weeklong spiritual leadership conference. The other speakers were Loren and Don Richardson. Don was well known for pioneering a powerful ministry in Papua New Guinea, and he had written a vital widely read book about it, titled "Peace Child." *

At the end of the week we were all being driven to the nearest international airport to catch a plane going to Denmark. Loren, Don, and I were to be the speakers at a Y.W.A.M. leadership conference there.

I was seated in the back seat of the car, having my daily reading of the Scriptures, when suddenly I was arrested by the Holy Spirit. The verse was Job 5:26, "You shall come to your grave in ripe old age, as a shock of grain comes up to the threshing floor in its season." The immediate understanding was that I would still be around in my really old age. I didn't tell anyone.

Some later time, again when having my daily time of reading the Scriptures, the Holy Spirit spoke clearly to me and said the same thing.

At no time have I ever asked God to give me a long life, but because of these times when God has sovereignly spoken to me,

* Don Richardson "PEACE CHILD" ©2005 by Regal Books.

I'm not surprised I am 94 years of age…and still fulfilling my destiny. I know there's still more for me to accomplish for the extension of God's kingdom…. despite the fact that Heaven gets more desirable by the day!!!

The Road Becomes Rough

One night in mid-February 1993 I awoke with lower back pain like I'd never had before. First I said to God, "Reveal to me the purposes and/or causes of this pain. Then, show me everything you are trying to teach me through it; and please tell me the next thing you want me to do. Lastly, please heal me when the maximum glory can come to Your wonderful Name. Thank you for the answers in Your way and time. Amen." Four months later God spoke clearly to me from the Book of Job that I was in a time of severe testing.

I believe undoubtedly that the revelation of God's character and understanding of His ways that I had studied for decades, was the main reason that I was able to maintain a life of worship, thankfulness, and praise, plus intercession for others through it all.

My public speaking was now limited, but God clearly directed me to write books at this time.

The eight books and three booklets I have written have been solely at God's clear directions to me to do so. While that ministry has inevitably involved a lot of work, I have always sensed the directions and enabling power of the Holy Spirit.

It has brought me a great sense of fulfillment and destiny purpose, as so many lives have attested to being permanently changed, as a result of applying the proven Biblical truths they contained. All glory to Jesus!

By the way, for two of my books, Jim did all the computer work, as he worked off my hand written scripts. Jim taught himself how to use a computer at 68. He always did an excellent job. I was very proud of him for that accomplishment.

September 1993

It was in September 1993 that I was speaking at a vital Lydia Fellowship Conference in Dallas, Texas.

Shelagh McAlpine was the leader, and her son Stewart was the other speaker; both dear friends of mine. Among others, I gave a series of two messages on the thought provoking, penetrating subject titled, "Inconsistency, phoneyism, and hypocrisy." It never ceases to amaze me what the Holy Spirit's probe brings to the surface, through presenting God's Word on these issues, in the power of the Holy Spirit.

On the last day, before we partook of communion, Stewart shared about the place of women's devotion who ministered to Jesus when He was on earth.

As we served the emblems to each other individually, the Holy Spirit came and melted our hearts, as He shared some of the depth of the price Jesus paid for our salvation. Quiet weeping came upon everyone.

This was particularly meaningful to me, as I grieve over the frequent shallowness associated with "remembering His death until He comes" at Communion services, particularly in America.

Three days later I was on a plane headed for New York, en route to Israel, where I was to speak at "The Feast of the Tabernacles Conference in Jerusalem. On arrival, I was wiped out with exhaustion and went straight to bed. I was scheduled to be the opening speaker the next morning!

Before I go any further, I need to report that during the last 24 hours my "wonderful Counselor," the Holy Spirit had been convicting me of having a wrong emphasis in my thinking regarding this ministry journey.

I had been mentally assessing the price I was paying to be able to fulfill my commitment to God to try to be "the right person, at the right time, in the right condition of heart, saying and doing the right things in the enabling power of the Holy Spirit, in order to get the right results." I had wondered why I had to be the first speaker in the morning of the first day, on jet-lag and coming from a heavy schedule???

Whereas, God wanted me to be thinking a lot more about His desires to bless and reward me, and turn on treats for me, like only He can, and had already done in the past.

I then responded by switching my thinking to God's way.... little dreaming of what lay ahead!

My opening message was on "Excitement and fulfillment, through holiness of life." Jim said the anointing of the Holy Spirit was very strong for 1 ½ hours of teaching. I slept all afternoon from exhaustion, while Jim counseled a married couple.

You may be wondering why I never mention Jim being on jet lag? It's a simple answer. He never had any! When Jim lay down to sleep, he was out like a light. I have often said that if I could drape him over a clothes line, this amazing man would still sleep. He never knew the meaning of insomnia! Maybe God figured that one in this partnership needed to be spared those hazards, and for that I was always grateful.... never resentful to God or to Jim. Thank you, Jesus.

During the course of Jim's counseling the couple, he shared about the time he was at the Kinshasa airport in Zaire, on the Congo River in Africa. God had un-expectedly arranged that Jim meet up with a godly man who was a missionary in that area. He had recently had to bury his wife and was in deep grief. Jim ministered the compassionate love of God to him, with faith filled prayers for the healing of his broken heart.

This incident deeply marked Jim and he broke down and wept when sharing it.

Now back to Israel. We toured all around Jerusalem one day and on the next day went to the Mount of Olives, and Nazareth. All very interesting and spiritually impacting. We stayed the night at a large new hotel at Tiberius, in a fabulous setting. The next day we all went for a boat ride on The Sea of Galilee and then to the mountainside where Jesus taught the Beatitudes.

After that we went to Metulla and on to The Voice of Hope Radio Station. This ministry was a powerful means of spreading the Good News in that region and far beyond. It was directed by George Otis Senior and his wife Virginia; both of whom were our dear friends.

This trip culminated in our spending quality time not only with them, but also with their Board members at a strategic ministry-oriented meeting held in a beautiful hotel overlooking the ocean in Tel Aviv.

The next day we flew into Frankfurt, Germany, and after a long layover, a mechanical delay caused us to miss our flight connection to Norfolk. Lufthansa Airlines finally put us up in a hotel in New York. It was 3:40 a.m. when we arrived!

The next day we flew into Norfolk, Virginia and were met by wonderfully kind Betsy Phillips, who drove us to her very beautiful home and lovely guest cottage with every convenience. The setting was fabulous! We were right on the river's edge, set in beautiful trees, with total privacy.

After being in eight different beds in eleven nights, it was wonderful to unpack our suitcases and settle in! We didn't have to catch a plane, or go on a bus; and we could be alone with NO PROGRAM.

We were overwhelmed with God's goodness!

I actually slept from 9 p.m. to 6 a.m. For me, that was truly AMAZING!! While reveling in the relaxation and privacy, I was pondering again what a life of extremes I live.

- While I receive no salary, my financial needs are always met.
- While I have to endure by God's grace alone, the heavy demands and tests that accompany an anointed International teaching ministry, I am in His time, lavished with rewards and special treats that only God could turn on…. like this one!

We daily worshiped God and read our Bibles, interceded for others, had long walks, read a vital book, "Shout it from the House tops" by Pat Robertson and Jamie Buckingham, had quality time with our godly friends Connolly and Betsy Phillips (our hosts) ……and slept and slept and then slept some more! So very needed. A million thanks to our magnificent Master, Jesus, for this gift of time.

I was soon up and running in ministry assignments again. This time it was being interviewed by Pat Robertson on The 700 Club. He asked me how we could know that a genuine, Holy Spirit energized Revival and Spiritual awakening was coming.

I answered by quoting the following Scriptures:

- Isaiah 61:11, "For as the earth brings forth its shoots, and as a garden causes what is sown in it to spring up, so the Lord God will cause righteousness and praise to spring forth before all the nations."
- Isaiah 52:10 "The Lord has bared his holy arm before the eyes of all the nations; and all the ends of the earth shall see the salvation of our God."
- Isaiah 59:19 "So they shall fear the name of the Lord from the west, and his glory from the rising sun; for he will come like a rushing stream, which the wind of the Lord drives."

I added a quote from one of Edwin Orr's books, pointing out that conditions were similar just prior to the 1905 Great Awakening. Edwin Orr was known for his deep understanding of the history of past revivals.

There were numerous other times that I was interviewed on The 700 Club and other Christian T.V. and radio stations. It was something I really enjoyed doing and always felt fulfilled.

But on this day, what was more fulfilling, was then being able to have an in-depth time of unhurried intercession for revival with Kelly Byrd, of the Freedom Council; and then later, another very powerful time of intercession with Kelly and four others, as we really stormed the gates of Heaven on the abortion issue, and other pertinent needs related to the Christian Broadcasting world in general. Believe me it was serious business, which ended with our strong declaration of faith that God's hand had been moved!

A Pivotal Time

I will now report from my diary on October 22nd, 1993. "I was feeling the strain of six months of broken sleep and little sleep, plus much pain. This is accompanied by all the travel and speaking responsibilities."

2 months later, I had a cat scan on my spine, which revealed I had spinal stenosis. This led to my going to a spine specialist who gave me an epidermal cortisone injection, which was complex and painful, and totally unsuccessful. He finally told me that surgery was my only recourse!

On December 28th my diary records, "Still in intensive pain, Jim and I sought God for directions and some understanding whether I'm to have surgery or **whatever**??

I then cried out to God to have mercy on me, and believed He would speak to me from His Word. He directed me to Isaiah 30:18-21, and verse 26:

"Moreover the light of the moon will be as the light of the sun, and the light of the sun will be sevenfold, as the light of seven days, in the day that the Lord binds up the bruise of His people and heals the stroke of their wound."

The Holy Spirit simply spoke to Jim, "WAIT."

A few days later, my precious family came together and prayed fervently for my healing, anointing me with oil. God also gave them comforting and assuring scriptures, along with ones that brought understanding. For example, Psalm 90:13-14, Job 2, and Mark 5:34.

God spoke to Jim, 1Peter 1:6-7 the testing of our faith through trials. Psalm 42 and 43; we're to keep waiting on God. Psalm 43:3-5, God's help assured in times of trouble. 1Peter 5:10-11, promises of restoration. Luke 9:1-2, our God given authority to expect healing.

I was also greatly encouraged a few days later to hear Paul Cain speak on "God leans toward mercy."

As the pain continued, I sought God diligently again as to the purpose of all this suffering. He answered me from my daily Bible reading in Jeremiah 11:20:

"But, O Lord of hosts, You who judge righteously, testing the mind and the heart, let me see Your vengeance on them, for to You I have revealed my cause."

This verse makes it crystal clear along with Jeremiah 12:3 and Jeremiah 20: 12-13 that the Holy Spirit was affirming again that I am being tested in the furnace of affliction.

I share again from my diary on January 16th, 1994, "I felt absolutely depleted to-day and was totally grounded. I was unable to go on our prayer walk .... again!

Jim and I sought God for understanding about my illness, which is progressively worse.

The Holy Spirit directed me to the 'Truth in action' pages at the end of the book of Job, in 'the Spirit filled life Bible'. Thomas Nelson publishers incorporated 1991.

God had the last word with Job's fiery trial of affliction and He will have the final word with mine.

We managed to intercede for America for an hour together, in the evening.

At 4:30 a.m., in exhaustion from lack of sleep and severe pain, I was sitting in the bathtub trying to get relief, telling God that I was at the end of my rope. I asked God to take me home to Heaven, if He's not going to give me relief, as I am useless like this!

Immediately, there was a 6.7 magnitude earthquake and all the power went out!!!" end of diary quote.

We didn't get the full force of it and were able to navigate the inconveniences, including a 5.5 after shock.

Later that day, as I enquired of God again for anything He had to say, He opened my Bible to Psalm 18:4-7 which exactly described what had just happened at 4:30 a.m.

"The pangs of death surrounded me, and the floods of ungodliness made me afraid. The sorrows of Sheol surrounded me, the snares of death confronted me. In my distress I called upon the Lord, and cried out to my God; He heard my voice from His temple, and my cry came before Him, even to His ears. Then the earth shook and trembled; the foundations of the hills also quaked and were shaken, because He was angry." **Truly Amazing!!**

I also pursued my best friend Jesus for an answer to my comments immediately before the earthquake. He responded to them by speaking to me from my daily readings in the "Daily Light" devotionals from Psalm 30:2-10:

"O Lord my God, I cried out to You and You healed me. O Lord, You brought my soul up from the grave; You have kept me alive, that I should not go down to the pit. Sing praise to the Lord, you saints of His, and give thanks at a remembrance of His holy name. For His anger is but for a moment, His favor is for life; weeping may endure for a night, but joy comes in the morning. Now in my prosperity I said, 'I shall never be moved.' Lord, by Your favor You have made my mountain stand strong; You hid your face, and I was troubled. I cried out to You, O Lord; and to the Lord I made supplication: 'What profit is there in my blood, when I go down to the pit? Will the dust praise You? Will it declare Your truth? Hear, O Lord, and have mercy on me; Lord, be my helper!' "

The Holy Spirit then confirmed every word again, by opening my Bible to that exact same Psalm, including the rest of the verses in it, which were **very pertinent** to my exact situation, and a glimpse into my future. Only God!

God directed Jim to 1Peter 5:11, "To Him be the glory and the dominion forever and ever. Amen."

The Holy Spirit then directed us both that I was to cancel some of my speaking engagements to be considered for later times. Everyone involved co-operated.

For months I was under the kindest possible care of dear Dr. Corinne Allen who is a PhD in holistic medicine, which I firmly believe in.

Later, I sought God again for more understanding of His perspective on the continued increase of much suffering which hindered me from going to church. He answered me from the "Daily Light" again. Scriptures were related to being refined by fire, rejoicing in sufferings, enduring hardship as discipline, inviting God to reveal to me my heart as He sees it and the importance of humility. I wholeheartedly embraced every scripture.

A friend told us that he had suffered spinal stenosis and had a complete recovery from it through surgery. We then seriously considered my having surgery… as a last resort.

A Doctor friend recommended I pursue a certain neuro surgeon, which I did. We sought God diligently for His directions.

Because I was so ill I became less confident in my ability to discern God's instructions clearly, so I relied heavily upon what He was saying to Jim and John. This was a very dark time for me.

They strongly believed I was to have surgery, and once again reassuring Scriptures were given to them connected to healing.

In our hour of deep need Jim and I cried out to God to say something to meet that need. He answered us from **Isaiah 66:13** "As one whom his mother comforts, so I will comfort you…" and **Job 23:10** "But He knows the way that I take: when He has tested me, I shall come forth as gold."

My precious husband received a very insightful scripture. It was Luke 22:31 "Satan has desired to sift you like wheat, but I have prayed for you that your faith will not fail." This was another reminder that I was in a Job test among other tests. My faith was being tested at every level.

Even Dr. Corinne Allan then believed I needed surgery. We contacted our intercessor friends for their vital prayer ministry to me.

On February 16th I had the surgery on my lower spine.

As soon as I came out of the anesthetic, I felt the same pain, and knew I wasn't healed!

Six days later I was discharged from the hospital, with the awareness that my nervous system was now negatively affected.

Due to a set of unusual circumstances, Jill had to drive me home in her van, and I had to be in the front seat. In my damaged condition it was unnerving, and I had to keep my head down because of apprehension. Jill started singing worship songs and I joined her. Then the Holy Spirit came upon me and I sang 3 stanzas of a new song to God with rhyme and music. I wept with wonder of this visitation under such a stressful condition and situation.

When we went back to the Neurosurgeon ten days later and I reported that my **whole nervous system had now been badly damaged**, his clinical reply was, "It's all in your mind."

I knew that my mind had been focused entirely and diligently on Isaiah 26:3"You will keep him in perfect peace whose mind is stayed upon You, because he trusts in You" God knew that to be 100% truth.

<u>I faced the facts.</u>

- The surgeon didn't want a possible law suit, so he totally avoided the truth.
- I had experienced faulty surgery.
- I needed to forgive him, which I did by God's grace.
- I was in a <u>worse</u> state physically than before the surgery.
- I was now living in a body that was totally foreign to me.
- I chose to trust God, when I couldn't trace Him "His ways are passed finding out."
- I would continue to praise and worship my precious Jesus.
- I would continue to ask God what He's trying to teach me through all this.

It wasn't long before I received some understanding on that question. I was stepping out of the shower, when as clear as could be, I heard the Holy Spirit say to me, "You have neglected your husband." Immediately, I understood what He meant, and quickly confessed and repented of my sin to God, and then to my dear Jim.

I had wrongly rationalized the following in my mind. Because I had by far the heaviest weight of responsibilities related to the ministry giftings God had entrusted to me, than Jim had, I concluded that he needed to help me as much as possible.

While there was a real measure of truth in that thinking.... I had taken it too far! Thank God, His mercy is always extended to a truly repentant heart. My precious husband soon noticed the results that came from it. I found a new joy in serving him.

Jim and I became very aware of the need to follow out the instructions given to those who are sick, from James 5:14. So we asked Pastor Jack Hayford to come to our home and pray for me. He brought his assistant Dan Hicks with him.

Part of the instructions that are required for healing in verse 16 are, "Confess your sins one to another." Unhesitatingly, I confessed before these spiritual elders and Jim the sin for which I had recently been forgiven. This was very humbling, but very necessary.

Healing still didn't come to my body, but I continued to trust God.

Very dear pastors Mike and Jan Gillman and their ladies' prayer group sent me a needed, lovely bed jacket. On a card they had written out Isaiah 40:28-31, personalized with my name written throughout the verses. It ministered life, hope, faith, and comfort to me, as I was having difficulty walking, following the surgery.

The following night (my diary records) "I had a terrible night with severe pain and **no** sleep. For the second time since this illness I felt I was going to die, as life was seeping away from me.

At 1 a.m. Jim phoned Jill and a deeply committed intercessor friend, Carolyn Alsup. As they and Jim prevailed, in desperate prayer, finally the crisis passed.

Very practical and meaningful deeds of kindness can flow out of intercession. This truth was remarkably demonstrated through our precious daughter Jill's sacrificial love.

During my prolonged and very painful illness following back surgery in February 1994, when healing didn't come as expected,

Jill's fervent and frequent intercession was matched only by her twenty-one months of meal preparations for us.

Words are totally inadequate to describe the depths of my gratitude. Only God can justly reward her.

The next morning as I sought the Lord about my critical condition, He clearly revealed to me that Satanic forces were trying to take my life. We knew from Job 42:2 that God was in the ultimate control of my life. But the intense spiritual warfare, combined with the severity of God's testings of my faith, caused Jim to call both John and Jill to my bedside. They came and both had powerful, Spirit directed intercession for me.

The next day the severe pain was again relentless, attended by great weakness. I had to keep battling against despair!!

On February 27th, 1994, it was my 68th birthday. It was one of my darkest days. I decided to relinquish all my rights to be healed. I simply said to God, "Be glorified however You choose, through my body." I said it before Jim and Jill as witnesses. We then worshipped and praised God together and did strong spiritual warfare. I threw whatever crowns I may receive at Jesus' feet.

The next day was our 46th wedding anniversary. Jim managed to get a prayer alert out to Y.W.A.M.ers related to my worsened condition, via our dear friend Paul Hawkins.

That night was one of the worst yet, with severe burning pain and minimal sleep. I quote directly from my diary again.

From 28th Feb 1994, page 2, "I embraced the cross and thanked God for the suffering which He was using to make me more like Jesus. I worshiped God passionately and threw Him kisses in the long night hours of pain as I walked around the room.

I did strong spiritual warfare from the sheepskin rug I stood on, representing the shed blood of the Lamb of God which covers and protects me. I want God to be glorified whether by life or death or pain.

I walked by faith the Via Dolorosa with Jesus, picking up my cross of suffering and going on with praise and worship to the One who had suffered infinitely more for me."

The next night, more severe pain and no sleep, but I engaged in the strongest spiritual warfare. Jill gave me **Psalm 71:20-21** and **John 12:27-28**. Glorify your name, Lord!

On Friday 4th March, "I had the worst pain <u>ever</u> in this illness, or any time in my life. I felt like I was being burnt at the stake. I interceded for the suffering individuals I've been praying for and the suffering multitudes of lost souls to be converted, delivered, and healed. I said I'd pay the price for a public healing ministry if that was what God wanted."

And from the next day, "More strong pain, which lifted after more than 2 hours of worship and prayers for others. Later my body went into violent shaking all over and precious Jill came again and helped me through it. I started to understand I'm to cancel all speaking engagements through July."

Monday March 7th was another real crisis point, (written up in my diary by Jill). The satanic attacks were unleashed upon my mind with unprecedented fury. Surely this must be the final blow of the enemy!

In desperation, physically, mentally and spiritually I again called for John and Jill to come to my bedside.

After John had held me close and ministered to me tenderly, he prophesized, "From the mouth of the Lord, I say, 'Be still and know that I am God,' you are to do **NOTHING** else at this time."

Pastor Dan Sneed came to our home and ministered to me and said, "You are to rest in Jesus arms and do **NOTHING** else."

Both Jim and Jill received Scriptural directions of confirmation to all of this. I received all these words from the Lord and actually had nearly 6 hours of (broken) sleep that night. Truly Amazing!

The next day was a day of celebration.

We were sure the battle was won and this was a new day. We were greatly rejoicing in the Lord.

As I continue to write this report in May 2018, it has now become very clear to me that there is a definite reoccurring pattern in what God allowed me to go through.

I would reach an all time low of suffering, accompanied by intense spiritual warfare and fervent faith filled intercession on my behalf. This was accompanied with varied medical and holistic means. We would be given a real measure of hope for a breakthrough… only to find I was **worse than ever**!

That's what happened the next day following the above report. As I have Jim's written account in my diary of Wednesday, March 9th. It's full of additional violent kinds of intense suffering, all night and day.

I question now in 2018, whether my faith in God's character would have remained strong at that time, had I not previously made a serious study of God's absolute justice.

All this caused Jill to have to leave her husband and two young children again and come and take over with me, as I was in great need, while Jim got some much needed sleep in another room.

From March 10th, my diary reports, "Jim spoke to Scott Bauer at The Church on the Way and he reported on the previous night's church prayer meeting where special fervent prayer was made on Joy's behalf. He is going to send a tape of the meeting.

Becky, Scott's wife, had a vision in the service where she saw a large Chinese Dragon attempting to bite and swallow Joy. 'The teeth were in Joy's back, but she has not been given to the teeth of a predator! The Lord is on her side.'

Scott was given Psalm 124 'If I had not been for the Lord who was on our side… they would have swallowed us alive when their wrath was kindled against us…. Blessed be the Lord, who has not given us **as prey to their teeth**.'"

Jill stayed with me all through that painful night. The next night I was so ill, that from a physical stand point alone, all I wanted was to die.

Jim phoned Pastor Jack Hayford and reported on my condition. He expressed great concern and quoted some comforting Scriptures. Then he commented on the tremendous time of fervent intercession the church had for me the night before. Both men wept as they prayed for me together.

A few days later it became evident that the strain all this was putting on Jim, had taken a heavy toll in every way. He was experiencing pain in his upper arms and was depleted.

At Jill's suggestion I moved into a bedroom at her house, where she and J.B. took care of me; and Jim remained at home to sleep at night; recuperating from the months of strain and stress.

My Christian Doctor was able to prescribe a new drug that helped give my nervous system a measure of relief.

I walked all around this property calling down God's blessings, like when the Ark of God was at Obed-Edom's house. The Bible says, "God blessed all his household." I blessed everyone and everything I could think of…. which was a heap.

Only God can adequately reward my precious, caring, unselfish daughter for ALL she was to me and did for me during those critical crisis times of my life. I honor her big time along with my dearly loved and greatly appreciated son in law, J.B. They were Jesus to me.

I actually got dressed for the first time in months and it felt wonderful; so significant was my gradual improvement at this particular time. But I was still not healed.

Mario Murrilo

I will be forever grateful to my dear friend Mario Murrilo who so kindly sent out a meaningful letter internationally, asking people who knew me to pray fervently for the healing of my severe back problems.

He set a specific date, so that everyone would be calling on God in unison. Because of the different time zones it was spread out over twenty four hours.

Jim and I were highly expectant that I would be experiencing God's miracle working power.

I vividly remember that when it came to the last ten minutes of that time frame, and no change had taken place, that I declared to Jim that my faith was still unwavering.

When I was finally left in the same condition, after all those earnest prayers, I just kept on worshiping, praising, and trusting God's character when I couldn't trace Him.

Mario is undoubtedly one of the most anointed evangelists of this era. Consistent reports of his meetings over many years, are similar to those in the book of Acts.

God Will Prevail Over The Enemy

In 1994, on September 7th, I was in severe pain and sensed that satanic forces were involved. As I took authority over them in Jesus' mighty Name, the pain thankfully subsided.

In the evening, Jim and I asked God to speak to us from His Word about this illness.

Jim was given 1 Samuel 17 – David's victory over Goliath, with an emphasis on verse 32, "Let no man's heart fail because of him."

I was given Psalm 44:5 "Through You we will push down our enemies. Through Your Name we will trample those who rise against us."

This battle will be won by the Lord. Then I was given Song of Solomon 5, 6, and 7, with the understanding that I am to keep an intimate relationship with the Lord.

We were encouraged, as we faced the long haul ahead of us.

On a later occasion when in severe pain, and Jim was seeking God on my behalf, the Holy Spirit directed him to Psalm 138: 7,8 "Though I walk in the midst of trouble, You will revive me; You will stretch out Your hand Against the wrath of my enemies, and Your right hand will save me. The LORD will perfect that which concerns me; Your mercy, O LORD, endures forever; Do not forsake the works of Your hands."

Reporting On My Condition By Letter

July, 20, 1995

Our dear Intercessor friends,

Praise God from whom all faithful friends flow. You certainly come into that category. You'll never know the significant part each one of you has played, in your ministry of continued prayer support and loving encouragement to us. We have needed it all.

The only way we can try to bless you in return, is with our regular fervent intercession that all your needs will be met by the great "I AM," the "One Who knows you best and loves you most," (from Bill Gaither's song.) We also often pray for the salvation of the unconverted loved ones of those who pray for us. Our hearts overflow with love and deepest appreciation to God for you.

The up-date on Joy's health is that there are days when the pain is severe, other days when it is more tolerable, and still other days when it is much less. Although her nervous system continues to improve, she has not fully recovered in this area. As she can still only sit walk or stand for relatively brief periods of time because it induces pain, she is almost solely confined to the home. Sitting to write is always painful.

The pain, coming from the pinched nerve in her spine (which must be affecting her nervous system), and the osteoarthritis which is in both hips, is only partially controlled with medications. For some months Joy has been taking the best that advanced nutritional advice offers. She also does some aquatic exercises. We have been inundated with advice and literature, (some of which we've been unable to read yet, and all related to bringing relief,) from very kind and caring people.

Jim is finally recovering from six months of having a severe allergy which turned into bronchial asthma. We praise God for His mercy in the release of His healing power. There are no words to adequately express the depth of gratitude in my (Joy's) heart, for the wonderful way Jim has so faithfully and lovingly ministered to me from such an unselfish, servant heart in these stressful confined circumstances. I'm believing God to raise me up so that I can minister back to him in every way that he deserves.

Great encouragement has come from several sensitive, mature people, who have given us strong confirming words from the Lord that He will completely heal Joy. God continues to say the same thing to us, as we diligently seek Him for understanding, and we are fully believing Him.

While we are aware that we are still experiencing the trial of our faith, and the intensity of the spiritual warfare that accompanies it, we are equally aware that we are on the Master Potter's wheel. He is doing a major re-shaping work on both of us, to which we are submitted with genuine deep gratitude and praise. We often sing together, the old chorus:

"He's changing me, He's changing me,
From earthly things to the Heavenly;
His likeness and image to perfect in me,
The love of God shown to the world."

For many years we've prayed Paul's prayer in Phil 3:10. We've never had more answers on the last half – "that we may know the fellowship of His sufferings, being conformed to His death." God's work and ways are perfect.

We would greatly appreciate along with your prayers for our complete recovery, Paul's prayer "that through endurance and the encouragement of the Scriptures, we might have (continued) hope."

Eternally lovingly and gratefully,

Joy and Jim

Expressed Gratitude

The following letter is very meaningful to report in our journey with Jesus, as it expresses often significant areas in our lives for which we are truly thankful…despite the difficult circumstances.

November 8, 1995

Dear Intercessor friends,

We lovingly greet you with Paul's words "We must forever **give thanks to God** for you, our friends loved by the Lord…" (2 Thess.2:13 LB), and by us. You are precious to us, and greatly appreciated.

We're thrilled and thankful to God that multitudes of the world's unevangelized in the 10/40 window are coming, and will continue to come into the Kingdom of God resulting from the additional and major prayer emphasis of God's people worldwide, during October.

We're also thrilled and thankful for the deeply significant moves of God's Spirit in reconciliation through identificational repentance, that are taking place all over the world, among estranged and sometimes hostile racial and ethnic groups, denominations and even nations. Jesus' prayer for unity is being dramatically answered. Hallelujah!

Now to the personal

We are deeply thankful that God has used this extended time of trial in our lives to draw us closer to Himself, and one another, (not that we were ever alienated.) But we can truly say, that as we've been together turning our eyes upon Jesus, and looking more fully and more frequently in His wonderful face, the things of earth have been growing more strangely dim, in the light of His glory and grace.

We are very thankful that as we have kept "looking unto Jesus, the author and finisher of our faith, "He has kept assuring us from His Word that the miracles of healing that are needed, both in Joy's body, and for Jim's bronchial asthma, will take place. We wait God's timing, exercising the rest of faith.

"We are having the same spirit of faith, according as it is written, 'I believed, and therefore have I spoken; we also believe, and therefore speak. (2Cor.4:13.) "I wait for the Lord, my soul waits, and in His Word do I hope." (Ps. 130:5)

We are also encouraged by the testings in the lives of Abraham and Job.

We are very thankful that God is continuing His refining work in both of us. How incredibly patient and merciful He is. How we love and worship Him for His pursuing love.

The following is an update on our health.

We are so thankful that with Joy, some days the pain is less, she feels stronger, and is able to do aquatic exercises at the YMCA pool nearby. And having been able to eliminate one of the medications she has been on for a long time, is progress. But there are still numbers of days of pain, pervading weakness, and an inability to sit, walk or stand for any length of time without the pain intensifying. We're still very confined. Jim's asthma, though much improved, continues to linger on.

When the pain in Joy's back started in April 1993, she asked God to do something through it that would bring the maximum glory to His name. By God's grace, through the ensuing two years and seven months of suffering, that request remains the same. **We are very thankful** that we can anticipate the glory that is coming to our precious and wonderful Savior, when His purposes for allowing the suffering are completed in both our lives.

We are aware that God is working out a plan to enable us to fulfill our destinies, in answer to our fervent prayers. We believe He's preparing us for the next ministry phase together – whatever that is. **We're more than thankful** for that hope. Hallelujah!

Your continued love, prayers of faith, and specific rhema words of encouragement some have received from the Lord for us during this long trial, have never been more needed or **appreciated.**

Please pray with us that God will accelerate the work that needs to be done in us. We so yearn to be in the flow of the end-time reviving of His Church, and to be actively used of Him in relation to the great ingathering of those yet to be reached for Christ before His return.

We pray that you will experience more of God's light in your darkness; more of the power of His life to energize and heal you; more of His grace in your trials; more of His comforting love in your pain; more understanding of His ways in your perplexities; and a more consuming passion for intimacy with Himself, in order to make Him more fully known to others in the power of the Holy Spirit. We also pray for any of your loved ones not yet in the Kingdom of God.

With warm love and deep gratitude.

Joy and Jim

God In Diversities

It was February 1996, and Jim and I had appropriately celebrated my 70th birthday with family members on the 27th. On the 28th Jim and I had celebrated our 48 years of marriage by going to a good, quiet hotel restaurant where we exchanged our written loving words and cards to each other.

We had thanksgiving prayers for the past, and then had prayer for God to use us more than ever for His glory in the future.

With that background, we came to February 29th. I had very little sleep the night before. By the evening, I felt ill, and became weak. The lower back pain was severe.

After interceding for others, I asked the Lord if He had anything to say to me.

He answered me by opening my Bible to 2 Kings 20 verse five, "I have heard your prayer. I have seen your tears. Surely, I will heal you."

For confirmation, I asked Him to speak a page number in my Bible that would have verses saying the same thing. He said, "Page 357."

When I looked it up it was 2 Kings 8:6 "Restore all that was hers." Then verses 9 and 10, "'Will I recover from this disease?' And Elisha said to him, 'Go say to him, 'You will certainly recover.'"

I wrote in my diary, "Thank You, praise You wonderful Jesus. I love You, believe You, and trust You."

Another Significant Letter

A letter Jim wrote in June 1996 to our faithful intercessor friends is worth reporting here. It includes my input:

"We are deeply grateful for your continued, loving, prayerful concern for us. So many of you have blessed us with encouraging notes and letters. We are very aware that all this input has greatly helped to sustain us during this long trial. The reason why we haven't written to you before now is that we haven't known how to report on Joy's health, due to its many vicissitudes.

The good news is that ever since Christmas the lower spinal pains are less intense. This has enabled her to attend church, which has been a wonderful blessing after <u>two years of absence</u>. Praise God for this direct answer to your prayers.

The not-so-good news is that a test done by a fine Christian neurologist/nutritionist has confirmed that her nervous system is still severely damaged. Joy is being treated with natural nutrients and homeopathics in an attempt to restore the substance which should be coating her nerves. The nutritionist said they are like wires without insulation; resulting in frequent pain, weakness and insomnia.

With God's help, Joy managed to work through her book on intercession again (after it having to lie dormant for two years), and it is now at a publisher.

Through this illness, God has highlighted again to me (Joy), the fact that Christ alone is the source of my strength. Without His enabling grace, I have nothing to offer.

Despite the long delay in the fulfillment of God's promises to bring healing, Jim and I are confident that our loving Father sees the big picture, and is working on us from that perspective. We haven't found it easy to wait on the Master Painter, with little or no understanding. But as we keep singing praises to Him for Who He is, He supernaturally lifts us up above the confinement, suffering and perplexities, and gives us His ability to keep on trusting and believing.

We're in a university course on "resting in the Lord and waiting patiently for Him." Sometimes it feels like we're going for a doctorate!

We're encouraged by veteran Paul's lessons in this course…. left for two years in a Caesarean prison awaiting trial, and years under house arrest in Rome. He understood perplexity ("we were perplexed"), insomnia ("in sleeplessness often"), and weakness ("in fear and trembling and much weakncss.")

We suspect that one of the purposes in all this, is that we may be able to identify with suffering humanity in order to more effectively reach them for Christ – a burning desire. Again, Paul mentors us. "To the weak I became weak that I may win the weak."

We believe that God's awesome holiness and unprecedented displays of power accompanied by His blazing glory are soon to be revealed among His people worldwide, to precede the great end-time harvest before His glorious appearing.

So we keep crying out to God for an acceleration of His mighty purposes in the earth, and praying "Don't pass us by." As Jesus is coming again for His Bride who will be "without spot or wrinkle," we also need and want our "cleaning and ironing" to be accelerated in order to be fully used of Him in His end-time purposes.

You are genuinely loved, greatly appreciated, and regularly prayed for.

Lovingly,

Joy and Jim"

The Eternal Perspective

On a Saturday morning in July of 1996, the sheriff from Bass Lake, (where we had our missionary families' vacation home) phoned us to report that it had been "trashed" by vandals who had broken into it. He said it could have possibly been done some months ago. He reported windows broken, all mirrors broken, everything overturned, the computer face broken, the shed broken into...John's trailer trashed. The sheriff said, "They've done a thorough job!"

My immediate reaction was to worship God and then trust Him to fulfill Romans 8:28 "We know that in everything God works for good with those who love Him, who are called according to His purpose."

Straight away, my deepest concern was for the lost souls of the vandals. They were obviously in deep need spiritually, so I cried out to God to have mercy on them and that they would have an opportunity to know the way of salvation and be converted…. and believed. I was in perfect peace.

Jim and J.B. drove up there and it took them two full days of cleaning up the awful mess and getting the place back into some order.

To our great joy, we heard that a few months later, one of the group of young guys who vandalized the place had gone to the police and confessed his sins. He was truly repentant, and the sheriff said he was being cared for by some "very good people."

We understood that to mean that God had answered our prayers for this teenager's salvation.

In God's great faithfulness, in time, He restored to us all that was taken from us.

I'm still believing for the salvation of each one of the vandals. They must have come from a background of pain and rejection to be so messed up. In prayer, I always called them, "those precious thieves."

Calcutta, India

On one of the occasions that I went to Calcutta, India to teach at the invitation of pioneer missionary Mark Buntain; Don Stephens was my ministry partner and dear friend.

On a day off from speaking at Mark and Huldah's church and Bible school, we visited Mother Teresa's ministry compound in Calcutta. Her passion was reaching out to human rejects of society found on the city streets, and ministering the love of God to them to meet their needs of body, soul, and spirit. She was a living legend.

After interviewing us, Mother Teresa gave us permission to minister the love of God to the poor and needy. As we approached one of the rooms where they were housed, I saw the back of a human form, which was squatted on the floor. It had no arms and no legs and was apart from the others in the room. I didn't know if it was male or female. The head was gyrating back and forth and barking sounds were coming from its mouth. I have never seen anything like it, before or since!

Instantly I knew what to do! I walked toward this desperately needy soul and put my arms lovingly around the shoulders, kissed the top of the head, and kept lovingly saying, "God loves you and I love you." I felt Jesus' compassion taking over, despite the fact of the language barrier. The weird noises stopped, the head became still, and the peace of God enveloped us. The language of God's pure love was penetrating the darkness and bringing healing. I was in awe of God.

The Price To Pay

You may be thinking that it must be a glamorous lifestyle to be travelling around the world, sharing platforms with mighty men of God, as I did for decades. I will address that myth! While it was a great privilege, it came with a high price tag.

In my bestselling book, "Intimate friendship with God" - through understanding the fear of the Lord, I teach in depth on how to navigate the inevitable tests from God and attacks from satanic forces that accompany our being linked together by God in ministry with the opposite sex.

**Joy Dawson "INTIMATE FRIENDSHIP WITH GOD" ©2008 by Chosen Books.*

If you haven't read it, I recommend that you do so.

The weight of my accountability before the Lord to be an in-depth intercessor, and Bible teacher with a prophetic mantle, bringing only the specific 'word of the Lord' for each occasion and living everything I teach as a way of life, was heavy enough. But the responsibility and accountability of being primarily a teacher of spiritual leaders, carries the greatest degree of responsibility I know. It has never left me. The Bible says in James 3:1, "Those who teach shall be judged with greater strictness."

One day, when on a long trip away, I said, "The nearest thing to Heaven would be a day at home, without having to prepare for the next one." It wasn't long before I had to repent deeply before the Lord, and then say, "The nearest thing to Heaven is being in the center of His will."

Here's a scenario.

My diary records on Monday May 11, 1987: "*On this trip of two and half weeks away,*

- *I taught the Word of God 13 times in meetings,*
- *did five T.V. interviews that included full messages,*
- *participated in three lengthy National Prayer Committee meetings,*
- *and travelled on 7 different airplanes.*

I've never worked harder. The pace has been incredible. But as always, it's been a great privilege."

Sharing God's truths off stage with spiritual leaders.

Here's another scenario:

Campbell McAlpine, a British Bible teacher/prophet and Loren and I were teamed together as the speakers at 13 spiritual leadership conferences in diverse places. In His great goodness and mercy, God always showed up powerfully.

At the close of one of those conferences, the conference leaders, who were a pastor and his wife, invited the 3 of us to stay in their home overnight, before leaving the next day to go our separate ways.

The first thing I did was to stretch out on a sofa in their living room and say, "This is the best part of the week for me!" (meaning, 'I am more than ready for a break from all the responsibilities that go with this ministry') My close friend God was totally unimpressed with that statement and let me know it, with deep conviction.

I had to repent before the Lord and my friends, and then declare that the privilege of serving God and His spiritual leaders, is always higher than the price.

I also broke one of my little toes, on the end of an iron bedstead. The next day I had to take a flight to my next destination in order to speak. This meant having to negotiate my luggage alone, while being on crutches with a throbbing foot. Mercifully some people saw my plight and helped me. I kept my speaking engagement only with God's help

As with many prominent leaders with strong personalities, with whom God gives us opportunities to be linked with in ministries, difficult circumstances will inevitably arise. That's life. God waits to see our reaction.

If we understand that God is testing us by them, we should want to pass the tests. Choosing humility is the only way through. There are no shortcuts. We simply say, "Lord, I want to learn what You're trying to teach me in this pain. Give me Your grace and power to unconditionally love this leader… NO MATTER WHAT. Thank you, Holy Spirit, for moving in my heart, to work this in me and through me, as only You can, and will. Amen."

If we harbor resentment and unforgiveness toward them, we will not only <u>not</u> be forgiven by God for our sins, but we will miss out on the many future blessings and promotions that God intended to give us through those same leaders.

At the same time, the reality is that some of those same leaders will need God's grace to cope with our idiosyncrasies and times we've caused them pain--- wittingly or unwittingly! I know that applies to me.

An Excerpt From My Book, "All Heaven Will Break Loose"

"All week long I had been teaching at a spiritual leadership conference at YWAM's University of the Nations campus in Kona, Hawaii. It came to Thursday evening, when all of the many schools, plus all of the staff and teachers come together for a communal meeting. Outside visitors also come to the campus for the meeting. One of the outside speakers from the many spheres of training brought in for that week would be the speaker, and I was told this would be my responsibility.

All day long, from the first minute I opened my eyes on that Thursday morning until the evening, I sought the face of God diligently to know what 'the word of the Lord' was that I was to speak to the whole community. I never went outside the bedroom door, but no answers were coming to me.

I was listening in silence, reading the Word of God, interceding for others; I was coming against the enemy and doing spiritual warfare, thanking God, praising Him and worshiping Him. There was not anything else I knew to do. Then it came to around 6:00 p.m. and I still was thinking, 'It will come any minute.'…Nothing!

Finally, I got a message through to Loren Cunningham, our leader, saying that I needed to speak to him. It took some time before he was able to get to me. He was thinking, of course, that I had a message to speak.

I said to him, 'I've sought God diligently all day, but I don't have a clue what I'm supposed to do tonight. All I know to do, is say, 'Will you pray for me?' Maybe I'll get it then.' That had happened in the past. Loren prayed earnestly for me, and we both expected the message title would come to me while we waited in silence…. Nothing.

Then Loren took on his role of responsibility, knowing that the ball was totally back in his court since there was nothing more I could do. **He and I both knew that I would never ever give anything other than what the Holy Spirit gave me to speak on specifically at any particular time.** That was a given! So Loren sought the Lord earnestly to see what he was to do. Maybe he was to speak? Maybe somebody else? Maybe he was to turn it into some other kind of meeting? My role was then to intercede for him, which I did.

By this time the meeting had actually started; the worship had begun and we still did not know what we were going to do. Loren kept seeking God diligently. He is big and tall, and I am small. Finally he looked down at my five-foot-one frame and gave me a directive by saying, 'You are to preach the Gospel.'

I immediately felt the witness of the Spirit to this instruction. I had no time to prepare; I had no clue how I was going to present the Gospel, but I knew it was one of the tests of teamwork. I just said, 'Okay! I will.'

As the worship continued, I lifted my heart to God and said, 'How do I do it?'

These thoughts then came into my mind from Jeremiah 9:23–24 (verses I was very familiar with) 'Thus says the Lord: Let not the wise man glory in his wisdom, let not the mighty man glory in his might, let not the rich man glory in his riches, but let him who glories, glory in this, that he understands and knows Me, that I am the Lord, who exercise <u>loving kindness</u>, <u>judgment</u>, and <u>righteousness</u> in the earth. For in these things I delight,' says the Lord.

The Holy Spirit then said, 'Preach the Gospel on the basis of My character. Explain Who I am from these three statements about myself.' And then He flashed into my mind 'Romans 10:9–10 (RSV),'

'If you confess with your lips that Jesus is Lord and believe in your heart that God raised him from the dead, you will be saved. For man believes with his heart and so is justified, and he confesses with his lips and so is saved.'

I only had time to send up a telegram prayer asking God to anoint me, declaring that without Him I could do nothing, when it was announced that I would speak. I was out "walking on the water," cast upon God, Who never fails.

After quoting Jeremiah 9:23–24, I said that I did not know a better commercial for God's character in all of God's Word other than from those verses—and I took off explaining each of those three main attributes.

Then I preached on making Jesus Lord of our lives and the need to publicly say it with our mouths if we have made that transaction. As a response to the appeal, fourteen people openly and boldly declared Jesus as Lord for the first time in their lives.

That response was worth everything God had required of me that whole day and evening! And God has never put me through that particular test again."

Constraints And Restraints

Numbers of times when I have been teaching God's Word, I have sensed His nudge and have stopped speaking and quietly listened to the voice of God. His explanations and directions have been different, with significant results in relation to the many and varied audiences to whom I have spoken.

They are called either the constraints or restraints of the Holy Spirit.

These methods can only be experienced when we are totally submitted to the control of the Holy Spirit in the fear of the Lord, which releases us from the fear of other people.

I had been speaking for about eight minutes at a national women's conference in the USA, when I sensed an increasingly strong restraint of the Holy Spirit. I stopped speaking the message I was giving titled "Jesus, the Master Soul Winner" and how the same principles He lived by could be applied to our lives.

As I sought God, He revealed to me that unbelief in many hearts was hindering the flow of God's Spirit. I spoke this out and called the people to repent of this sin, giving them time to follow through.

Then the Holy Spirit released me to give the rest of the message. The atmosphere became as different as night from day and the people were then able to receive, and later apply the word of the Lord to their lives.

Another time I had received an invitation from a pastor friend to hold a series of meetings at his church. I sought God and He said, "Yes." The pastor had asked me to start on a Monday night and go through to the Sunday night, but whenever I sought God about this schedule, I became aware of a constraint in my spirit about speaking at the Sunday services.

God's direction did not make a grain of sense to my human reasoning. The largest number of people always attended the two Sunday services and I was available on that date. When I shared my impressions by phone with the pastor, he too had zero understanding, so we agreed that I would go and speak from Monday through Friday night and keep seeking God throughout the week. I did, although the pastor was urging me to continue through Sunday.

Because the whole thing seemed so illogical, I actually sought God three different times, and each time He spoke the same answer into my spirit: "Return to your home on Saturday morning."

That was it, despite the pastor's comments on how very strange it all seemed to him. I assured him that it wasn't all that strange to me because on many occasions God had told me to do things that were contrary to my human reasonings and/or desires, and every time, through obedience to His voice, the outcome was perfect. I told the pastor my mission at his church would be completed on Friday night.

The next day my husband phoned me to say that a young spiritual leader whom I had never met, had phoned and left a message that he felt he was to spend some time with me. He explained that he had only partial understanding of God's purposes, and that he was coming to Los Angeles from another country and would only be available for a few hours on Saturday morning before he had to fly out again. The young leader had no idea of my itinerary, but said he would do anything to meet with me anywhere.

The Holy Spirit let me know in a hurry that this was the reason for sending me home. It was obviously more important to God for me to spend time with this little-known young man than to speak to many hundreds of people in two church services. I took the first flight home on Saturday morning and was able to have quality time ministering to him. It was a crisis time directionally for his life.

Later, he was God's instrument to open up strategic doors of ministry in Afghanistan for me. That visit was the start of a lifelong close friendship. His name is Floyd McClung. After serving in a senior leadership position in Y.W.A.M. for many years, he became the senior pastor of the Metro Christian Fellowship in Kansas City. Later he and his wife Sally headed up a powerful evangelism and discipleship ministry in South Africa. He is a missionary statesman of the first order and the author of a number of vital books.

Can you imagine how it disappoints and hurts the heart of God when He has planned to bless us and others in ways beyond our imagination, and then we choose not to take some simple step of obedience to His directions because with our little finite minds it doesn't make sense. So then, God has to withhold all those benefits. This scenario is being repeated all too frequently.

The more implications involved with large steps of obedience and faith to God, the more glory will be brought to the Lord Jesus, the more His Kingdom will be extended, and the greater blessings will be ultimately showered upon us. However, we seldom see those blessings immediately.

As I have previously mentioned, in 1971 God called us to leave our home in New Zealand to become missionaries with YWAM. This meant living entirely by faith with two teenage children. We had very little money and not one person guaranteed us one penny of support, although our friends and church believed in our call from God. We were totally "out on a limb," with nothing but God's call, God's character, and God's promises.

That's when we chose to tell God, that for the rest of our lives, every bit of money He would give us would belong to Him, and that we would give any amount, any time, to anyone He indicated. We went from tithing 10 percent to giving Him the right to have it all. Now nearly fifty years later, at the time of writing this book, I can say that consistently living at that radical level of commitment and faith, by His grace, we have been greatly blessed in every way.

Of course there have been times of severe testings when God required us to give everything, when we were in desperate need ourselves. But that is God's way of strengthening and increasing our faith. God has never failed us, simply because He cannot fail. Faithfulness is part of His character. But I know for certain that obedience to Him because of Who He is, is the key to this level of obedience and faith.

One of the times when I was tested by God in relation to finances, was when I was due to leave on several overseas ministry assignments in two days time, and I had absolutely no money for the needed expenses.

Then, out of the blue, a couple from South Africa mailed me a check for $1000. They shared that they had never spoken to me, but had heard me speak at a spiritual leadership conference a few years earlier.

They wrote that they were very reluctant to obey repeated impressions by the Holy Spirit during the last three weeks, that they were to send me this amount of money.

Finally, in order to get some peace of mind they mailed it to me!! It met my needs at that time. Hallelujah!

I quickly wrote back to them a letter of deep gratitude, explaining the reasons why they were receiving those impressions from God.

More Fun

On one occasion, I had completed a week's teaching at a large outdoor festival co-lead by John called "Jesus West Coast," and was taking a 45-minute flight on a small plane from Chico heading for the San Francisco airport.

As I was the only passenger, I asked the Captain if I could fly the plane under His directions, assuring him that I had absolutely no fear! I was probably in my late fifties. He sized me up and said, "Sure."

To my sheer delight he let me fly it all the way under his instructions, until he took over to bring it in to land. There was some turbulence, which made it all the more exciting for me. This produced more praise, worship, and thanksgiving to my fabulous friend Jesus.

Connecting The Ministries

Jim served on Y.W.A.M.'s International Council from its inception and continued on for many years. He also served as

Y.W.A.M.'s international staff pastor, having an anointed ministry with people one on one. Everyone loved him!

Then there came a time when the Holy Spirit made it clear to both of us that Jim was to resign from the International Council and fulfill yet another role. This was a hard decision for Jim to make, but God in His faithfulness gave him strong Scriptural confirmation from Psalm 81:6. "I relieved your shoulder of the burden; your hands were freed from the basket." R.S.V.

The purpose was to be linked with my ministry giftings. I definitely needed help, and Jim was the perfect answer. We functioned together as the knife and the fork, but we never found out who was the knife or who was the fork.

I did the teaching and book writing, while he looked after our business affairs and did all the computer work. At 68, Jim taught himself computer skills. I was impressed! He took my handwritten scripts for two of my books and put them into the computer. I then had excellent scripts for both of the publishers involved.

My Methods Of Reading The Bible

I've had a few different methods of reading the Bible.

The one I have used the most is to start at Genesis and read through until Malachi; at the same time reading from Matthew until Revelation. Usually a chapter or more at a time. I also include the Psalms and Proverbs in the same way. I underline what the Holy Spirit enlightens to me as important, as I go.

Another method is to ask God to tell me which specific book of the Bible He wants me to be reading at any given time, and believe He will speak to me.

Finally, I wouldn't be without the "Daily Light," which is a compilation of Scriptures only, and their references around a given theme. One for the morning and one for the evening.

A.W. Tozer's writings of depth have been significantly used by God to help shape my life. I have kept a copy of the lengthy, historic, and extremely powerful prayer he prayed the day he was ordained. I keep reading it as a refresher course.

Andrew Murray's writings have also had a profound effect on shaping my destiny. I am deeply grateful to God for these priceless ministry pearls of truth.

God's Mercy And Grace

For most of my earlier adult life I had a love affair with speed. Along with that, came an abnormal lack of fear!!! Consequently, I often severely broke the speed limit.

When I studied the subject of the fear of the Lord from the Bible, I found it said, "The fear of the Lord is to hate evil" Proverbs 8:13. I obviously didn't hate breaking the law when breaking speed limits was a way of life.

A radical change took place when I deeply repented of this sin. At the same time, God knew how he had created me, and in His love and mercy set me up for a great treat.

It was 1972 and I was in Lausanne, Switzerland, teaching for weeks on end, morning and evening through the week at Y.W.A.M.'s School of Evangelism. By Saturday I was more than ready for a break in schedule.

My good friend Rudy Lack who was a Swiss, and a bit older than the other students, very kindly took me out in his Mercedes Benz to varied places for all of Saturday. Did I ever love that!

One Saturday he told me that just across the Swiss border, there is the Autobahn freeway in Germany where there is no speed limit. He asked me if I'd like to go on it and drive his car! I jumped at the offer and off we went.

There were no other cars around, as I gradually increased the speed until I pushed the pedal right to the floor boards. Was that ever exhilarating! Specially seeing it was in a Mercedes Benz! I later eased back a bit and then let Rudy drive the rest of the way to France for the day.

I thanked God for fulfilling a deep desire, at the right place, and at the right time, and with the right person (who was possibly praying), and with the fear of God on me! Throw in a couple of my guardian angels to complete the scenario! Before anyone thinks of doing the same thing, make sure you are fulfilling all the right conditions.

An Unusual Surprise

In 1996 on Monday, September 30th, Jim and I went to Anaheim Stadium in Southern California. Pastor Benny Hinn was having a gospel Campaign and it was packed out.

My introduction to this man of God is a good illustration of what was to come. I was in great need of God to heal me from debilitating back pain, which was compounded by my recently having had faulty surgery done in that area.

Ron Haus had placed us in the front row. We had never met Benny Hinn. During the preliminaries he suddenly announced to the 22 thousand people that I was there and asked me to stand and led in an applause. Then he came forward and sat down on the edge of the stage and chatted away with me. He said he'd seen me and knew my ministry of teaching and intercession, and was expecting the Lord to strengthen me today. He then encouraged me to believe that God would touch me and quoted, Matthew 7:7a, "Ask and you shall receive."

All this utterly amazed me, as I never knew the man of God knew I existed!! Later in the service, he came down from the platform and spoke to Jim and me personally. I then told him I had been ill for three and a half years, and he was surprised. I explained that I was going through a Job test, and that both of us needed healing.

Pastor Benny then said, "I sense such a rich deposit of the Spirit in you both." He then laid his hands on our heads and the power of God pushed us back into our seats, as we'd been standing.

The four hour service was a wonderful experience. After Benny had preached the Gospel, many hundreds responded to the appeal and came forward for Salvation. A young boy was healed of blindness from birth, along with many other miracles of healing and deliverances. To God be the glory!

After the service we were invited to meet Pastor Benny in a private room with a few others. This, and many more privileges continued for many years.

We bonded closely in the Spirit, and in heart not only with him, but with his platform personnel… and his family. To this day, his son-in-law Michael Koulianos, and his eldest daughter Jessica are among my very closest friends!

One of my greatest ministry privileges and opportunities has been doing thirty television programs where Benny has interviewed me, and aired them extensively internationally. I brought specific Biblical teachings every time.

That was so fulfilling and rewarding. I will be forever grateful to God and His anointed servant for releasing me to teach in that extensive way.

Updated Letter

April 28, 1997

Our dear Intercessor friends,

"Oh, give thanks to the Lord, for He is good! For His mercy endures forever. Let the redeemed of the Lord say so…" And we wholeheartedly do!

We are deeply grateful to so many of you who have faithfully prayed for us during this continuing trial. We are acutely aware of the resultant spiritual impact upon our lives.

Healing has not yet come to me. However, we're very thankful for a recent improvement in my strength level, and that some days the pain is less than on others. But I am still restricted from returning to a normal lifestyle. Regular doctors have nothing to offer me. We believe God has directed us to continue to be under the supervision of the highly qualified Christian nutritionist that we wrote about in our last letter, while looking to God as the source of healing. Jim's health has greatly improved which is a cause for praise and thanksgiving.

Our burden in prayer increases in intensity for a revived Church and spiritual awakening among the lost; for this nation and the nations worldwide. We're praying much for the hearts of the spiritual leaders to be prepared for the outpouring of the fire, wind, and rain of the Spirit that is coming. It won't be a picnic. As someone has said, "When we pray for rain, we need to be prepared to deal with some mud."

God ploughs deeply in the hearts of those who **want** to be prepared. Let us not flinch at the pain of the blades, but look forward to the display of His glory and the mighty harvest that will also result to the praise of His glory.

God has brought us encouragement, confirmation, and enlightenment from the reading of Bob Sorge's remarkably insightful book, "The Fire of Delayed Answers." * We're all either in a prolonged trial, heading for one, been in one and could do with more understanding, or know someone who is in the same boat.

We don't know anything better to recommend than this book that has been written in the furnace of affliction.

Understanding of some of God's purposes in our trial has gradually surfaced over the years.

(1) The testing of our faith in God's character and ways (as with Job, Joseph, David, Abraham.)

(2) Entering into the fellowship of Christ's sufferings as a result of having frequently prayed Paul's prayer in Phil. 3:10.

(3) Being refined and more conformed to the image of the Lord Jesus (a) in preparation for being part of the Bride of Christ. (b) in answer to our many prayers to be more prepared for the Judgement Seat of Christ.

(4) Enabling us to be more identified with suffering humanity in order to more effectively minister to them.

(5) The possibility of being called by God to suffer, as an example to others. Paul had this revelation and made numbers of references to this concept.

**Bob Sorge "THE FIRE OF DELAYED ANSWERS" ©1996 Oasis House Publishers.*

> 2 Cor 1:6, Ephes. 3:13. James refers to the same thing in his epistle, chapter 5 verses 10 and 11. We're still pondering this aspect, and are willing to remain submitted to Jesus' Lordship if that is part of His plan.

We're all living in challenging, amazing days. We personally don't want to miss anything that God has for us, so that we can truly fulfill our destinies regardless of the cost.

We have rich fulfillment in our daily times of meaningful intercession together, and our love for the Lord and each other is

more precious than ever. My book, "Intercession, Thrilling and Fulfilling," should be published next month. Bringing this project to birth during the four years of illness, can only be likened to my carrying and giving birth to our two children. Neither of them came quickly or easily!!

We've also worked on updating my resource catalog.

Many blessings have come to us through this long illness. We can only worship and praise our wonderful Lord for His unfathomable love, infinite wisdom, and unending grace. In His unswerving faithfulness, He will yet fulfill His continued assurances from His Word to us for full restoration of health.

In the meantime we're learning lots about endurance, patience, and deeper dimensions of faith. We deeply desire that our greatest fulfillment at all times will come from an increasingly intimate, passionate love relationship with our Heavenly Bridegroom, rather than in ministry accomplishments.

**Joy Dawson "INTERCESSION, THRILLING AND FULLFILLING" ©1997 by Y.W.A.M. Publishing.*

We trust Emily Matthew's poem will encourage you as it has us:

Waiting is the hardest
When we feel our need is great,
But it helps if we remember
That our God is never late
He knows our deepest longings,
And He times things perfectly,
For in His love, He only does
What's best for you and me.

Lovingly and gratefully,

Joy and Jim"

Revival Praying

In January of 1998, I was speaking at an all day prayer meeting being held at Melodyland (Church), opposite to Disneyland in Southern California. Benny Hinn was in charge. The three subjects were related to different aspects of praying for genuine revival and spiritual awakenings.

Application in powerful times of intercession followed each session. During one of them while praying for the Holy Spirit to be poured out upon Southern California, the Holy Spirit clearly spoke to me from Zechariah 10:1 "Ask the Lord for rain…"

This was an added confirmation of the three times God had previously spoken to me from Hosea 6:3 b, promising an outpouring of the Spirit in Southern California.

I shared this with Pastor Benny and then publicly. I closed with reading a report of the unusual events surrounding the Cane Ridge

Revival. This was followed by leading the audience in interceding for spiritual leaders who would become desperate in prayer for revival and would then pay the price to lead the people when the unexpected and the unusual was the normal, in the fear of the Lord.

Only yesterday, I watched on Daystar Television a man with an apostolic ministry from Brazil, prophesying with the deepest conviction that genuine revival is coming to America.

Isaiah 59:19 says, "When the enemy comes in like a flood, the Lord will raise up a standard against him."

That first part surely fits this scenario here in Southern California and encourages me to keep on keeping on in desperate faith filled prayers for the fire, the wind, and the rain of the Spirit to break forth in my territory, for the glory of God, and salvation of many thousands of lost souls.

A Spirit Filled Life Conference

On Saturday, June 13th, 1998, I spoke at the Spirit Filled Life Conference at The Church On The Way, under Dr. Scott Bauer's leadership on "The Fire of God."

At the close of the message, I invited the audience to either kneel or lie on the floor and cry out to God for the fire of God to invade us with His awesome presence.

Scott, led the packed-out audience in the main auditorium to respond to the message by crying out at the top of his lungs, "Send the fire, send the fire." He then lay face down on the floor in front of the platform beside his serious son, Kyle.

Later, Scott led in fervent praying, naming categories of bondages that needed the fire of God, until 5 pm.

Waiting On God Pays Off

It was Saturday December 19th, 1998 and Benny Hinn was scheduled to be ministering at the Dream Center in Los Angeles for an outdoor Christmas event, with gifts for the people. It started at 5pm and Jim and I wanted to go.

As we sought God about it He repeatedly spoke to us from His Word to wait. This continued for many hours. It wasn't easy!

Finally, at 5:20 p.m. God spoke to Jim from Judges 19, "the journey on which you go is blessed by the Lord. Go in peace."

Because we were suitably dressed and ready to go, we shot out of the house like jack rabbits. I prayed for miracle parking right outside the gates; and when we arrived a van pulled out and we went right in. Thank You Lord! By this time, Benny Hinn's event had come and gone!! We then concluded that God had another plan and we were on full alert for His directions.

We were buying a copy of Jim Baker's new book, from his book stand, when an attendant recognized me and asked if we would like to visit with Jim and his new wife of 3 ½ months, Lori Beth, who were upstairs. I had a long standing good relationship with Jim, so we immediately accepted. We were very warmly welcomed.

Jim Baker and his lovely wife were now on the staff at the Dream Center and had their own small apartment.

Jim Baker had on a denim jacket complete with jeans and a blue baseball cap, and was as relaxed as a poached egg.

At one point in the lively conversion, he casually mentioned that at some stage tonight he was going to perform a marriage ceremony. When we told him that we would slip away whenever he gave us the signal, he assured us there was no need as it was going to be held right here!!

When I asked the obvious question, "Where are the bride and groom?" Jim pointed to a quiet couple sitting in the corner of the room, who were also part of the Dream Center staff. They were also in jeans.

Jim Baker returned to sharing with enthusiasm about his radically new life ministering to the poor and needy. We listened with rapt attention.

Another lovely married couple were there who had ministered for years alongside Jim Baker in his "Praise The Lord" Television days before going to prison. The husband was a top notch violin player, so he provided a fabulous musical background for the occasion.

Jim Baker finally asked the couple to come forward.

As soon as they did, Lori pulled some red roses out of a vase on top of a table and put them in the bride's hands for a bouquet.

Jim Baker then started to conduct the wedding ceremony, complete with the baseball cap still in place. Despite the casual surroundings, I was very moved by the anointed, simple and sincere way he reverently conducted the whole service. It was beautiful.

After the exchanging of the vows, this officiating spiritual leader smilingly announced that "our dear sister Joy will now bring a word from the Lord."

I had no time to do anything but cry out silently to the Lord, "help me." Instantly He flashed into my mind the main principles by which Jim and I operated on in our very successful marriage. I simply shared them and then prayed for the couple.

The entire two hours was refreshingly different to say the least. However, it would never have eventuated had we not learned to wait on God.... without having understanding <u>why</u>, but understanding <u>Who</u> was in charge.

Significant Intercession

In June of 1999, I was in intercession for the persecuted Church, when the Holy Spirit directed me to ask God to arrest many religious leaders like Saul of Tarsus, and reveal Himself to them, and they'd then be given apostolic ministries. I did this and believed.

Then I had a message spoken in tongues with an interpretation, which said God had answered my prayers and I was to mark this date, because God would let me know who they were.

That has all come to pass. I've listened to numerous testimonies from strong apostolic ministries who have shared that their past was anti-Christ and His claims.

Vision For Hispanics

I had been interceding for years for God to raise up anointed leadership to spearhead a very vital ministry to reach the vast number of Hispanics in the greater Los Angeles area. I was waiting in faith for the answer. On December 19th, 1999, God suddenly imparted to me His vision of how this was to be done.

As a result, I met with Jim Tolle for an hour, following an 11 a.m. Sunday service at The Church on the Way, and shared it with him. He was in a painful time of major transition related to his ministry and had just accepted Pastor Scott Bauer's invitation to oversee a small ministry to Hispanics at our home church. Jim Tolle spoke Spanish as a second language. He made it clear to me that he had zero vision for his future, at this time.

I have always had a deep love and appreciation for this genuine, gifted man of God, who was a recognized elder at The Church on the Way.

The vision was as follows:

1. The multitudes of Hispanics in Los Angeles are like the Israelites in Egypt, where God sovereignly

multiplied them profusely.

2. God has a plan to reach this large needy people group of Hispanics. Just as He raised up Moses to lead the children of Israel out of bondage, God has now raised up Jim Tolle to lead these Los Angeles Hispanics into their God given freedom, and full potential. The good sized West Campus Church will become too small for the great numbers God will send you.

3. God has heard my repeated cries for the five fold ministries mentioned in Ephesians 4 to be brought forth among them. This will come to pass in time.

4. It will take both of the Apostolic leadership anointings that are on Scott Bauer and Jim Tolle to lead the people of The Church on the Way, and help prepare them for the mighty moves of God's Spirit ahead.

I had shared this ahead of time with Pastor Scott Bauer who confirmed it all, as God had given him a similar vision.

The ministry to the Hispanics soon multiplied and flourished at every dimension. It was truly remarkable, and could only be explained by being under a visitation of the Holy Spirit at unusual dimensions being led by God's appointed anointed leader, Pastor Jim.

There were many couples who were living together in the church and some had children, but had never married. This included a number of those who had recently given their lives to Christ.

The solution was having a **HUGE** wedding; all the couples getting married on the same day at the same time!!

A lady member of our church had a business renting out lovely bridal gowns. She generously supplied free of charge, a bridal gown for every woman getting married.

What an historic day! What an amazing ministry! What an awesome God!

The numbers grew to such proportions that multiple services each week became the norm, and this church actually became the largest Spanish speaking church in America at that time.

Pastor Jim Tolle took frequent airline trips to the White House, where he was asked to give his input on how best to solve the many issues related to the Hispanic people in the U.S.A.

This ministry became the subject of much fervent, faith filled intercession from Jim and myself. Much later, God directed Jim Tolle to start from scratch, and start a ministry to Hispanics on his own, with a few of his staff members. They rented school facilities.

That ministry thrived and again became a formidable force against the enemies' plans and power over the Hispanics in Los Angeles. A special school for ministry training was also added, directed by Dr. Paul Chappel.

As of this writing, this ministry has again greatly expanded in breadth of anointed pastoral staff and in spiritual dimensions of intrinsic depth for the extension of God's Kingdom. All glory to God.

In recent years God has burdened my heart in prayer for the large contingency of Armenians that live in Los Angeles. I am believing God to raise up foundational ministries to reach them with the gospel message and disciple them. It's an urgent project!

Rewards

The Lord Jesus makes it very clear in Mark 10:29,30 that He has a reward system.

"Jesus said, 'Truly I say to you, there is no one who has left house or brothers or sisters or mother or father or children or lands, for my sake and for the gospel, who will not receive a hundredfold now in this time, houses and brothers and sisters and mothers and children and lands, with persecutions, and in the age to come eternal life.'"

There are specific rewards for those who have obeyed His commands to be sent anywhere, anytime, under any conditions, to spread the truths about Him from His Word.

He also states that this includes those who have had to leave the securities of a home and lands, father and mother, and brothers and sisters and children.

The rewards are a **hundred-fold return in this life**; -- houses, plus all the relationships, with persecutions added. Jim and I and our children and grandchildren have lived to see this reward system work in marvelous and miraculous ways.

Because there are three generations of adult Dawsons that have, and most still are, living as unsalaried missionaries around the world, there came the need for this clan to have a place to have some much needed rest and relaxation.

We experienced the promises of Mark 10:29,30 come alive. God directed us clearly from His Word to own a double wide mobile home that we were able to add on to, in a remarkable situation.

It was at Bass Lake, in Northern California; 8 minutes to the nearest appealing shopping center; with diversely quaint little shops. It was set back from the highway, with a winding road that led up to the house with a big verandah across the front, and a good-sized deck at the side, which we added.

We looked out on to an unobstructed panoramic view, with no noise and no neighbors in site.

It was also a bit of Heaven on earth to revel in the magnificent and unique beauty of the nearby big blue lake, which was surrounded by native forests, and a snowcapped mountain glistening at the top end of it.

There were times when Jim and I were sitting in our deck chairs at the edge of the lake with the forest at our backs, having our many daily readings of the Bible, when we would find the beauty of our surroundings a distraction, and have to discipline ourselves to keep focused.

At a later time, we were able to purchase an older model speedboat. This proved to be a wonderful asset in providing hours of fun for those who loved to water ski – adults and grandchildren alike, or for just cruising around.

When I would be jumping off our boat and go swimming around some beautiful cove in the warm lake, thinking, "How does this get any better?" I would remember Jesus' promises in Mark 10:29,30.

I would also remember all the superb outdoor beauty and beaches and home we left behind in New Zealand, as we gladly "left all to follow Him" …and I was not missing any of it.

Jim and I had endless numbers of vital prayer walks together, plus many bike rides around the lake, and lots of picnic lunches.

There was a very special walk through thick forest which ended up at a beautiful stream flowing over rocks which "wowed" us every time. We would sit on a rock and marvel at God's creation.

Bass Lake was also the place where I would climb up the side of a 42 feet waterfall with my grandsons. With our arms linked together we would then go over the top and hurtling down, yelling out exuberantly with sheer joy, into the lake below.

Then we would repeat the process. What fun!

A never to be forgotten memory was driving around the lake on a Christmas Sunday morning after church, with snow falling everywhere. J.B. and Jill and little Jenny and Justin were with us.

For Californians it was a very rare experience for us to have snow. To have it in this unusually beautiful setting on this special day, caused me to erupt with exuberant bursts of praise to God.

Our children and grandchildren, proved again in a tangible way, that God is neither poor nor mean when He asks us to live entirely by faith in Him alone.

These times of intense pleasure could only be compared with some of the things I did back in the seventies.

Having Fun

On one my birthdays in my sixties, I asked Jim to buy me a skateboard. He readily complied, so I was now ready to have fun joining in with my three grandsons David, Paul, and Mathew as they went skateboarding.

I loved going down sloping places, doing my best to keep up with them. I kept getting new boards, in order to keep up with the boys, as the styles kept changing. The only reason I had to give up this fun thing at 68 years young was because of lower back pain that had developed. (Nothing to do with skateboarding.)

At 68, I learned to snow ski with these same boys. Mathew was learning with me, but David and Paul were already adept at the sport. When Jim was well into his seventies, we frequently took Jenny and Justin on interesting bike rides when they were young.

I think the cutest thing a grandchild ever said to me was when Rachel was four years old. She said, "If I was as old as you, I'd be a dinosaur!" That was on April 20th 2001, when I was 83. Rachel is John and Julie's fourth child, who came much later than their boys.

Rewards Continued

The Bass Lake house proved to be a wonderful asset to me when writing my book "Intercession, Thrilling and Fulfilling." * I desperately needed to get away from all the demands attached to my office and home.

It was a very difficult time for us when we had to finally give it all up. Bass Lake was a five hour drive from our home, and the severity of my back condition meant I couldn't cope with the pain that went with all that driving. It was also very hard on the rest of our families to have to give it up. Such is the reality of life.

**Joy Dawson "INTERCESSION, THRILLING AND FULLFILLING" ©1997 by Y.W.A.M. Publishing.*

The Holy Spirit had made it very clear to me that I was to prioritize my ministry time in getting a lot of my Bible teachings into books that I would write.

This meant we needed another place near home for us to accomplish that task. The answer to our prayers came when we found a mobile home park, with a mobile home for sale, at Newport Beach, California, very near the ocean.

Jim did a great job while there, putting all my hand written notes of "Forever Ruined for the Ordinary" * the adventure of hearing and obeying God's voice, into the computer. This became a best seller.

This was followed by Jim doing all the computer work from my handwritten notes of my book, "The Fire of God,"**

This location was only an hour's drive in the car from home, which made it possible for me to handle with my continued back pain.

To get a break from the intensity of writing books and the many TV teaching interviews and other ministry assignments I had with Benny Hinn from that location, we badly needed some rest and relaxation.

God provided it with a small electric boat that was for sale at a nearby docking sight that became available. We would slowly cruise around the harbor and see the numbers of ships worth millions of dollars, that were docked alongside many others of varying degrees of wealth and wonders.

* *Joy Dawson "FOREVER RUINED FOR THE ORDINARY" ©2001 Thomas Nelson Publishers.*

**Joy Dawson "THE FIRE OF GOD" 2005 Published by Destiny Image.

Then we would cruise on to different sights of natural beauty, which we much preferred. Our family was also to benefit at times from this needed provision from the Lord.

However, the time came when Jim was not able to maintain two properties because of his age, so this one had to go.

It sold at the exact time that Jim was putting up the "For Sale" sign outside the house. Plus a realtor friend opposite, to whom we had witnessed many times, took care of the needed ramifications.

Our heavenly Father was watching over us as He promised in Psalm 31:19 "O how abundant is Your goodness which You have laid up for those who fear you and wrought for those who take refuge in You in the sight of the sons of men."

The 2000s And Beyond

Matthew 6:13 …for Yours is the Kingdom and the power and the glory forever.

Jim's Letter To The Sisk's

I found the following letter which had been filed away, written by Jim to some of our very close friends. I'm including it in this book for two reasons. First, because it reveals the gracious way Jim communicated as a way of life, and it also gives a unique glimpse of his perspective on some of our darkest days.

December 29, 2000

Beloved Mary Lance and Bob,

By the time you receive this, 2000 will be a memory, with 2001 dawning with fascinating possibilities. Our prayers and desires for you both are that you'll have the most fulfilling year ever, and that you'll experience God's precious anointing on all your worship and service to our wonderful Master.

I'm so grateful for your prayers. The delicate surgery to remove numbers of polyps inside my nose went well, but then, twelve days later at 3 a.m. on Sunday morning Dec. 17th, I woke to find my nose gushing blood everywhere. Joy immediately phoned 911 and we were soon in the ambulance on our way to the hospital. However, by the time the emergency doctor got to me I had lost so much blood that I passed out.

(I, Joy, was shocked to see him look like death warmed up, and faced the worst scenario or outcome. It was very sobering. I had been warned that the implications could be very serious. I placed him in God's hands in faith.)

Anyway, they plugged up my nose and stopped the bleeding but kept me in the hospital to monitor me for the rest of that day and the following night. Apparently, an artery, exposed during the surgery, decided to "protest." Well, that was over a week ago, and I'm now feeling almost back to normal. (Whatever that is for a 78 year old.)

It's nearly eight years since Joy began experiencing daily pain from lower back disorders. The pain levels have increased, and the non-addictive moderate medications she takes three times a day don't help much anymore. Some days all she can do is lie down, worship, read the Word and intercede; and wait for the pain and weakness to subside enough to function in her other ministry responsibilities and daily chores. She never wastes a minute.

Joy struggles to try to cope with the large volume of correspondence she receives, which often contains peoples' unrealistic requests and expectations of her. This load increases every time she writes a new book, which is the area of ministry that God has made clear she is to prioritize over travelling and speaking. She is also presently working on writing a 1500 word contribution to a book co-authored by Tommy and Thetus Tenney, at their request.

Every time we seek God diligently to say anything He wants to say about her health, He always directs us to scriptures assuring us of complete healing in HIS TIME. We are in total trust that the Lord is in control, and in faith that He will one day fulfill these many promises to us. In the waiting time, your prayers for grace and strength to endure are needed and greatly appreciated.

Because we don't mention Joy's physical condition any more unless people ask, many have concluded that she is healed, which is far from the truth.

It's so good to have a little chat with you precious friends. We trust you are both doing well in every way. You're greatly loved and prayed for, including your family and businesses.

Always, your friend and brother in the Lord,

Jim

More About My Sweetheart

On a much lighter note; I always loved the fact that in Jim's early forties his grey hair topped his handsome face. Then in his fifties I delighted even more in his white hair doing the same.

It was also very practical, because I could always quickly spot him in a crowd when I was on a platform as the speaker. I would never start preaching until I located him. He was my greatest earthly friend and intercessor.

By the way, God understood my positive reaction to Jim's distinctive hair tones. Proverbs 20:21 says, "The beauty (or the splendor) of old men is their grey head." One translation says, "The ornament of old men is a hoary head." Hoary means white!

My sweetheart had these distinctions much earlier than most.

Jim was spontaneously funny. We never knew what he'd say next, and we loved it as a family.

One day grandson Justin and his Papa (Jim) were together in the motor home, which was to the right of the driveway. A young man Y.W.A.M.er was doing yard work, just below a motor home window.

Papa, out of sight, and from the inside of the window, said in a deep voice to the young man, "Hello, this is God speaking."

To which the young man replied, "Hello God, what should I do with my life?"

Papa, without skipping a beat said, "Do what you're doing now, only faster."

Perhaps this is as good a place as any to share that Jim was uniquely anointed by the Holy Spirit whenever he conducted a wedding or a funeral. I loved watching him function in these capacities, and was so proud of him. His pastoral ministry was never stronger than when counseling people one on one. He was a strong father figure to countless numbers, who needed just that.

On Sunday, January 27th, 2002, I noticed a very meaningful entry in my diary. I quote, "I was in unusually strong pain today. Despite that, Jim and I had a precious time of close fellowship, sharing our hearts and encouraging each other in the Lord, which is not unusual for us. I wouldn't trade our close deep relationship and level of love and trust for each other for anything in the world."

At the time of that entry Jim would have been 79 and I would have been 76.

Proverbs 9 was in my Bible reading that day. I noticed again in verses 10 and 11 the direct promises of years being added to the lives of those who fear the Lord, and pursue the knowledge of God's character.

Jim lived to be 90 and I am 94.

Seeking God

In January of 2001, with continued increased daily joint and pinched nerve pain, Jim and I sought God diligently if He had anything to say to us concerning this.

Jim was directed by God to read Pastor Charles Blair's commentary preceding the book of Job, in the Spirit filled life Bible. He said there are times when God cannot explain why we are suffering, because it would defeat the purposes for it.

This confirmed what I have believed; that the greatest test is the perplexity test. However because God is just, He has a reward system for those who will trust Him when we cannot trace Him.

We also need to accept the possibility of being among those in Hebrews 11 who had to wait until they went to Heaven to obtain their freedom from much suffering.

This was the time I went to the piano and sang the following song, as the Holy Spirit gave it to me, line by line:

"I trust You Lord, I trust You Lord
When I can't see the way ahead that's best for me.
I rest in You, I rest in You
I know your wisdom proves You true.

So I'll keep my eyes on Your dear face,
And trust You Lord for all the grace
To rest in Your unfailing power to see me through.
I'll trust Your Word which cannot fail,
And then one day You'll lift the veil,
And I will see that what You did was best for me.

Your mighty power is still the same
In this dark hour as when You came
To earth to show mankind You care,
And that Your heart will always bear
Our burdens, pain and sorrows too,

For on the cross was where You bore
Our sin and sickness; ours no more.

I want Your glory to be shown
That Your Name may be fully known
So when Your purposes are complete,
I'll lay the glory at Your feet."

Leaning On Jesus

It was October of 2001. For three days and nights before going to speak at a spiritual leadership conference in El Paso, Texas, I had very little sleep and was in severe pain. I knew what to do.... phone some of my intercessor friends for their help....and trust God for His enabling power. I did both.

I then went and spoke to 150 spiritual leaders at a city Pastor's luncheon on "Preparation for being the Bride of Christ."

Jim said this was the most anointed of the times I've given this message. I too, sensed the grip of the Holy Spirit on the leaders as I spoke, "Thank you Lord for answering our desperate prayers." "When I'm weak, then You are strong" (In the Spirit) says Paul in 2 Corinthians 12:10b.

The next day I spoke to 150 missionaries, as well as other Christian leaders, at an Episcopalian Church. My message was, "Waiting for the fulfillment of promises, visions, and destinies."

My diary reports, "There was a strong sense of God's awesome presence as I spoke." Thank You, Holy Spirit.

I continued in pain and broken sleep, but continued to bring the word of the Lord for two more days, until Saturday night when I crashed and slept. God is faithful. "His strength was made perfect in my weakness," so He gets all the glory.

On Sunday afternoon we drove out to George and Melanie Wayne's fabulous Georgian English Mansion and Grounds for a beautiful dinner with about 22 precious Believers whom it was a delight to be with. The Wayne's proved to be the dearest friends of ours with whom we kept in touch for many years. I still love them and will never forget them.

An Unanswered Question

It remains an enigma to me that numerous times God has used me over my long lifetime to pray for people who needed healing whether in mind, body, soul, or spirit and God answered in remarkable ways....and yet I still remain unhealed and am in a lot of pain.

I am thinking of a Sunday morning in March of 2002 at the close of the 11 a.m. service at The Church On The Way. Dr. Scott Bauer had invited people who needed to respond to the challenging message on discipleship he had just given, to come forward. Dozens responded. Elders prayed for them.

I counseled a middle age woman who was full of resentment and anger toward people close to her who had harassed her. After leading her through the Biblical steps she needed to take in order to forgive them, I then laid my hands on her head and asked the Holy Spirit to free her with His love for those who had offended her.

Immediately she was slain in the Spirit and lay on her back on the floor. Everybody around us soon departed and we were left entirely alone. I continued praying for the healing of her mind, body, and emotions, and fully believed God to do it.

She then told me that God had released her from all pain, cleared her mind, filled her with peace, and that she felt the Holy Spirit moving gently through her whole being. I could feel this movement under my hands as I kept praying in faith with my hands on her stomach, as I bent over her with pain in my back. This lasted for an hour and we were the last to leave the building, knowing that God had done a mighty work.

Weeks later she testified to having been healed mentally, physically, emotionally, and spiritually, and has never needed her cane again for walking. We praised and thanked God for His mighty miraculous power on her behalf.

Disappointment ??

"Disappointment – His appointment,"
  Change one letter then I see
That the thwarting of my purpose
  Is God's better choice for me.

His appointment must be blessing,
  Though it may come in disguise
For the end, from the beginning,
  Open to His vision lies.

"Disappointment – His appointment,"
  Whose? The Lord's who loves me best,
Understands and knows me fully,
  Who my faith and love would test;

For, like loving, earthly parents,
  He rejoices when He knows
That His child accepts unquestioned
  All that from His wisdom flows.

"Disappointment – His appointment,"
"No good things will He withhold."
From denials oft we gather
Treasures of His love untold.

Well He knows each broken purpose
Leads to fuller, deeper trust;
And the end of all His dealings
Proves our God is wise and just.

– author unknown

Three Prophetic Words

On Saturday, June 13th in 2002, God gave me a strong prophetic word for The Church On The Way, which I spoke only to the senior Pastor, Scott Bauer. It was just before I was to speak at a Spirit Filled Life Conference on a Saturday afternoon that he had convened. It was, "Scott, our church is at a definite place of change, and this very day God wants to take us to a whole new dimension or plateau. As a people, we won't be the same again." A little later, I repeated it again to him.

In his powerful book titled, "The new Church On The Way,"* Scott tells about this, and then how God sovereignly spoke in essence the same thing through Pastor Jack Hayford at the next service on Sunday morning. At the Sunday evening service Rev. Jim Tolle flew in from ministering in China and came straight to the church. He gave a strong prophetic word before he gave the message, which in essence was exactly the same thing. Neither of the

**Scott G. Bauer "THE NEW CHURCH ON THE WAY" ©2002 by The Church On The Way.*

three of us had any opportunity to confer with each other! God had made His statement.

Soon after, I gave the message titled "Our greatest need." It's all about seeing our many and diverse ways that pride operates through our lives. At the close, I asked the people to respond to the Holy Spirit.

The Holy Spirit deeply penetrated the peoples' hearts. Over a thousand people fell on their faces before God in repentance. The ministry of the Spirit continued late into the afternoon. To God be the glory.

I recommend every member of T.C.O.T.W., past or present, to read Scott Bauer's book.

Understanding During Suffering

I am recording the following for those who are in similar circumstances to what mine were. I am hoping that you will have a greater understanding of God's character and His ways. Never stop seeking Him, when you are suffering the most. Keep believing Him for answers from His Word.

Jesus is "The Wonderful Counselor."

In 2002, on the 17th and 18th of June, my diary records in large letters across the top of the pages:

These are the two worst days of intense pain in 9¼ years.

This follows: - "I am perplexed at the increased pain and deterioration in my body. I keep asking God for understanding, and relief of pain to function.

- In my Bible reading today in Genesis 40, I noticed the last verse, 'Joseph remained in prison until God's time of deliverance came.'
- The Holy Spirit spoke to Jim, 'The fellowship of His sufferings,' which was confirmed by directing him to Mathew 10:24,38 & 39.
- Being like Jesus our Teacher, we are to take up our cross and follow him. A cross is painful.
- I then opened my Bible at Matthew 15:21-28 where the Canaanite woman had delayed answers when she came to Jesus in great need of His help.

Psalm 18:30 says, "As for God, His way is perfect." We worship Him and trust Him. He is trustworthy. He will come through to meet our needs in His way and time.

Later, on the same day I wrote, "I worshiped God and then asked Him if He had anything to say to me. He said, "How you pass these severe tests, determines not only what I will do through you when they are lifted, but what I'll be able to trust you with in eternity. Look at this testing time through the "BIG PICTURE."

This Word from God marked me! He then said, "Read Ezekiel 44," which I did. It's a very significant chapter.

I then wrote. "I confessed my lack of praising God today."

First thing the next morning, after reading Psalms 49 and 50, I was singing praises to God, when He birthed the following song in me. I went to the piano and sang and played it.

I have every reason to praise You
    For You are God
I have every reason to praise You
    For You're my Lord
I have every reason to love You
    That's why I bring
My offering of praises to You my King

I have every reason to thank You
For what You've done
I have every reason to trust You
The unfailing One
I have every reason to tell You
That's why I bring
My offering of praises and choose to sing.

On November 11th in 2001, when I was having difficulty in walking because of stabbing pains in my joints, the Holy Spirit directed me three times to Scriptures that spoke about having faith and patience. Hebrews 6:11-12 was one. Also Luke 21:19 was another. "By your endurance you will gain your life" and verse 13 says, "This will turn out for you as an occasion for testimony."

I wonder whether God had this book in mind when He spoke those words to me that day.

God spoke to Jim, "What I have promised, I have promised and I haven't changed My mind. You are learning patience and endurance."

Finally, I asked God twice to direct me by His Spirit to one of the women in the Bible who had long standing illnesses and then had a miraculous healing. Immediately God opened my Bible to Luke 13:10-17 It was the woman who had been bent over for 18 years who was instantly healed.

I am trusting that these accounts that I have shared with you from my experience will help give you understanding of some of God's ways and encourage you.

A Memorable Evening In 2003

There were times without numbers when Jim and I would have significantly powerful times of intercession together. One such time was on Sunday evening March 30th, 2003.

We were fulfilling my vow to spend at least one hour's intercession per week for America.

As usual, we waited on God to tell us what was heaviest on His heart that He wanted to share with us.

The Holy Spirit directed us to spend most of the hour praying for the desperate need for God to bring the U.S.A. back to the Bible. He revealed that suffering would be part of that answer, as only then would we find that our greatest means of comfort was in God's Word.

Then the Holy Spirit shared His grief over the unbelief in the hearts of many, that the Bible was the Word of God. We wept with God, over that undeniable fact.

Then we were shown the great grief in God's heart over the unbelief in His children's hearts that He would speak to them personally through His Word. We wept again for and with God.

Finally, we were shown the immense grief in God's heart because of the disobedience in the lives of His people, when they knew the truth's of His Word but never acted on them. By this time we were undone with weeping with and for God's pain. It's impossible to have God share His heart with you and not have a spiritual heart transplant.

We were then reminded that it was twenty years ago that Dr. Bill Bright and Senator Armstrong asked President Ronald Reagan to declare 1983 as The Year of the Bible; which he did! So we then asked God to move on President George W Bush to declare another year of the Bible in the U.S.A. ….we didn't get that answer.

Jesus' Manifest Presence

On September 20th in 2003, Jim and I were up in Big Bear; a resort in the San Bernardino mountains of Los Angeles. I was a speaker at a Singles Retreat of The Church On The Way.

I believe that so often, God cannot release the outpouring of His Spirit upon on us in deeper dimensions, while we are consciously or subconsciously bound to our liturgy.

This Saturday night the liturgy was at zero dimensions. I understand that the flexibility of programming which a Retreat setting offers, made it much easier for the breakthrough we experienced.

After I had given the message on "The Justice of God," I gave opportunity for the audience to openly respond. Several shared genuine deep needs to which I responded with compassionate counsel, while calling everyone to participate by being conduits of the caring love of God towards the hurting individuals; the love of God being the most powerful healing source.

God then directed me to these Scriptures.

<u>Psalm 99:1</u> "The Lord reigns; let the people <u>tremble</u>!"

<u>Ezra 9:4</u> "Then everyone who <u>trembled</u> at the words of the God of Israel assembled to me…"(Ezra)

<u>Ezra 10:3 b</u> "………those who <u>tremble</u> at the commandment of our God; and let it be done according to the law."

Next, the Holy Spirit directed me to call everyone to stand at full attention, as we would if an earthly monarch were entering the room. We did this with our eyes closed for about 15 to 20 minutes, while focusing in worship, in total silence on God's majestic splendor, awesome holiness, and blazing glory.

This resulted in a visitation of the Lord's awesome Presence which was manifest in numbers of ways to His waiting people. Several, including the leader, (Doug Anderson, the associate pastor) had a vision of the Lord Jesus in a long robe, walking between the rows of people, while His robe brushed up against each person to bless them. (It was in contrast to the woman in the Bible who had to press through the crowds in order to touch the hem of Jesus' robe.) How gracious and merciful Jesus is. Other people had visions of the Lord as a protector and warrior leader. Elizabeth Ewing, the children's pastor, had an instantaneous healing from four years of numbness in both feet.

About five minutes into this prolonged silent worship, strong trembling took over in my body and head, and with my teeth chattering. Nearing the end of this protracted time, I clearly heard the Holy Spirit say to me twice, "I am coming to visit My people, and this is preparation."

I was acutely aware that the Holy Spirit was referring to The Church On The Way, although a number of other churches were represented in that audience. If God had spoken to me in an audible voice it could not have been more real, so I broke the silence by telling the audience exactly what God had said to me.

According to the many meaningful testimonies that followed, **all with depth of content**, it was truly a life-changing experience. I heard comments like, "I've been to other Singles Retreats, but **never** like this one." Doug Anderson said he agreed with that statement. All glory to King Jesus who visited us.

The Body of Christ understands so little of the fear of the Lord and experiences so little of what it means to tremble in the presence of our awesome God. Could it partly be because we know so little of the discipline of silent, focused worship? I often ponder with awe and wonder what thirty minutes of silent worship in Heaven will be like as described in Revelation 8:1.

Dr. Scott Bauer's Promotion

It was on October 22nd, 2003, on a Wednesday night church service which Scott had led. He had called the church to pray for me as I was about to have a hysterectomy surgery in a few days. Pastor Jack and Anna Hayford joined Scott as they laid their hands on me and prayed in faith. (The surgery was 100% successful.) We then had a guest speaker; after which Scott asked one of the staff pastors to close in prayer.

As Scott was leaving the platform, his son Kyle noticed that his dad was unsteady on his feet and immediately grabbed him by his right arm, while another staff member grabbed him by his left arm, and they steered him out through a side door into a narrow hallway.

I followed closely behind, along with his wife Rebecca, as I had an appointment with Scott immediately following the service.

When senior staff personnel found their pastor lying in Kyle's arms on the floor, saying, "My head is hurting," they soon called 911, and it wasn't long before they came and had him on a stretcher. Before this, Scott had repeatedly told Rebecca that he loved her.

During this time, I stood close by silently praying fervently. We were later informed that Scott went to be with the Lord on his way out of the church to the nearest hospital. He was diagnosed as having had an aneurysm over one of his temples, which is fatal.

Pastor Jack and I were believing God to raise him from the dead, and were separately praying accordingly. We later heard at the memorial service that others were praying the same way. But God had another plan. Scott's memorial service exuded God's Presence. Although lengthy, I didn't want it to stop! God knows.

God only knows the deep grief and tremendous sense of loss, when Scott went so suddenly to be with Jesus; because only God knows how close Jim and I were to this remarkably gifted and precious servant of God. He was one of a kind.

Dear Pastor Jack nobly stepped in, and lead the church again as many months that it took before Pastor Jim Tolle then took over. He remained leading the large Spanish speaking congregation at the same time, which was a mammoth task.

A Significant Day

The 19th of September, 2004, was a significant day for The Church On The Way and for me. Rev. Jim Tolle was being inaugurated as the senior pastor. The Holy Spirit had given me directions to share, and Pastor Jack Hayford who was leading the ceremony, had released me.

The Scriptures God had given me for Jim were 2 Chronicles 27:2 &6 referring to Jotham. Verse 2 says, "He did what was right in the eyes of the Lord, according to all that his father Uzziah had done." This means he had a deep respect for his spiritual father. This parallels with Jim Tolle's respect for Pastor Jack's mentoring.

Verse 6 says, "So Jotham became mighty, because he ordered his ways before the Lord his God."

The Message Bible, which is a paraphrased version says, "Jotham's strength was rooted in his steady and determined life of obedience to God."

In addition I was giving 2 Samuel 23:3, King David's last words, "He who rules over men must be just, ruling in the fear of God." Verse 4, the results are, "And he shall be like the light of the morning when the sun rises."

These Scriptures were designed by God to affirm and encourage dear Jim Tolle.

Trials

You may recall that when this lower back pain first occurred, I asked God to only heal me when the maximum glory would come to His name through it.

I have never withdrawn that request I made 27 years ago, as I continue to suffer a lot in this area of my body.

"As for God, His way is perfect" expresses my heart in this fiery trial.

I have a framed list of powerful Biblical promises related to Divine healing that I fully believe in, and often declare fervently.

For many decades, I've been challenged by insomnia. Consistently being on jet lag from long distance ministry trips only aggravated the problem. My diaries also record frequent times of absolute exhaustion from the consistently heavy schedule associated with the ministry entrusted to me.

Praise and worship always helped to get me through. Murmuring has not been an option.

After repeated bouts of very severe pain in September of 2004, I asked God to speak to me again from His Word, as I continued to wait on Him for a release.

He answered me from Colossians 1:11, "Strengthened with all might, according to His glorious power, for all **patience** and **long suffering** with joy." Nothing had changed.

There are numerous times recorded in my diaries during the past twenty-six years, where I have sought God diligently for understanding as to why I have not yet been healed of the severe lower back pain; despite repeated promises from Him to do so.

In July 2004, I asked God the following questions:

1. Am I to keep on believing for healing; or have you changed your mind for any reason?

2. Has the time come yet for You to heal me when the maximum glory can come to your Name?
3. If not, do I just keep waiting in full faith?

The Holy Spirit answered me by saying, "Turn in your Bible to page #949." It was Lamentations chapter 3. Verses 23, 26 speak of God's faithfulness, as we seek Him, hope in Him **and wait for His deliverance**!

Here's a written snapshot of a normal day in our lives. I haven't changed the script.

October 2nd 2004, my prayer journal records the usual questions and answers about numbers of ministry related things in the future.

"In the evening we took communion; expressing much love and gratitude to Jesus for the incredible price He paid for our redemption, followed by praise and worship… and then intercession for genuine revival to come for our home church, the Church On The Way.

As I was incapacitated to do anything that required physical exertion due to extreme pain, I worshiped the Lord again. I told Him that if it took more pain to conform me more to His image… it was OK with me. But, if in His mercy He could still achieve that goal, relieve me of the intensity of my pain, I'd be more than grateful.

I then told Jesus that I **utterly trusted Him**, in my great complexity of understanding His purposes for all this suffering.

Sunday, the next day in my daily Scripture reading the Holy Spirit spoke to me from Psalm 105:19, "Until the time that His Word came to pass, the word of the Lord tested him. (Joseph). I wrote, "I saw the parallel. I wait for God's fulfillment of repeated promises for deliverance over many years, from this affliction."

-We then interceded for America for over an hour, praying desperate prayers for genuine revival… our only hope for survival!

I trust God to give you, the reader, at least some understanding as I've tried to give you some glimpses of this side of my life. I also pray that it will bring more understanding to those who suffer similarly. It's a great day when we learn to worship and praise God as a God of mystery.

If you have read my book, "Some of the ways of God in healing" you will know that I fully believe in God's miracle working power to heal today… and have experienced it many times over in my lifetime.

Ministering in Tauranga, New Zealand

In 2004 trusted spiritual leaders in the Tauranga area of the North Island of New Zealand, invited me to come and share with a group of seasoned intercessors.

The Holy Spirit kept speaking to us from His Word that it was connected with my teaching about aspects of genuine revival and spiritual awakening. I accepted the invitation.

June Dooney, a dear friend, and the New Zealand leader for the Lydia Prayer Fellowship International at that time, became the Convener.

In January of 2005 we arrived. As there was limited space in the only venue that was available for housing, the numbers of attendees were restricted. But the Holy Spirit wasn't! Nor were the open hearts of the seriously committed intercessors who came to hear the word of the Lord. The event was called "A Word in Season."

For two days I poured out my heart on one of the subjects most dearest to me. "The preparation needed, and then the price to pay, for genuine revival and spiritual awakening to come according to the Word of God," with many illustrations.

This was serious Kingdom business we were on and the people welcomed it and responded accordingly. It was a privilege and joy to minister to them, despite the inevitable lower back pain that caused me to have to sit, when speaking.

On the morning of the third day, our son John took the final session. He has an intense love for New Zealand and has been given God ordained favor throughout the land at many levels, for the extension of God's Kingdom.

I fully believe there will be a sovereign outpouring of the Holy Spirit that sweeps across this nation in these end times.

While there, I learned that New Zealand, like the U.S.A., had its foundations laid on Biblical Principles that came from missionaries who were sent there from God!

That was very meaningful to me. Perhaps that helps to explain why there is such a significantly sovereign love and appreciation for Americans by the majority of New Zealanders.

Consistent with God's character, He had made it very clear to us that we were also to have some quality time enjoying a beautiful hotel overlooking the mountain and beach area of Tauranga, with John and Julie and our granddaughter Rachel.

John's youngest son Mathew, with his lovely wife Cora and their children, who are Y.W.A.M. missionaries based in Tauranga, also joined the party.

Looking back, I see the goodness of God in all this, as it was the last time we would be in our beautiful homeland.

One day June Dooney interviewed me for an hour over Radio Rhema, on my teaching about "Some of the ways of God in healing."

That night Jim and I watched some Maoris do a redemptive haka on the death and resurrection of the Lord Jesus, which was extremely powerful.

A Maori haka is a war dance with a spiritual meaning. When some Maoris did a haka to welcome Billy Graham to Auckland, New Zealand, he said it was the most impressive welcome he had ever had before doing a Campaign, than anywhere else in the world!

I love watching a Maori haka, with a passion! I think it's great that my grandson Matthew, and the father of four beautiful children, does the haka like a native and speaks the Maori language.

Ever since Mathew was a little boy, I have called him "My joy germ." Now, as a strong spiritual leader, that title still applies!

In earlier days, Jim and I had taken our grandsons David, Paul, and Mathew to Redondo Beach in the Los Angeles area. At one point we all energetically built a huge sand castle with tunnels that ran inside and outside of it. Then we repeatedly ran three tennis balls through them. It was a spectacle!

Later in the day Jim said to the boys, "I'm getting old. What am I going to do?" Immediately, Matthew the 8-year-old said, "Live with it!" We all roared laughing.

My Years With Benny Hinn

I am very aware that my dear friend Benny Hinn is a controversial figure. And I totally understand that reaction. The closer you get to him, the more you understand that the unpredictable is the absolute normal. A small framed plaque in my bedroom gives the solution to this phenomenon. "Blessed are the flexible, for they shall not be broken."

Now for some behind and in front scenes, not before told.

This incident was in the ballroom of a large hotel in Orange County, S. California, at a Benny Hinn Partners' Conference, with approximately 2,000 in attendance. It was near the close of the second day, and Benny had been giving out powerful teachings from the Word of God.

His last message was on "How to be free from repeated satanic attacks and or bondages in your life".

At the end of the teaching, he asked me to come up and join him on the platform. I immediately went and stood beside him. He then invited anyone in the audience who wanted to be prayed for in this regard, to come forward, and he would pray over them.

In minutes, people were four rows deep all across the front of the large stage. I quietly said to Benny. "For those who may have satanic bondages, they first need to repent of all known sin."

In genuine humility, Benny quickly agreed and then privately asked, "Will you take over now? I'm really tired!" I said, "Sure," and he slipped away behind the stage curtain.... without any explanation to the audience! I was deeply touched that this dear man of God trusted me.

I became aware of the Lord's enabling power, as I instructed the people for the need to first ask the Holy Spirit to reveal any undealt with sin in their lives and if so, to repent of it.

I gave them unhurried time, explaining the importance of this time of preparation. Only when everyone had indicated by an upraised hand that they were now ready did I proceed.

I did strong spiritual warfare over those many people, using the weapons of the Word of God (which I had memorized), the shed blood of Christ, the name of the Lord Jesus, and in the power of the Holy Spirit.

God in His faithfulness came through, as the people then acknowledged their need to be totally under His control. We concluded with strong praises to Him as our Deliverer.

I proved once again, that my wonderful Lord will never fail me, when I'm out on a limb but in His will. Hallelujah!

Another occasion was during the end part of a large Campaign meeting, when Benny invited people to come forward and testify to their miracle healing during the service, and when he would pray for more miracles to take place.

A young widow came onto the platform with her twelve-year-old son who had an incurable disease. Benny was trying to discern how to pray for him, but was having difficulty getting a clear signal from the Holy Spirit. I so appreciated that he didn't move in presumption.

In genuine humility, He then asked me to come up onto the platform and share what God was showing me. I readily complied, because God was giving me the understanding that the highest point of prayer for this particular mother was to pray the prayer of total relinquishment of her son into God's hands, and leave the outcome with Him.

I explained this to the mother and then led her in a prayer which she then repeated after me. I had perfect peace that God would reveal to her the truth of Psalm 145:17 "God is just in all His ways and kind in all His doings." To God be all the glory. He is awesome and full of wisdom!

Undoubtedly one of my most priceless, precious, and tender memories were when Jim and I would stand close together with his arm wrapped around me in the center front row of a Benny Hinn Campaign, during the lengthy praise and worship times. Dear David Palmquist, in charge of the partners, would always look after us and get us the best seats.

For a full hour Benny would stand with his eyes closed, while he led out spontaneously in one powerful worship song after another---totally unrehearsed.

He had the musical gift of perfect pitch, while Bruce Hughes the pianist, and Sheryl Palmquist the organist, devoid of any sheet music would automatically follow him in perfect harmony on their instruments. Truly remarkable! It was undoubtedly quintessential team work in the Spirit.

Jim and I would have one arm each reached up toward Heaven, singing out our heartfelt pure worship to The Lover of our souls together. We were totally one with the Godhead and each other. Fabulous.

We always loved being invited to the unpredictable staff Christmas parties. Benny's birthday is in December, so we celebrated that at the same time. At peak times of enjoyment, I would always throw my shoes in the air....and catch them....to express my joy.

On Saturday, November 24th, 2001, Jim and I went to Rock Harvest Church in Pasadena, Los Angeles where Benny Hinn was to be conducting a four hour prayer meeting for America. He had asked me to help lead it.

Despite the fact that the elements were pouring down heavy consistent rain, 3,000 people showed up.

After Benny had spoken, we all went into serious intercession from 3:30 p.m. until 7 p.m., covering a number of vital subjects.

At one stage he asked me to lead out in prayer for the Muslims; which I found to be fulfilling as I had been praying for them for many years.

This unusual afternoon meeting was very powerful for the extension of God's Kingdom. All glory to God.

At the close, a converted Muslim who was now a pastor, shared at length with Pastor Benny, Ralph Wilkerson, Pastor Che Ahn, Lou Engle, and Jim and myself. It was very interesting!

In 2006, I had received a phone call from Pastor Benny Hinn's secretary, inviting me to come to his studio in four days time for a TV interview related to my book "The Fire of God," which had recently been published. The invitation included joining him afterward to attend his Monday evening Bible class, where he taught several hundred people who came for an eight-week course of in-depth teaching.

I responded by saying that Jim and I would seek God and get His answer back to her as soon as possible. When we waited on God, having died out to our human reasonings and desires, and resisted the enemy's voice in Jesus' name, we both had impressions that I was to accept, accompanied by God's peace.

The next day, we sought Him again specifically to know if God had a purpose for us to attend Pastor Benny's teaching class. We did not want to presume anything. The Holy Spirit's answer to us both was "yes." To me, the additional words, "It is important," were clearly spoken into my spirit.

From many years of having the great privilege of being linked with Pastor Benny in ministry assignments, I have learned to be prepared for the unexpected and the unusual. So the next day I sought God diligently to know what God would have me share from His Word, should Benny spontaneously ask me to do so. This had happened on previous occasions!

As a result of my waiting on God, everywhere I turned in my Bible, verses on the control of the tongue and the importance of our words were standing out and being quickened to me by the Holy Spirit. Because of severe time constraints, all I could do was to find the message I had recently worked on and given, titled "The implications of our words and how they shape our destinies." I put the big notebook in my bag and took it with me, wondering how in the world this lengthy new message would ever work with Benny's program—and why? We then traveled down to Laguna Beach.

The next day we taped the TV interview at his studios. That evening, we arrived at the packed-out Bible class, with Pastor Benny announcing our arrival and saying, "I know Joy Dawson has something to share with us this evening. Come and sit right up here at the front, Joy and Jim." We did.

Pastor Benny was speaking under a strong anointing, a very powerful message on the blood of the Lord Jesus and how it should be applied to every area of our lives. The more he taught, the more I wondered what on earth the word of the Lord about the tongue had to do with what he was teaching.

I asked God to confirm to me from His Word if I was still to share with this audience about the importance of our words. When I opened my Bible, I found it was at Matthew 12 and my eyes immediately fell on verses 36 and 37. They were some of the exact same verses God had spoken to me from the night before. "But I say to you that for every idle word men may speak, they will give account of it in the day of judgment. For by your words you will be justified, and by your words you will be condemned" (NKJV).

I was extremely thankful that I had done my homework, to be somewhat prepared in case this scenario eventuated. But I didn't have a clue how much time I was going to be given to share, or what I was to share from this hour and a half of teaching material I had. Was I just to start at the beginning?

I distinctly remember repeatedly thinking that everything about my situation was insane in the natural reasoning. Here I was, seated right under the speaker's nose on the front row with my large teaching notebook, not taking notes, but seeking God as if my life depended on it. "Where do I start in this message, Lord?" I inquired (interspersed with fervent, whispered requests to Jim to pray for wisdom and direction to be given me). Finally, I received clear direction from the Holy Spirit where I was to start. It was somewhere in the middle of my notes. That direction brought tremendous relief—believe me.

At the end of two hours of teaching, Pastor Benny simply said, "Now Joy Dawson will come and pray" (not speak). What was I to do? Do the only logical thing, and what appeared to be the only right thing, by doing only what I was asked to do? Fear man and disobey God's clear directions, or fear God and follow through in obedience to that voice that has led me throughout my long lifetime?

I went to the platform with my awkward-looking big notebook in hand, stood by my dear friend Benny and said to him, "I'm so glad we really know each other as friends after all these years, because I need to ask you if you would release me to share what God has spoken to me from His Word in relation to this class." Benny said, "Yes, you may."

I taught for about five minutes on the link between the fear of God and the words we speak. I showed the emphasis God's Word places on the evidences of the fear of the Lord operating in a person's life. It is to the degree that person speaks 100 percent of the truth 100 percent of the time.

I read from Psalm 34:11–13 where the first lesson on the fear of the Lord is related to having our "lips free from deceit." I said that God has a lot to say in His Word about the sin of deceit.

Deceit manifests itself in overstatement or understatement. By adding a few words or leaving a few words out we can distort the truth. In failing to report the setting or the context in which the words were spoken, we can give a distortion of truth. The words spoken could have been in humor.

Our standard for living and speaking is the life of the Lord Jesus. When describing Jesus as our example, 1 Peter 2:21–22 says, "that you should follow His steps: 'Who committed no sin, nor was deceit found in His mouth'" (NKJV). Also, Revelation 14:5 says, "In their mouth was found no deceit, for they are without fault before the throne of God" (NKJV).

At that point Pastor Benny said, "I think you should stop now, Joy. But I want you to come back and be the guest speaker at the banquet we are having at the close of this school. I want you to speak from your new book, "The Fire of God." I felt complete peace with Benny's leadership instructions.

I believe I had shared exactly what God wanted me to say, and that dear Benny had been given a clear signal from the Holy Spirit to say what he did. I replied that I would seek the Lord about Benny's invitation, and immediately did.

Before he had finished closing the meeting in prayer, God had answered me with the words, "Yes, I have opened this door." So I committed myself publicly by accepting the invitation as I shared what God had spoken. Then Benny greatly encouraged me by announcing that he was giving a copy of my book, "The Fire of God" to the four hundred class members, as a gift.

The sequel to all this is that at the class banquet, after I had spoken on "The Preparation and Price for Revival (which is part of The Fire of God), a man came and spoke to me privately. He said he had been a Christian for many years and was a practicing lawyer of many years. But when I spoke following Benny Hinn's teaching at the Bible class about the importance and implications of our words and quoted the Scriptures related to that subject, he had a totally life-changing experience. He kept repeating, "I will never be the same." He conveyed with deep conviction that the Holy Spirit had powerfully impacted his life in those five minutes. He said, "I cannot thank you enough for your obedience to say exactly what I needed to hear. Thank you. Thank you."

Wow! Can you imagine what that kind of encouragement brought to me? I never had the opportunity to explain to him what testings from God I had gone through to be the instrument to bless him in such a profound way. But I was deeply grateful for his sharing his testimony.

Some weeks later I was sitting in my home church, The Church On The Way, in Van Nuys, California. It was at the end of a Wednesday evening prayer service, and I was waiting for the executive pastor to come and have the arranged appointment with me.

A young woman came to me and started to share how God had significantly spoken to her when I had briefly shared about the fear of the Lord and the words we speak at the Benny Hinn Bible class (a ninety-minute drive away). The pastor arrived just as she was speaking to me, terminating her account. I would love to have heard more. But it was enough for God to assure me that He was working out His purposes in the lives of others, through my times of testing.

To close this section, I want to make it clear that I have never heard the message of the gospel presented more clearly and Biblically; accompanied by what it really means to commit your life to Christ in response, than through this servant of God, Benny Hinn.

A typical entry in my diary, reports on a Benny Hinn Crusade in July, 2004:

"The sense of God's presence during the worship was very strong. This was followed by the clearest gospel message ever, with many hundreds responding for salvation. Then many more reported on receiving wonderful miracles of healing. God was certainly glorified!

It has been a privilege and calling from God, to be a committed intercessor for my dear friend Benny....to this day. He is still being greatly used of God for the extension of His Kingdom among the nations. All glory to Jesus!

Michael Koulianos

During 2008 we were at a powerfully anointed Benny Hinn Crusade in Long Beach, California, where many responded to the crystal clear presentation of the gospel, and remarkable miracles of healings were evident. This was proceeded by the usual one hour of Holy Spirit directed praise and worship. We appreciated and loved it all.

I had known and loved Benny's oldest, beautiful daughter Jessica since she was just a girl. But I had never met Michael Koulianos, who was now her husband of 2 years.

Prompted by the Holy Spirit, I walked over to him and asked him questions about his life and ministry. We connected warmly. After a meaningful conversation, I gave him my phone number if he should want further contact. He did! We scheduled a time and that conversation lasted two hours.

As a result of that first life changing call for Michael, the Holy Spirit revealed to me that this relatively unknown 30 year old man, would one day be given a powerfully anointed ministry to the nations. I was also given the understanding that I was to respond to every time he enquired of me for spiritual insights related to God's character and ways. The times have been numerous.

The results are ten remarkable years of sheer joy and enormous fulfillment for me (and five for Jim.) Michael has become exactly what God showed me prophetically he would be.

However this has not been without a high price for Michael as he has had to face major tests related to relationships, and still does.

Michael has his story, recorded in his remarkable book, "Holy Spirit. The one who makes Jesus real" about what I've meant to him during these years. I am deeply moved by what he has so passionately shared.

My story is that I have been given one of the richest and most precious friendships of a lifetime with both Michael and his God ordained, anointed, wonderful wife Jessica. They and their three lovely, unique children are special to me. I love them dearly.

Intercession For Los Angeles

Over our many years of being elders at The Church On The Way, it has become a way of life for God to give me specific Scriptures that I would submit to the Pastor and then share with the congregation. He then would lead the people in making application of that truth. On March of 2008, the following is written within that context.

Pastor Jim Tolle had called the church to a week of consecration. At the close of that time, on Saturday morning March 15th, he asked us to come together from 8:30 a.m. to 10:00 a.m.

About 1,000 showed up. He then lead us with a Holy Spirit anointing and passion, to have a vital time of intercession for our City of Los Angeles.

I asked God if there was something from His Word that He wanted me to share. Immediately He opened my Bible to Ezekiel chapter nine, with understanding. As soon as Pastor Jim put us into prayer circles, I submitted this to him, and he released me. I read forcefully the eight verses where we are exhorted to cry out to God to be "marked by God" as a people who sigh and cry over the city, as clean hearted, desperate intercessors. I exhorted them to pray accordingly.

The audience responded with the most fervent, sustained intercession I had ever heard in this church, which went on and on and on. To God be all the glory.

Poignant Moments

On Sunday July 6th, 2008, I found a poignant entry in my diary that I want to share.

"We went to church and Pastor Jack Hayford gave a profound unfolding of Psalm 16, which was a great treat. He and I had a mutual very warm exchange of greetings.

I told him how much his messages had brought comfort and tender shepherding to me from the Holy Spirit, during these 15 years of pain and perplexity. I expressed my gratitude for the wonderful message today.

I was always wanting God to do a deeper work of His Spirit in me, so that a greater work of His Spirit would flow through me. This is reflected in a quote from my diary on September 2nd, 2008.

"I am determined to go after the following attributes until they become part of my spiritual bloodstream."

- 1 Peter 3:4 "the incorruptible beauty of a gentle and quiet spirit, which is very precious in the sight of God"

- Zephaniah 2:3 "seek the Lord, seek righteousness, seek humility."

- 1 Timothy 6:11 "Pursue godliness, righteousness, faith, love, patience, gentleness."

Desperate Praying

There were numerous times over the years when I sought God desperately for understanding as to why I continued to live with strong back pain. All are recorded in my diaries.

One example, was in May of 2009.

In my daily reading of the Scriptures, I read in Matthew 21:20-22 that Jesus said, "if you have faith and do not doubt," (miracles will happen) and "whatever things you ask in prayer, believing, you will receive."

I sought God diligently for over an hour to speak directly to me TO-DAY from His Word, as I wept and wept with anguish to be assured that all that I am doing to obey the teachings from His Word, will end in a deliverance from this horrible affliction.

The silence from God was awful! But I wouldn't stop seeking and weeping.

Finally the Holy Spirit directed me to Jeremiah 33:6, "Behold, I will bring to it health and healing, and I will heal them and reveal to them abundance of prosperity and security."

This greatly encouraged me.

Further Understanding

There was a time in the beginning of 2009 where I sent my D.V.D.'s on individual subjects when I was asked to speak, instead of having to travel, because of severe back pain.

In January of 2010, I was seeking God earnestly again, for fresh revelation or for some further understanding as to why there was no breakthrough with the severity and frequency of the pain I endured, when I was in full faith for the promises He had given me for deliverance and healing.

The Holy Spirit responded by saying, "Isaiah 49." The message was to "wait for Him," He also said, "I'm going to speak to you through Joyce Myer tonight." Her T.V. program centered around long suffering and endurance with patience under great trial, and the need to persevere.

My deeper answers came a week later, as Joyce shared that at age nine she was converted and had subsequently prayed frequently for God to deliver her from her father's sexual abuse of her. Those prayers were not answered.

She believes that God allowed it, so that she could now minister with understanding to millions via T.V., who are suffering severely from all kinds of traumatic experiences. She shares that there is hope and healing in surrendering their lives completely to the Lord Jesus and living for Him and for others in the power of the Holy Spirit as she had learned to do. She is living proof that God's Holy Word, has the answer to every need, when we obey it!

Subsequently I'm encouraged to believe that large numbers of people will be inspired to keep on believing and obeying God, regardless of the extent of their sufferings, as they read this book.

We are not promised that we will always have understanding as to why God allows some things to happen. Remember that God demonstrated His dramatic miracle working power to release Peter from prison, while John the Baptist was murdered in prison....

without an explanation! That's when we trust God when we can't trace Him!

Unusual Visitations

On December 13th of 2010, I was woken early, with the Holy Spirit speaking into my spirit, "Isaiah 55:8." I got up and read it. "For My thoughts are not your thoughts, neither are My ways your ways says the Lord."

I went on to read verse 9, "For as the Heavens are higher than the earth, so are My ways higher than your ways and My thoughts than your thoughts.

I was sitting perfectly still, alone, with my Bible across my knees, when to my total amazement an unseen hand carefully folded over a number of pages until they came to Jeremiah 29.

Verses 10-14 were immediately quickened to me by the Holy Spirit.

This brought great encouragement to me and I worshipped and thanked God.

I also need to recall that I had discovered a reference to the above incident in one of my diaries, which put me on a search to find the correct dates and an accurate account of what took place.

I prayed earnestly, repeatedly, in faith and searched at length diligently, and found nothing. I was very perplexed!

I was in my bedroom at 11:20 p.m., when to my amazement and intense relief. I looked at a diary sitting on my dressing table that was open just inside the cover. It had all the facts I needed at the top of a page, which had nothing else on it!!! Then I noticed that it was thirteen pages away from the diary section, because of it preceding the section for names, addresses, and telephone numbers.

I was at a total loss to come up with any logical explanation of this experience. All I can think of is that unseen hands had been at work again to meet my needs to record these phenomena.

There are times in the Bible where Angels were visible and other times when they were invisible! It's the same today. I'll take their services with deep gratitude to God who commissioned them, whether I can see them or I can't see them.

A Prophetic Dream

Somewhere around 2011, I had a vivid dream which was obviously from God. I dreamt that I was in a room with Christians who were seeking God. It was a small church like setting.

I was sitting up the front asking people around me to tell me what they were asking and what God was saying, but no one answered me.

This disturbed me, so I got up and went among the people asking the same questions – all to no avail. No one could tell me.

Finally I went right to the back of the room where a young man was high up and in a corner, involved with various technologies.

In desperation I asked him, "What is this all about? I must know! Tell me!"

That's when I heard a booming voice saying repeatedly, "He forgives all your iniquities and heals all your diseases."

Then I woke up.... knowing God was assuring me again that one day I would be completely healed of all my pain! I thanked Him and believed.

Book Writing

In the numbers of times that I've been interviewed in relation to the books I've written, the same question often comes up. "Why did you write this book?" My answer is predictable, "Because God directed me to."

Putting some of the major truths God has entrusted to me, into book form, has been undoubtedly one of the greatest fulfilling aspects of my life and ministry.

My first book, "Intimate Friendship with God" – through understanding the fear of the Lord – is obviously God's favorite of the eight books. It has had the least publicity, yet it has been translated into at least twenty-six languages.

It was first published in 1986, and a revised edition was published in 2008. It is still going strong and outsells all the others. I think I can understand why. The fear of the Lord is the most life changing subject I know of in the whole Bible. It has certainly proved to be that for me. My spiritual life can be easily summarized. Before the fear of the Lord, and after the fear of the Lord.

Mrs. Vonette Bright, co-founder with Dr. Bill Bright of Campus Crusade for Christ International, published a book titled, "The Greatest Lesson I've Ever Learned." It was compiled of a number of prominent women's stories related to that subject.

When she invited me to contribute to it, it didn't take me long to know what my allocated chapter would be about. It was the fear of the Lord, and the wisdom that comes from it.

This unique book is not only very interesting, it's very revealing. There are times we may wonder what caused God to promote some ministries more than others?

As these well known women open up their hearts and share some of the greatest learning curves of their lives, it can be a major incentive for humble readers to make any adjustments the Holy

Spirit may require of them. This book makes a great gift to give to other women.

Dr. Bill Bright published an equivalent one for men, with the same title.

My second book, "Some of the Ways of God in Healing," came as a surprise to me. It was only after initially preparing a message on that subject, that the Holy Spirit indicated I was to expand my material related to making a book.

I vividly remember the impasse I reached half way through, when writing "Intercession, Thrilling and Fulfilling." I had so much material, (probably enough for two books) I couldn't discern what to include and what to leave out…no matter how hard I prayed.

Finally, I sent out letters to a lot of my intercessor friends, sharing my dilemma and asking them to pray me through to clarity. Those precious (to God and to me) people took my request seriously, and only then did I get the needed breakthrough.

Pastor Benny Hinn was so impressed with the depth of content in the chapter titles, that he said he wanted to read it; and then he promoted the finished product extensively over his daily Telecast program, and it **really took off**. Thank You Lord. It's still selling and being used by God to greatly extend His Kingdom. I use it frequently as a manual.

I greatly enjoyed writing "Jesus the Model" because it's all about the lover of my soul, and my fascinating, awesome, other worldly, holy, Almighty, best friend, Jesus…. who not only came to die on a cross to give me eternal life, but who **is** my life.

I use this book as a refresher course for my mind, soul, and spirit. I'm rereading it again right now.

It saddens me to think that so many Christians think they could never live like Jesus did. That stone of unbelief needs rolling away. The person of the Holy Spirit possessing us makes it possible.

My dear friend, Pastor John Whelan says: "If I only had one book, besides the New Testament, I would choose "Jesus the Model." I believe that becoming conformed to the image of the Lord Jesus Christ is the primary call of God on my life.... not that of being a pastor."

The hardest one of my books to write was the one titled "The Fire of God." I was utterly cast upon God to inspire, direct, and anoint me to write on this difficult subject. I was painfully aware that if I didn't, there would be no book from me. It was a challenging adventure of submission, obedience, and faith.

However I am fully aware that the Holy Spirit wrote it through me, therefore He must be given **ALL THE GLORY**. It was a big relief to me when it was completed.

There are some aspects of God's character that are seldom taught because they're unpopular. Sometimes they are avoided all together. Although I've written on only nine different aspects of the fire of God, I haven't dodged facing the whole truth on this important but controversial subject. This book is not for spiritual wimps.

Jim and I had difficulty coming up with the right title, and finally decided on the simplest. But I have since regretted it, as it conveys a negative connotation.

When I sent the manuscript to one of my previous book publishers, they turned it down on the basis that "it was too deep in content." They suggested that I reconstruct it, and make it into bite size proportions as a Daily Devotional. This did not witness with my spirit as the answer.

When I sent the manuscript to Destiny Image Publishers, it was immediately received and subsequently published. I was greatly encouraged when I received a report from my very dear pastor friends, John and Debbie Whelan, who were reading this book together as a couple. They shared that they would often have to stop and digest the truths slowly, before being able to apply them to their lives, which was then transformable. Praise God!

My most significant encouragement was still to come. Following Easter, Jim and I were attending an annual conference in the Harvest Rock Church in Pasadena. Che Ahn was the Senior Pastor at the time.

Kenny Peavy came and shared with me. He had previously been the worship leader at our Y.W.A.M. base in Los Angeles, before becoming the worship leader for Harvest Rock Church. He had been exposed to a lot of truth.

He said he had recently read "The Fire of God." It took him a whole year to read it very slowly, to digest its contents, and then apply everything he'd learned to his life. He said it was absolutely life changing, and expressed real gratitude to me for writing it.

Although my book "Forever Ruined for the Ordinary," published by Thomas Nelson, has a lot of vital and interesting content and has done well, I have always regretted that I gave into the real pressure from the editor and his staff to have that title.

I wanted the title to be, "The Adventure of Hearing and Obeying God's Voice," which is what the book is all about. It ended up as a subtitle. It was fulfilling to share from a lifetime of experiencing the contents at a deep level.

During my many years of counseling sincere people, I have frequently recommended this highly informative, interesting book.

Writing my book, "Influencing Children to Become World Changers" was a joyful, fulfilling experience… It flowed out of having seen the Biblical principles I've shared on the subject, fleshed out in the lives of two generations of Dawsons… with their partners and children, along with a third generation of 15 great great grandchildren, all heading in the same direction.

I've never been interested in influencing children to become just good church going people. There's an overdose of them! And the world remains unreached with the gospel.

While this is the smallest sized book I've written, it's not small on dynamic, workable content, that if applied will eventually help change the world.

2012 was the year that I put so much work into launching my eighth book, which was on unity in the Body of Christ, titled, "All Heaven Will Break Loose."

According to Psalm 133:3, "God commands His blessings," when we're in Biblical unity. This means it's imperative that we understand from God's Word what He requires of us. In a very interesting and practical way, this book explains that, with varied illustrations from my life.

My beloved friend Jessica Hoover did a remarkable job of putting my handwritten notes into the computer for me. She was so fast and competent, and a delight to work with. Jim then did every practical thing that needed to be done, to get my manuscript ready for the publisher.

The three booklets I have written are:

- "Knowing God" which is my favorite life message,
- "The Character of the One Who says 'Go.'" When you really get revelation from God's Word about His justice and faithfulness, you'll want to go wherever He sends you.
- "How to pray for someone near you who is away from God." These principles really work. Test them!

My Statement Of Faith

In August of 2012, I made a Statement of Faith related to the fact that I was still not healed of the strong arthritic pain in my hips and the pinched nerve in my lower spine, and the numerous times that God has clearly spoken that I would be healed. It was simple and direct:

"Dear God, I praise You and worship You. I thank You for multitudinous blessings. I love You. I trust You completely. You are just. I believe You will heal me when the maximum glory can come to Your wonderful name."

I am still standing in faith on this statement, after 27 years of suffering, which varies in intensity. The arthritis has gone into a shoulder and my hands as well. I have done spiritual warfare against this disease many times.

For many years I have repeated in faith the ten verses on Divine healing that I have framed.

It was also a tough year of seeing my precious Jim suffer many health issues. He had a premonition that it wouldn't be long before Jesus took him home to Heaven, which he shared with a few close family members, but never with me. He didn't want to hurt me. His premonition was correct.

Jim in his eighties.

February 2013

At 90 years of age, in the last six months of Jim's life, cancer sores had broken out on the top of his head. Repeated surgeries didn't bring relief, and he finally had to wear bandages from the top of his head to under his chin and back. He also sensed that his heart was weakening.

I never once heard him complain!

Because of a deteriorated heart condition, he spent a few days in hospital where he was being monitored.

J.B. and Jill took the responsibility of being with him most of that time. They were remarkably committed.

A few months later, on February 20th, 2013, Jim was back in the hospital and placed in the intensive care unit, because of the frailty of his heart.

During this time John was in Australia, dealing with the Y.W.A.M. medical ships deployed in Papua New Guinea.

At one time a new doctor walked in, and cheerfully said, "Hello Mr. Dawson, who is your hero?" Without missing a beat, Jim replied, "My wife." The doctor responded with a question, demanding an answer, "Your **wife**?" Jim said, "Yes! Because she has such strong faith in God." It brought me such encouragement that he would say that to a stranger! Jim and I had a very tender time alone together that day. Normally there were doctors and nurses, or J.B. and Jill around.

The next day as J.B. was driving me to the hospital, having warned me that there were signs of Jim's further deterioration, I asked God to speak to me from His Word, which I had in my hands. Immediately He spoke into my spirit, "Isaiah 41." When I turned to it, verses 10 and 13 were my precious Savior's comforting assuring promises for whatever I was to face. I was so grateful to Him.

Verse 10, "fear not, for I am with you, be not dismayed, for I am your God; I will strengthen you, I will help you, I will uphold you with my victorious right hand."

Verse 13, "For I the Lord your God, hold your right hand; it is I who say to you, "Fear not, I will help you."

The third day, as I was holding Jim's hand, and he was in a very critical condition, I said, "Darling, would you prefer that we relinquish you into God's hands?" (As he knew that we had been praying fervently for God to bring him through this crisis.)

Immediately he nodded his head affirmatively! At that moment I knew that the most loving thing I could do for him was to co-operate with his deepest desire.

So by faith I placed my darling into God's hands, to do with him whatever would bring the most glory to His wonderful name.

Then I lead J.B. and Jill and myself in singing worship songs to Jesus, with a shaky voice and silent tears running down my face.

Jim's response with his eyes closed, was a clearly spoken, "AMEN."

We kept this up, until God's angels fairly soon came and took him into Jesus' arms.

A remarkable report was soon given to us directly by our precious daughter in law Julie Dawson in California, and the same report from our dear friends Marty and Kelly Myers in Ohio. It was right at the time of Jim's passing that both parties, though far apart, had seen into the Spirit's realm, as they were praying for him.

They saw a **great** time of rejoicing going on in Heaven, as Jim was being joyously welcomed Home.

After my sweetheart went to be with Jesus, I made a deliberate choice not to focus on myself and my enormous loss. That would produce grief and pain. Instead, I wholeheartedly focused my attention on the Lord Jesus, and kept audibly praising Him throughout the day.

At night I went to bed listening to Terry McAlmon's worship C.D.'s as I'd done many times with Jim. This time I chose to make my praise and worship more abandoned, more ardent, more extravagantly expressed to Jesus the lover of my soul. It was noisy. As I live alone, I wasn't disturbing anyone.

This way of life has resulted in an absence of the grieving processes that I'd read about when losing a loved one. Did I initially miss Jim? Terribly! Seven years later, do I still miss him? More than ever!

But the Bible says that when we "put on the garment of praise we don't have to deal with a spirit of heaviness." It's our choice. Vocal praises to God for WHO HE IS is so therapeutic! ☺ My Bible is heavily marked with verses telling us to make it a way of life.

Jim and I were linked together as one, in so many ways. I probably miss him the most as my most treasured, powerfully anointed prayer partner. What a priceless gift!

Jim's Memorial Service (A copy of what I shared)

"I am so deeply grateful for everyone who has come today. May the Lord reward you in ways that only He can.

James Allen said, "You will become as small as your controlling desire; as great as your dominant aspiration."

Jim's dominant aspiration was unquestionably found in Romans 8:29 "to be conformed to the image of the Lord Jesus Christ." He would often say to me, "I just want to be like Jesus." He had the right goal.

He was a man of strong faith who understood the character of God.

At 48 years of age, in 1971, Jim answered the call of God to come into Y.W.A.M. as an unsalaried missionary. This meant literally leaving everything to follow Jesus; including leaving New Zealand with his family and coming to live in Los Angeles. He did this gladly, with absolutely no known monetary support. He cashed in his life insurance to get us out of debt.

His life of living entirely by faith was fulfilled by living out Matthew 6:33, "Seek first the kingdom of God (making God's priorities from God's Word, Jim's priorities) and His righteousness (making sure of having purity in thoughts, words and deeds. He lived in the deepest sense of the fear of the Lord) and all these things shall be added unto you."

Jim was an anointed servant of others. He truly had a servant's heart.

His ministry giftings were both Pastoral and the ministry of helps. He would often come up with a practical solution in a time of ministry need. He could fix anything – very gifted with his hands. At 68 he taught himself how to work a computer, and with two fingers he typed two of the eight books I've written, onto the computer, from my handwritten notes, and he did an excellent job. I was so proud of him for these achievements.

In order to fulfill our callings to be missionaries to the nations of the world, there were many years of frequently being separated – twice, for three months at a time. He went to 50 nations. I went to 55, many times alone, many times together.

1) He was an avid true worshiper of Jesus. He worshipped Him "in spirit and truth." It was expressed worship that came from the depth of his heartfelt devotion to the Lord, at the start of every day. Time alone with Jesus was always his first priority – expressing thankfulness and love to Him. He became so like Mary of Bethany sitting at the feet of Jesus.

2) He had a passionate love for God's Word. I noticed that he was always underlining it. It was amazing a few days ago when looking through a modern version of the Bible called, "The Message" that he loved to read, to find that I couldn't find **one page of it** that he hadn't underlined – not one! And I looked at length! He also loved and heavily marked "The Spirit Filled Life Bible."

3) He was a mighty intercessor. He took very seriously the ministry of praying for others as directed and energized by the Holy Spirit. Only God knows and will ultimately reward him for his faithfulness, diligence, and faith in that powerful ministry.

One word sum's up our relationship as a couple.

It's **TOGETHER.**

As a way of life, we loved to **worship Jesus together**, in church and in every other worship setting, as well as in our home. We'd play Terry McAlmon's worship C.D.'s and just revel in pouring out our hearts in love to Jesus together at length.

How we loved standing close together with Jim's arm around me in the front row of many Benny Hinn's campaigns, when dear Benny would spontaneously lead out in worship for an hour or more with wonderful worship songs. We were totally one in heart, mind, soul, and spirit as we were totally focused on Jesus. Fabulous memories!

We interceded together regularly for every nation of the world.... for needy individuals, and masses of projects in between.... spiritual leaders, unity, abused children, spiritual awakening and revival, being in the top bracket.

We waited on God together – seeking His directions about decisions large and small and always came to total agreement.

We loved being in the outdoors together. For 45 years we played golf together. We loved camping together, swimming together, boating together, fishing together and having endless long prayer walks together. We did personal evangelism together in many nations. We shopped together, shared household chores together, we looked after each other.

We shared our hearts with each other. We were each other's best friend. But most of all we were sweethearts. Every morning his normal greeting to me was "Good morning treasure girl," and I would reply, "Hi precious sweetheart."

Numbers of times over our lifetime when worshiping God together, and when seeking God for directions, I strongly sensed "the smile of God" upon us as a couple. That our marriage put a smile on God's face was very awesome to me.

The deepest desire of our hearts as a couple is found in **Romans 15:3**, "May the God of steadfastness and encouragement grant you to live in such harmony with one another, in accord with Christ

Jesus, that **together** you may with one voice glorify the God and Father of our Lord Jesus Christ."

I lived with a holy and very humble man of God who would quickly say "I'm sorry, I was wrong," and he was **so** quick to forgive.

He didn't like talking a lot, but "Well done" is better than "Well said." That's my precious sweetheart.

"The Lord gave. The Lord has taken away. Blessed be the name of the Lord." Job 1:21.

Jesus is the number one Lover of my soul.

"He is just in all His ways and kind in all His doings." Psalm 145:17.

An Interesting Discovery

When coming near to the end of writing this book, I happened to pick up the well worn Bible Jim used for most of his adult life. It is the Revised Standard Version.

I was immediately intrigued and impressed by the obvious way he had studied and then heavily marked it throughout. He had not just underlined it, but there is a complete marking system of arrows that cross over the page or pages as he was connecting relevant truths to one another.

This is a consistent pattern on many well marked pages. I always knew that Jim loved God's Word and read it diligently and daily; and God frequently spoke to him from it about subjects big and small as a way of life. But I didn't know he was such a personal student of it.

This man was a serious <u>student</u> of the Word of God, but for some reason kept it to himself!

I'm so glad that I discovered this reality so that his descendants can benefit from it. What an heirloom for one of them!

A Very Different Day

On the 10th of June in 2013 Brian and Christy Brentt came and took me to Lou and Therese Engle's home in Pasadena, where 25 young women were jam packed into their living room.

The Brentt's had handpicked them from Y.W.A.M., as they were demonstrating spiritual leadership qualities and were influencing other young women significantly.

The Holy Spirit had withheld all knowledge from me as to what I was to say or teach. I was totally depending on Him, moment by moment. He faithfully came through every time with the Biblical truths He wanted me to share.

This continued on for 8 hours without any notes; as I was clothed with the fear of God and totally under the Holy Spirit's control.

We started at 2:15 p.m. and ended at 11:30 p.m. with one bathroom break, and a 1¾ hour break for a meal and to listen to Lou Engle share.

Christy gave a profound encouraging prophecy for me. Therese wrote it down.

God's manifest presence was awesome. At one point my body shook violently. At another point, I looked to my left and saw an African American girl and started prophesying over her life. (I have just heard that God is presently using her mightily for His glory.) At another point a young woman fell on her face on the floor and stayed there a long time as God did a deep work in her.

It was as if time stood still, and we were only aware that the Holy Spirit was in complete control, and that God was being both glorified by the pure truths from His Word that were being both shared and received. What an amazing historic day! What pure love flowed in that room!

To God be the glory!

A Night To Remember

In July of 2013, when I was eighty-seven years young God set up an exhilarating ministry time for me. I spoke to about one thousand young people in their early twenties, who were serious about knowing God, in order to make Him known. Some were from the Circuit Riders, some were from a group of Christian musicians, and both were under the leadership of Andy Byrd, a Y.W.A.M. leader based in Kona, Hawaii, and Brian Brentt from Southern California.

We were blessed to be able to fill a good-sized Korean Church in Irvine, Los Angeles. We already had a very good relationship with the Pastor, Dave Gibbons. A lot of prayers proceeded this meeting, as I had sent letters out to 90 plus intercessors asking for their serious involvement with me in this meeting. That resulted in a strong sense of God's presence permeating the church.

I was filled with the strength and joy of the Lord when we started at 7:00 p.m. and right through until 10 p.m. when we finished. My message title was "Desperate Praying."

At no time did I ever feel a day over 50. I felt like Joan Baez, a U.S. singer, who said, "When somebody says to me, 'How does it feel to be over the hill?' I respond, 'I'm just heading up the mountain.'"

Frequently I would throw out questions for anyone in the crowd to stand up and answer. This brought a great sense of unity and freedom amongst us, with plenty of humor thrown in. But I always kept our focus on the word of the Lord that God had given me, and the serious implications involved.

At times we would stop and intercede in small groups for needy people groups. Neither I nor my wonderfully responsive audience knew what the Holy Spirit would direct me to do next.

I could easily have gone on past 10:00 p.m. I marveled at the way the Holy Spirit took a really serious subject and made it palatable to be absorbed and applied.

The leadership thought it was a historic night. All glory to the Lord Jesus!

In November of 2013, I noticed in my diary that God had spoken to me from Psalm 71:17-18 in my Daily Light devotional. The same verses were in my daily Bible readings.

I quote, "O God, from my youth You have taught me, and I still proclaim Your wondrous deeds. So even to old age and gray hairs, O God, do not forsake me, till I proclaim Your might to all the generations to come."

This whole chapter is heavily marked in my Bible, confirming my deep desire to teach 20-30 year olds the truths about God's character and His ways.

I have recorded, "My destiny will be fulfilled, regardless of my age of 87."

Here I am, seven years later, still going towards that goal, like Gideon's men, "faint but pursuing."

I need to back track here and record a little history from behind the scenes.

Unhurried time studying God's character and ways, as I daily read His Word, and then living it; produced a steady flow of new messages. I would work on putting them together under the direction of the Holy Spirit during my travels. I never had to struggle to get messages...they flowed from my lifestyle.

A Significant Answer

There was a period of time during 2013 and 2014 at The Church On The Way when we were without a senior pastor. I interceded fervently and frequently during that time, that God would bring us a "little David" to fulfill that role. By that I meant someone who had a heart like young David when he approached his enemy, the giant Goliath.

It was Saturday the first of February, and we were at the church for a service. During the course of the meeting, an unassuming youngish man who was on the platform was asked to pray, which he did.

Immediately the Holy Spirit said to me with great clarity, "That's your little David." It was a spiritually electric moment for me! He was later introduced as our new pastor.

A little time later, I asked God to speak to me from my Bible that David Timothy Clark was a type of David when he slew Goliath. He immediately did by opening my Bible at the exact same page. It was 1 Samuel 16:18…….and "The Lord was with him." I knew we were in for a treat. A few days later, I saw Acts 10:38 "For God was with Him" referring to Jesus as Son of man!

That was over five years ago from the time I am writing this. I am still deeply committed to ministering alongside humble hearted Timothy, in any way that God requires of me. It is a genuine privilege.

The Bible clearly states in 1 Corinthians 14:1 that we are to "earnestly desire the spiritual gifts, especially that we may prophecy."

With that in mind, I was praying earnestly that God would release the gift of a word of knowledge amongst us as a church, so it wasn't surprising when He did!

I was praying specifically that the gift of the word of knowledge would operate at the Sunday morning services, as it uniquely pin pointed individuals' needs and helped bring about their speedy release.

About this time, one morning at the 11 a.m. service, Pastor Timothy had a word of knowledge that there was someone in the service who had just been diagnosed as having pancreatic cancer. He said that God wanted to miraculously heal them, if they would believe.

What made this so remarkable, is that just that very morning, our Pastor had announced that Anna Hayford, Jack Hayford's lovely wife, had just died of cancer of the pancreas!!

Pastor Timothy told the person to whom this word of the Lord applied, to identify themselves by phoning the church office and testifying that they had believed God for this miracle and were now pancreatic cancer free!!

The next Sunday morning our pastor reported that everything had happened exactly as he had spoken it out by faith. What a mighty, miraculous God!

On another Sunday morning at the 11 a.m. service, the Holy Spirit gave me a clear word of knowledge. It was this, "There are people here today who had a frightening experience at age four, that was related to being with your mother. If you will acknowledge that relates to you, and you have suffered as a result of it, please stand. I will pray for your healing and give you the strictest confidentiality, as you share your story.

Immediately nine people stood to their feet! It took a full hour to listen to them and then pray for them individually until they were set free. Praise God for the wonder of His ways!

Another Sunday morning at the 11 a.m. service at T.C.O.T.W., I was given a word of knowledge that there was someone in the service who had been contemplating committing suicide. I asked them to come forward at the end of the service, where they would be given the counsel that would set them free from this horrible temptation.

Three people came forward and two of them identified that it applied to them, and were then subsequently fully counseled into freedom.

The third person acknowledged that the night before, she had experienced strong spiritual warfare from satanic forces who were trying to get her to commit suicide. However, she strongly quoted

God's Word pronouncing her authority over all the powers of darkness and finally came to peace.

Praise God for this wonderful gift of a word of knowledge that brings deliverance to the needy.

God Given Tribes

There are two tribes to which God has called us to be committed. One is Youth With A Mission and the other is the local church of His choosing.

Jim and I have always been convinced of the Biblical importance of being committed and accountable to the Church family of God's directions.

This is especially important for your family's children. Friendship choices are usually formed out of the environment to which they are most familiar with. The friendship choices they make in these impressionable years can strongly influence their future destinies for good or for bad. I cannot emphasize this too strongly.

When we came to America in the early seventies, God directed us to join the Osborne Neighborhood church, in Pacoima, California. The pastors were very supportive of Y.W.A.M.'s vision and many were sent out into Y.W.A.M.'s Discipleship Training Schools from there.

In 1976 we were equally clearly directed by God to leave, and become part of The Church on the Way in Van Nuys, California, which has remained our church home. It has been a joyous fulfillment to serve under Dr. Jack Hayford, Dr. Scott Bauer, Pastor Jim Tolle, and Dr. Ricky Temple's leadership.

My dear friend, Scott Bauer, understood the prophetic teaching ministry God had given me, and released me to regularly bring the

Word of the Lord to the powerful Spirit Filled Life conferences that he lead yearly.

We have found that the greatest tests from God have come through these tribes. Conversely, as we've passed those tests by God's grace, the greatest blessings have come from Him through them.

Both our children met their life partners when serving God in Youth With A Mission, and four of our grandchildren met their life partners in the same way. If there is resistance to God's directions to join a tribe or tribes, frustration and lack of fulfillment will be the result.

As the Church On The Way is my home church, it becomes an automatic responsibility to be seriously committed in intercession to this Tribe of Believers.

It has always started with the senior pastor, who has the greatest accountability toward the Lord. As I have always had a warm, close relationship with each one of them since the 1970's, this has been a joyous privilege, which I've taken very seriously. God alone knows.

Divine Intervention

In August of 2014, I went with my close friend Daina House, to a The Church On The Way mid-week prayer meeting in the Prayer Chapel. During the worship Rick Segall was leading in a song about God being the "I AM," when the Holy Spirit stirred me about Jesus being our lover and took me to verses in Song of Solomon that powerfully express that. I often quote them to Jesus, passionately as I worship Him at the end of the day,

I submitted my impressions to Pastor Timothy Clarke, that I was to share this with the audience. He then released me.

After I had quoted the poignant verses (chapters 2:16, 5:10, 6:3, and 7:10) I then said, "No one can totally fulfill you like Jesus," and quoted Colossians 2:10, "You are complete in Him."

I then poured out my heart in fervent love talk to Jesus, with my arms raised, and then said, "I adore You."

Suddenly I was slain in the Spirit; and as I started to fall backwards Pastor Timothy caught me and laid me down on the platform. I was totally out of it. I didn't know a thing until later, when he helped me get up.

Later, Daina told me that Timothy stayed down beside me all that time, and continued to lead the service. It changed the course of the meeting.

The next day after thanking God for touching me, I poured out again, the deep yearnings of my heart to see His glory. How I long for that.

I also asked God to reveal to me why He had slain me in the Spirit during that church service. He responded by saying that, "It was a sign that He is coming to manifest His power; and prophets are often given signs among the people."

When I asked for Scriptural confirmation on this statement, the Holy Spirit opened my Bible to Amos 3:7-8, "Surely the Lord GOD does nothing, without revealing his secrets to his servants the prophets. The lion has roared; who will not fear? The Lord GOD has spoken; who can but prophesy?" In reverential awe, I quietly said, "I worship You."

I was soon to discover that it was nothing unusual to see my pastor Timothy ministering to the people from the platform, while squatting on his heels on the floor. He does it as a way of life, when preaching, and when praying; whenever he feels the need to humble himself before the Lord. Being regularly on the internet doesn't alter anything. I love this genuine humility, and pray he will never change!

I deeply regret that my beloved Jim never had a chance to know Timothy....and vice versa. How they would have loved and enjoyed each other! I'll have to wait until Heaven to see that worked out.

I am committed to being an intercessor for Timothy, and his lovely wife and co-pastor Deborah, along with their three lovable teenage children.

Foundational Ministries

Ever since Pastor Timothy has been the senior pastor of our Church, I have sought God diligently for His direction in relation to fulfilling my complimentary ministry role to his.

Ephesians 2:20 says "the foundational ministries are built upon the apostles and prophets." When these two ministry gifts operate in the fear of the Lord, in trinity unity and genuine humility, God's full purposes are able to come forth among His people. It's an awesome responsibility, as well as a high privilege.

As with the linking of all ministries for the extension of God's Kingdom, there will be trials and testings. We've had them both; but they are not to be compared with the joyous fulfillment that always overshadows them.

Being foundation ministries, God shares His visions, for where He's taking His Church, with both ministries.

An Unusual Intervention

One Saturday evening around 2014, I switched on my television set which was automatically set on the Daystar Television Network.

To my surprise I found that it was now showing the Roman Catholic channel's documentaries. I then tried to switch it back to Daystar, but it wouldn't budge.

I thought, "O.K. I'll see what this is about," as I stopped to watch. Immediately I was gripped by watching the powerful testimony of a man who was formerly in great need, and far away from God, who had a radical conversion in a Roman Catholic setting. I rejoiced in that and tried to get back to Daystar. However, I could not get back; the channel would not change no matter what I did.

The second evening I tried again, only to have the same experience; only this time I was watching and listening to an outstanding conversion to the Lord in a Roman Catholic setting, from a woman who was formerly totally anti-Christianity. She only ever wore black clothing and former pictures showed her face to be very dark. She was now radiant and loved testifying about her transformed life. It had a vital impact! I rejoiced again, and then tried to get Daystar. Again, the channel wouldn't move.

On the third night at the same time, I watched the same Catholic documentary. This time it was even more arresting. It showed a classroom of teenage boys in a Catholic school.

One teenage boy was out the front asking his classmates where they were hurting the most. When each one spoke it out, he was then prayed for openly, with the rest in prayerful agreement.

Several responded. Their vulnerability was on full display for anyone to see. I have never seen anything like it!! Their age group is the most sensitive to this kind of exposure. But the wonder working power of God's tender love over ruled all this.

I was deeply moved and vocally praised the Lord.

On the fourth evening, my Television set easily switched back to normal! God's sovereign purposes were completed. I had a renewed and deepened appreciation of the powerful workings of the Holy Spirit among my dear Catholic brothers and sisters in Christ. Jim and I have never had a prejudice towards them.

I also had a reminder that "God's ways are higher than our ways," He can invade my space and alter my plans anytime He wants to, because every day I ask Him to take over completely.

"The Call" Event April 9th 2016

God had given Lou Engle the vision of gathering thousands of Christians together in the Los Angeles Memorial Coliseum which seats nearly 80,000 people. It was a colossus event. The stadium was electrified with at least 66,000 in attendance and another 20,000 watching online.

On Contend Global's YouTube channel the entire event can be viewed with subtitles in 4 additional languages. It has been watched over 785,000 times as of this writing and still counting.

The purpose was to believe God for genuine revival and a spiritual awakening to break out in Southern California, as a result of all the previous intercession, and the unity of the Body of Christ that this historic event produced.

The program included lots of worship, the proclamation of the gospel, and key spiritual leaders briefly bringing the word of the Lord.

God manifest His power with many people being converted, as well as signs and wonders as the gifts of the Spirit operated.

I personally experienced a bit of Heaven that memorable day. I was there from about 10:30 a.m. until 10:30 p.m., on the platform surrounded by very anointed spiritual leaders most of whom I knew well.

I had previously given Lou Engle an encouraging word from the Lord, affirming this event, so he asked me to share it that day, which I did; also stating that I firmly believed God for genuine revival to come to Los Angeles.

The twelve hours I was there, all desire for water or food completely left me and I was charged with supernatural energy. Also, my usual back pain temporarily ceased. Wonder of wonders!

After Todd White had been introduced to me, he voluntarily stayed beside me, which I enjoyed. At one point we were out of range from the front of the platform, and were worshiping Jesus along with the crowd, when I grabbed Todd's right arm and said, "Let's dance." He immediately co-operated and we took off singing and praising God as we went round in circles. Much later, when I had the pleasure of meeting Todd's beautiful eldest daughter, she told me that her dad had never danced one step in his entire life, and that she was amazed that no one would have ever known! I loved it.

Little did I know that one of the Y.W.A.M.ers from our Los Angeles Base, who was out among the crowd, spotted us and quickly photographed us. That photo went viral. It didn't bother me, just amused me, as I'm sure it did God.

At 10:30 p.m., after hearing Daniel Kolenda preach one of the most clear, succinct, powerfully anointed gospel messages, to which many responded, I was told I'd have to leave. If I stayed, I 'd get caught in the huge crowds of people exiting the stadium. I hated to leave!

When I was driven home at 11 p.m., I was still shouting Hallelujahs as I exited my car.

John Bills – Iraq

I have asked my son in law, John Bills to give me a report on his ministry with the refugees in Iraq, as he is an integral part of my life. Here it is:

"Because of the devastation created by the I.S. (Islamic State), thousands of men, women and children have been forced from their homes, slaughtered or taken into captivity to be abused. Most fled for safety within Iraq. Over 27 camps contain the estimated 2 million refugees and Internally Displaced Persons in Iraq.

I have had the amazing privilege to provide care to many who live in these camps. With the severe winter weather in Iraq, we're busy organizing the distribution of winter coats, shoes, and socks for the 300+ refugee orphans from I.S. along with food baskets for the 300+ widows along the Syrian border. This is a huge undertaking. We are thankful to have had outreach teams come and serve with us.

Part of the responsibility I carry is to recruit teams and to make the need of the refugees known in this part of the world. In one camp alone, there are over 250,000 refugees from Syria. When we get the visual of what war has created, it helps to bring us to desperate prayer for so many who are suffering so severely.

I have been entrusted with around 400 orphans as a result of I.S. The parents of these orphans were murdered by I.S. soldiers. Most of the children range in the ages of 4 to 17. All of them are suffering from various degrees of Post Traumatic Stress Disorder. We are establishing the first permanent trauma center in the camp for orphans and children captured by ISIS. We will have counselors working with them through their trauma. 50 of the most traumatized children will be in the first round of counseling. I am working closely with this team providing oversight and training for the director and his staff through Skype. I will be returning to Iraq to continue work with the counseling team.

Some of the other areas that we are creating for the refugees are:

- *A teen drop-in center for them in one of the larger camps entrusted to us.*
- *Discipleship training among three unreached People Groups here in Iraq.*

- *Opening a new English language/computer school for adults and young adults.*

I have also been involved in recruiting English teachers, art therapists, music teachers as well as sports development teams to come and help out. Whatever we do, we do in the name of Jesus Christ to see His love poured out through our lives to those who are hurting and abused.

One of the ways we are impacting the lives of the refugees is through the Discovery Bible Program. We have them sitting in small groups, sharing a Bible story, having them discuss the story and how they will implement that story into their lives the following week. Jesus is moving deeply in the hearts of many through this program. We have seen many come to Christ already by simply sharing the power of the Word of God."

I Choose Fun

My dear pastor, Timothy Clark, was due at my home in about five minutes, for Kingdom related purposes. I knew he loved coffee so I was trying to make him some.

I need to explain that it was many years since I had made any, as I only made herbal tea drinks for myself and others. Anyway I was trying hard to remember how I worked my coffee maker.

My best efforts were an obvious disaster, as hot water was spilling out over my kitchen bench just as the doorbell rang.

I decided to have fun instead of wallowing in embarrassment; so I immediately laughingly shared my dilemma, as I invited my pastor into my kitchen. By this time the hot water was now on my kitchen floor. Pastor Timothy was not only laughing heartily with me, but he asked my permission before tearing off some paper towels. He then got down on his hands and knees and wiped up the overflow!

How about that for being such an incredibly humble great sport!! Then he showed me where I was supposed to have poured the water, and I started again. When he was drinking the final product, while still in my kitchen, he said, "I've tasted better cups of coffee, but I've never had one that was more memorable." We both laughed heartily.

Believe me, after that day I made sure I was thoroughly tutored in how to work a coffee maker.

Today, on the 25th of March 2019, I phoned my dear friend Glenn Sheppard who was on the National Prayer Committee, to ask him some questions about events surrounding the N.P.C. and being at the White House. I needed accuracy for including reports in this book.

I hadn't seen either him or his lovely wife Jackie for many years, but Glenn and I chatted away as warmly and as freely as ever. At one point Glenn asked, "Do you still do cartwheels on your birthday?" I replied, "I did my last cartwheels when I was in my sixties."

I concluded the conversation by telling Glenn to give every one of his family members a huge enough hug from me that they'd need to consider having chiropractor treatment afterwards! ☺

The next day, Jackie returned the compliment. Thank God for old friends.

I need to explain that I haven't been able to renew my driver's license since my mid-eighties due to the severity of my arthritic back pain, so I have to rely on different people to drive me anywhere. <u>This remains a real challenge</u>. <u>It's been very hard to lose my independence</u>, since I lost my precious husband who drove me everywhere. I need more of God's grace on this issue, than any other challenges.

For many years before Jim went to be with the Lord. Mycol Shumpert, who was on the staff of The Church On The Way, was so often so very kind to meet whatever needs that we may have, that I named him "Our Black Angel." And the name has stuck. Jim loved it and used it.

Since Jim's passing, "My Black Angel" has always been right there by my side whenever I've needed him at the church. It's been truly amazing. I stand in awe of God!

One time when I had to climb a lot of steps that were almost vertical, in order to reach Pastor Timothy Clark's office, "My Black Angel" showed up. He just scooped up my 108 pounds in his super strong black arms and speedily landed me at the top. I was so impressed and very grateful! I wouldn't be a bit surprised if one day "My Black Angel" sprouted wings!!

Because of the severity of the pain from my arthritic hips, I would have had to proceed super slowly, one step at a time, with someone else helping to take some of my weight.

To my great loss, but with my blessing, My Black Angel and his wife have moved on to another assignment after 22 years of faithful service at our church.

God has greatly blessed me in my late eighties and early nineties, with having Reid Jones to help me for 2 afternoons per week in many and varied practical ways. There's very little that he can't do or fix! He's a strong Christian who has done three extended ministry trips to Africa with Y.W.A.M. He was raised in Y.W.A.M. I love him dearly, but as from the end of April 2019 he leaves me to further fulfill God's purposes for his life. He goes with my blessing.

I want to make a point of honoring Sandy Miller, who has the unique record of having faithfully served as personal secretary to four of the five pastors of T.C.O.T.W. over 31 ½ years. She has since retired.

God has seen the tireless, diligent, wise way she has pursued this inconspicuous ministry as unto the Lord, and I'm thrilled to have this opportunity to salute and honor her now.

One of the great benefits that come from being committed to the tribe of God's choosing is the priceless gift of dear friends whom God gives us.

At the risk of not naming them all, and causing offense, I can only state they are an enormous blessing, and are regularly prayed for.

God and you, the reader of this book, know who you are! I am well aware that some will think, "I can't believe that Joy never mentioned my name in her biography." I can only pray that God will give you understanding of how God directed me in this very difficult decision.

I would be remiss if I did not mention the following. In the early seventies I was ministering in a church in Fort Worth, Texas, when a married couple named Bob and Betty Mann asked me out to lunch. That started a lifelong, close friendship which has been an enormous blessing to Jim and me.

Only God can reward them for their nearly 50 years of faithfully praying for us and their unique generosity in ongoingly helping us financially.

For two very enjoyable summers in the seventies, Bob and Betty paid all our expenses to join their family of three children at a beautiful resort in Acapulco, Mexico. We were waited on from morning 'till night.

I call them "My American Family" and to this day Bob calls me "Sis." I delight to honor them.

Another exception to my sharing the names of dear friends is Dr. Vena Ricketts. She is an advanced medical doctor who has been a very special and uniquely generous friend. On numbers of occasions she has been right there to help me medically. My gratitude is deep. We have great spiritual affinity, and it's a joy to be together. She calls me her spiritual mother.

The longer it took to finalize the writing of this book, the more I would state that I was going to have a celebration when it was completed. I had no idea how. Little did I know that God had a surprise plan!

I had completed the manuscript on Saturday, October, 5, 2019. The next day at church, a beautiful young woman named Sarah introduced herself to me and told me how much she and her husband Adam had appreciated the ministry God had given me. As soon as I met, Adam, I sensed the presence of God upon him.

He quickly stated that the Holy Spirit had told him during the service that he was to bless someone, and he now believed it was for me and asked me to explain in what way? Immediately I said I needed to be taken to a mall to get some shoes. We made a date for during that week and took off.

It was genuine "love at first sight" for the three of us. Most unusual! We realized it came as a gift from the heart of God, via the Holy Spirit. The next week we repeated this assignment with much joy and fulfillment, realizing that I was celebrating the first milestone of writing my life's story. Hallelujah. God is so good!

Renewed Teamwork And New Messages

The last time Andrew, Loren, and I were teamed together, was in April of 2017 when each of us spoke over the internet at a conference Loren had convened. I was very grateful for that privilege. My message title was, "How much is eternity on your mind?" The international response was extremely encouraging!

It was Andrew's last public ministry assignment at 86 years of age, and our unity as a team was as strong as ever. All glory to our wonderful Lord Jesus.

In 2018, Loren asked me to team up with him again by bringing "the word of the Lord" in a videoed message that he wanted to play, where he would be speaking.

It was at an alumni plus gathering at Y.W.A.M.'s University of the Nations in Kona, Hawaii as they celebrated their 40th Anniversary.

As always, I took this assignment, which the Lord strongly affirmed, very seriously. This resulted in preparing another new message entitled, "STRONG FAITH ON TRIAL." I identified personally.

After I had delivered it, Loren and Darlene sent me a very encouraging letter as feedback. All glory to God.

Each time, I have had the messages videoed it has been done at The Church on the Way. My dear pastor friend, Timothy Clark has very kindly and generously authorized this, and the media department director, Julian Webb has graciously cooperated. I deeply appreciate these God given gifts to me.

A Significant Introduction

When God links together any two anointed international ministries, there is always an increase of Divine explosive purposes in the earth.

I was very aware of this, when Benny Hinn kept telling me that he wanted to personally meet Loren Cunningham. Benny had, much earlier in his life, been impacted by the Holy Spirit when he heard Loren speak at a youth rally.

As Benny was aware of my close relationship with Loren in Y.W.A.M., he made it very clear to me that he wanted me to be there when they both met. I was happy to comply.

Jim and I flew with Benny and his Crusade leadership team members to Kona, Hawaii, where Benny was having taped interviews with me for his T.V. programs. He was also having public nightly meetings.

The introduction to Loren was very natural and very warm and resulted among other things, in Loren doing a whole week's very powerful teachings for Benny's T.V. programs.

These God ordained friendships have stood the test of time. Recently, Benny and Loren were powerfully linked together at the close of that massively, spiritually strategic, one-of-a-kind events called, "THE SEND.

The Challenge of North Korea

It's July of 2019, and the nation of North Korea has once again been brought to my attention by the Holy Spirit.

There are many and varied factors that call for serious intercession in this needy nation that I've been involved in since the seventies.

One of them is related to the Communist Concentration Camps where Christians are severely tortured. One particular camp is located in a forest in North Korea.

Some years ago a young man prisoner, totally miraculously managed to escape to South Korea, and publicly told about some of the horrors. One of them was stringing people upside down with their hands cuffed and leaving them hanging for inordinate amounts of time....in agony.

I have cried out to God repeatedly in desperation for Him to destroy that <u>Hell hole</u>, and set them all free.

If that prayer hasn't yet been answered, I'm now praying that the Christian prisoners will be so endued with the power of the Holy Spirit's love and faith and be given the boldness of a lion.... that a spiritual awakening (revolution) will break out as a result of theirs' and our united prayers.

Also, that the glory of God will invade and disrupt the whole prison, causing numerous conversions. All this applies to every other Korean Concentration Camp.

My faith is based upon the Word of God.

- "Greater is He that is in you than he that is in the world." 1John 4:4
- "For this purpose was the Son of God manifest, that the works of satan may be destroyed." 1John 3:8
- "I will build My Church and the gates of hell will not prevail against it." Mathew 16:18
- "Resist the devil and he will flee from you." James 4:7
- "They overcame him by the blood of the Lamb and the word of their testimony and loved not their lives to the death." Revelation 12:11
- "His dominion is an everlasting dominion, and His Kingdom endures from generation to generation; all the inhabitants of the earth are accounted as nothing; and He does according to His will in the host of heaven and among the inhabitants of the earth; and none can stay His hand or say to Him, "What have You done?" Daniel 4:34,35

I am convinced that when we read in the Word of God about God's mighty power being demonstrated in the early Church, that we should expect to see God do it again in our day.

There was a price to pay then. They so operated in the fear of the Lord that people didn't quickly join them. Acts 5:13.

There was such an outpouring of the Holy Spirit's power in people being converted and healed that it came to the attention of the jealous leading Rabbi's, who put them back in prison. God then moved in and sent an angel to open the prison doors, and told them to keep on preaching.

I'm longing for the day this sort of Christianity is on display again. I believe it will be, the nearer we get to the time when Jesus comes to rapture all true Believers and we meet Him in the clouds en route to Heaven. See 2 Thessalonians 4:16-17.

In my daily Bible reading the next day, I was greatly encouraged as I read Habakuk 1:5 which confirmed what I had just written. "Look among the nations, and see; wonder and be astounded. For I am doing a work in your days that you would not believe if told."

Major Prayer Points

The closer we are in friendship to God, the more we will want to know what is burdening His heart the most. As we seek Him, He will reveal that to us. We then discharge those burdens back to Him in intercession, with full faith that He is working.

In that context and in recent years, the Holy Spirit has been burdening my heart especially but not at all inclusively, for the following:

- Unity in the worldwide Body of Christ
- For a Heaven sent genuine revival, that will convict and revive the CHURCH of Jesus Christ worldwide.
- For a spiritual awakening that will bring millions of lost souls into God's Kingdom.

- The millions of young women and children enslaved in sex trafficking to be delivered and healed.

- The millions of men who are the perpetrators to be convicted, and converted.

- The millions of Christians worldwide, being persecuted for their faith in Jesus Christ. – many requests.

- The 65.3 million refugees in different parts of the world.

- For the Bible to be translated and distributed into every people group worldwide.

- For the Jesus Film to be translated and distributed into the language of every people group in the world.

- For every nation in the world, naming three at a time, systematically.

- In the times without number that I have prevailed in prayer for the spiritual leaders worldwide, my greatest desire is that they would be recognized and known by Acts 4:13, "....and they recognized that they had been with Jesus." The more quality time we spend alone with our fabulous friend Jesus, the more we'll become like Him.

I have also been sharing what God says from His Word about these desperate needs, and how we can be a part of the answers. They arc all signs that we are living in the last days before Jesus comes in the Heavens to take His true followers Home with Him. 1 Thessalonians 4:16-17.

I love the heavy drama surrounding this epic event. The ruling reigning Monarch of the universe will take center stage in the heavens; accompanied by the awesome shout which only an archangel could render, with trumpets blaring simultaneously.

Grave yards will then erupt as the dead disciples of Christ will be the first to be given new bodies and then be caught up into the air to join King Jesus.

The unprecedented, mindboggling spectacle then takes place as multiplied millions of true Disciples of Christ worldwide, will instantly join them by “being caught up to meet the Lord in the air” as 1 Thessalonians describes it.

Those left behind worldwide will experience total chaos. For example, disciples of Christ who are actively engaged airline pilots, as well as the passengers who fit that criteria, will instantly be evicted from their planes to meet Jesus in the clouds.

If you are not sure that you are ready to spend eternity with the Lord Jesus, you can be, by carefully reading through and fulfilling the conditions from the Bible as are stated in the back of this book. It is under the heading, “A commitment of life to the Lord Jesus Christ.”

My Testimony

At the front of my Bible I have written the following:

Emanuel – God is with me.

He says He will help me – Isaiah 41:13
He says He will strengthen me – Isaiah 41:10
He says He will guide me – Psalm 32:4
He says He will speak to me – John 10:3,4,21
He holds my right hand – Isaiah 41:13
He’s the lover of my soul – Song of Solomon 2:16

His desire is for me – Song of Solomon 7:10

In 2 Corinthians 11:11,25 I am reminded that the Apostle Paul suffered a lot of pain throughout his ministry, and in 2 Corinthians 16:27 it says he was "in many sleepless nights."

This knowledge helps me to understand that God 's ways are so much higher than our ways, and at times are past finding out. With these thoughts in mind I will now share the following.

From reading through so much of my diaries, a pattern has emerged.

On numerous occasions, because of severe lower back pain, and a lot of sleeplessness, I have cried out to God for understanding as to what He was trying to teach me. When I asked if He wanted to heal me and bring glory to His name through it all, the answers from His Word were always "Yes," and at times, followed by "Wait." This pattern has continued for twenty-seven years.

The most prevalent verse from which God has spoken to me has been Luke 1:45 "Blessed is she who believed, for there will be a performance of those things which were told her from the Lord."

As the pain and insomnia have continued, I have found myself again wondering if I come into the category of those in Hebrews 11:13 that Paul refers to. The reward for their faith wasn't manifest in this life, but in eternity.... Whatever the outcome, I trust God's character. God is faithful! I will keep praising, worshiping, loving, trusting, and obeying Him.

Miracle Moments In Mundane Things

My conception of God's greatness is not so much in the epic things He does; amazingly and spectacular as they are. I'm apt to expect the ruling reigning Monarch of the Universe to roll back the waters of the Red Sea, and send down fire from Heaven. That goes with His territory!

But what blows me away and I stand in great awe, is when the Creator and sustainer of the Universe stoops down into my tiny little world and performs series of miracles in front of my eyes....as a way of life. As well as when He shows five year old Johnny where his five cent piece is that he just lost in the grass, because he asked God to show him.

I'll now illustrate from my everyday life.

Living alone in my nineties in a big house, with lots of grounds, gives me unique opportunities to prove that my God delights in turning on His wonder working power for this little widow.

A couple of days ago, I found to my amazement that one of my T.V. sets had changed channels, without my having touched it!!

I keep it set on Daystar Television Network, which broadcasts Christian programs all the time. I watch them sporadically, as needed. Just recently I found it was now suddenly set on some commercial channel that was advertising some product at length and <u>nothing I could do would change it back.</u>

So....... I said to God, "I'm now asking you to go into action with Your miracle working power, and put my Christian T.V. station back to where it was. This is no big deal to You. You can do ANYTHING! And I thanked and praised Him.

A little while later, I checked it out, and there it was, right back to where it needed to be. I shouted "Hallelujah!"

Because my eyesight is not as sharp as it used to be, I sometimes have difficulty threading my sewing machine needle, when I'm doing clothing alterations…or just when I need to thread a needle or when I can't pick up something from the floor….or when I can't open something….or when I can't read the small print when I desperately need to. That's when I call on the Lord for help. He always comes through and helps me in these little things. That's part of the enormity of His greatness.

There are also times when a shelf loaded with heavy files and Bible related materials suddenly starts giving way and falling on top of me as I'm working at my desk. I yell out in desperation, "Holy Spirit, H-E-L-P! And He does. Miraculously in front of my eyes! Things go into reversed gear, and I am spared from what could have been a bad accident.

I've kept my best miracle for the last. As I do 99% of my clothing alterations, I was able to detect that the length of the stitches had become unusually small. When I checked with the manual, everything on the machine was in perfect place for a normal stitch.

My son-in-law J.B. is extraordinarily gifted with his hands and was familiar with my machine, so I asked him to check it out. He did…at great length, and found nothing that would change it. I then phoned the shop that had previously serviced this machine, and left a message for them to call me back. They didn't respond.

So I laid my hands on my machine, and by faith, I deliberately placed it in God's hands, stating my full faith in His ability to take it and fix it! I then thanked Him that He would.

Several weeks later, when I needed to use the machine, I found that the horribly small stitch had changed to a normal size.

Hallelujah! I stood in awe of God.

Joy in her home at age 93.

Giving God The Glory

We all need to agree with King David when he declared, "My goodness is nothing apart from You" (Psalm 16:2). We need to also agree with Jesus when He said, "…for without Me you can do nothing" (John 15:5). Nothing means zero. Zero is a circle with a hole in the middle. So that's who we are.

The rim of each circle has a personal name on it for identification purposes. That's your name and mine and everyone else's. And we need to agree with Paul when he stated, "For I know that in me (that is, in my flesh) nothing good dwells; for to will is present with me, but how to perform what is good I do not find" (Romans 7:18). That's the bad news.

The good news is that all that we're not, Jesus is, and that He lives within us. So let's look at the other side of the coin of truth.

"I can do all things through Christ who strengthens me" (Philippians 4:13). This verse gets even clearer when Paul explains, "I have been crucified with Christ. My ego is no longer central. It is no longer important that I appear righteous before you or need to have your good opinions. Christ lives in me. The life you see me living is not mine, but it is lived by faith in the Son of God, who loved me and gave himself for me." (Galatians 2:20 The Message Translation)

We need to again agree with Paul when he states, "…Christ in you, the hope of glory" (Colossians 1:27). The "glory of God" is all of God's characteristics. Only God Himself can display those through us. Jesus Christ gave up His life for us on the cross, so that by His resurrected life, He could enter into the life of each one of us who receives Him and makes Him Lord. His intention and desire is to then live His life through us as we die to our own rights and desires.

It's a fabulous exchange. It's a daily deal, where we invite the Lord Jesus who is within each one of us who are truly born again to:

- think through our minds.
- look through our eyes.
- speak through our mouths.
- listen through our ears.
- love through our hearts.
- touch through our hands.
- walk through our feet.

Now, back to the circle with the hole in the middle (that's us). As we thank the Lord Jesus that He will do and is doing the above, His life goes into action, and the empty circle is filled with Him.

The beautiful person of the Holy Spirit within us will then convict us if we have usurped the Lord's authority in any area of our lives. Through confession, repentance, and restitution, we allow Jesus to take full control again.

The Holy Spirit's empowerment enables us to keep the Lord Jesus on the throne of our hearts. That's why it is so important that we do not resist the Holy Spirit, grieve Him, quench Him, or disobey Him. Our safest place is to invite and believe for His total control (see Ephesians 5:18) "...the Holy Spirit whom God has given to those who obey Him" (Acts 5:32).

When we understand that Jesus Christ lives His life through us as we are daily under His lordship, and empowered by the Holy Spirit, the sweat is taken out of living and the striving stops. Before doing anything God has shown us to do, we simply say, "I can't, but You can and will, now. Thank You." That's what I call the miracle takeover! The Bible calls it "the rest of faith" (see Hebrews 4).

Now, who alone must logically get all the glory from the spiritual things that take place in us and through us? Certainly not us! We're only a rim surrounding a hole! This makes it so liberating and wonderfully easy to give all the glory, all the time to the only One worthy to receive it—King God, the Lover of our souls. "For of Him and through Him and to Him are all things, to whom be glory forever. Amen" (Romans 11:36).

I rejoice in the unfailing character of God even when His ways are past finding out. This assurance, plus God's amazing grace, along with the prayers of many faithful intercessors, enables me to live above the trials, mentally, emotionally, and spiritually. Through it all I find my greatest comfort and satisfaction in my intimate relationship with God.

I can say with the Psalmist in Psalm 116:10 "I kept my faith, even when I said, "I am greatly afflicted."

Also, for many years before Jim passed, he and I had powerful times of intercession together almost every evening, for vital issues. I believe that the Kingdom of God is extended more through the ministry of intercession than any other ministry. I have that vision and conviction, so it's been a priority with us.

G.F. Vallance, Goodmayes once said, "You can do more than pray after you have prayed, but you cannot do more until you have prayed."

My dear friend Reona Jolly sent me the following quote, which I love, "When my arms can't reach people who are close to my heart…I always hug them with my prayers."

I maintain that there are no excuses to keep us from the ministry of intercession. I have prayed fervently alone; as a way of life with Jim and our children; regularly in groups with Christian leaders; with different prayer partners; with my precious life partner; in regular prayer groups at The Church on the Way, and with countless others as opportunities have arisen.

It's no wonder that I feel more fulfilled after an effective time of intercession than after I preached a message. When I speak to people about God I have no guarantee they will act upon the truth's I've spoken. But when I pray to God about people, I know He'll always act in response to my cries as I pray according to His ways from His Word.

If all our other faculties were taken from us and all we had left were a sound mind and a beating heart, we could still be mightily used of God to affect the history of the nations through the marvelous ministry of intercession.

In my life, the greatest times of dynamic spiritual action, revelation, and the sense of God's presence and power have been during times of worship and prayer. That's when I've experienced

- the deepest moves of God's Spirit to change me.
- the greatest revelation of my own heart.
- the greatest revelation of the heart of God.
- the greatest spiritual unity with others.
- the deepest moves of God's Spirit through me on behalf of others.
- the greatest spiritual authority.
- the greatest victories over the powers of darkness.
- the greatest releases of faith.
- the moments of greatest intimacy of friendship with God.

Worship and prayer dull? Hardly! They lead to adventure and friendship with God.

"For many years Jim and I have had a C.D. player beside our bed for worship purposes. By far our favorite C.D.s were seven of Terry McAlman leading worship in a variety of settings. He's a brilliant pianist with an anointed tenor voice. Because each tape is so powerful, I've continued to play them sporadically every night since Jim's passing. I live alone so I can sing and shout my praises to my wonderful Lord. I love it.

The following Psalm has been given to me by the Holy Spirit. It has ministered life to me at 94.

Psalm 71: 17-21 "O God, from my youth You have taught me, and I still proclaim Your wondrous deeds. So even to old age and gray hairs, O God, do not forsake me, till I proclaim Your might to all the generations to come. Your power and Your righteousness, O God, reach to the high heavens. You have done great things, O God, who is like You? You have made me see many sore troubles will revive me again; from the depths of the earth You will bring me up again. You will increase my honor and comfort me again."

I have in no way been able to record all the vital ministry assignments that God has given me over the many years. There are still diaries full of them.... unshared.

I have attempted to follow God's directions in the fear of the Lord as to the content of this book; written in total dependence on the person of the Holy Spirit, that my precious Jesus alone be glorified.

During the final stages of completing this book, I have been under the restrictions related to the covid-19 virus...a worldwide pandemic. My deepest prayer concerns have been that the glory of God be increasingly manifest at all times.

The following song was given to me by the Holy Spirit. It sums up my life's message.

I know dear Lord
that You love me,
You've proved it so
at Calvary.
My love for You
is proved You've said,
By my obedience
to your Word.

I'll trust You Lord
when I can't see
The way ahead
that's best for me.
I know You'll guide
me all the way.
Just tell me Lord
and I'll obey.

I put my life
in Your dear hands.
With joy I'll follow
your commands.
I know it's only
by Your grace
I will endure
and run the race.

And when I look
into Your eyes
That burn with love
and Holy Fire.
My deep desire
is that You'll see
You truly had
Your way with me.

David Thompson, who is also a photographer, took this photo when I was 94.

My goal in writing this book is found in Colossians 1:18 "That in everything He may be pre-eminent." I have been In pursuit of giving God all the glory while needing to record some of how He has worked through this little life of mine.

In II Thessalonians 1:11-12 the Apostle Paul prays a comprehensive prayer that echoes in my heart. "To this end we always pray for you, that our God may make you worthy of His call, and may fulfill every good resolve and work of faith by His power, so that the name of our Lord Jesus may be glorified in you, and you in Him, according to the grace of our God and the Lord Jesus Christ."

I have needed to be reminded to always say quietly to the Lord, "It's You Lord," whenever He uses me in some way, or others make reference to how He has used me. This has been a way of life.

John 3:34 "He whom God has sent, speaks the Word of God for God does not give the Spirit by measure," has been a foundation verse for me. By God's grace, I have always done my best to be the right person, at the right place, in the right time, saying and doing the right things in order to get the right results....so that Jesus can be glorified.

This includes every time I have taught the Word of God. It also includes total dependence on the Holy Spirit for every aspect of my life. Period.

In Colossians 1:25 NIV it states, "I have become (the Church's) servant by the commission God gave me to present the Word of God in its fullness."

"Him we proclaim, warning every man and teaching every man in all wisdom, that we may present every man mature in Christ. For this I toil, striving with all the energy which He mightily inspires within me." Colossians 1:28,29 RSV.

An Unexpected Ending

It was about 8:00 p.m. on May 13, 2021, and I had locked the front and back doors of my home for the close of the day. I lived alone at 95. I had received a small floor rug back from the Cleaners and had just put it back down in my walk-in closet. Immediately I walked on it, I slipped and fell and broke my left shoulder. The non-slip backing of the carpet had unknowingly to me been removed!!

I somehow managed to inch by inch maneuver my body out of my closet into my bedroom, and to within 3" of my phone on the wall. I had three very painful unsuccessful attempts to reach it. While feeling very abandoned, I kept crying out to God, "You said You would never leave me or forsake me."

I couldn't activate the device on the leather strap on my right wrist that would bring me help. My fingers were damaged, so I bit the device with my teeth. I then kept hearing, "Signal received. Stand by."

After what seemed the longest time, I finally heard a voice saying, "Where is your outside key?" I called out the instructions and 3 men came to rescue me.

After they had lifted me off the floor (where I almost blacked out with the pain) they put me on my bed. It was then I saw the beautiful face of another man as I turned my head. Immediately I said, "You are different!! Are you a Christian?" His face lit up with the most beautiful smile as he replied, "Yes!" His name was Mike.

I was comforted and felt blessed of the Lord. It was a poignant moment!!

After my daughter and son in law arrived, I was taken in an ambulance to the nearest hospital. Mike the paramedic stayed by my side all the way to the hospital where they thoroughly X-rayed me. I was very relieved to know my back was not broken.

My daughter and son in law took me to their nearby home, where they have given me the very best of care. I will be eternally deeply grateful to the Lord and to them. This is my fifth month. I don't know what my future holds but I completely trust my loving heavenly Father who does know.

Due to the extent of the trauma I had experienced, I was in great need of the healing of my memories.

God mightily used my son in law John Bills, who prayed a most comprehensive and compassionate, powerful prayer of faith over me. God then released that specific healing.

This painful major upheaval has been very challenging for all concerned, but made possible through God's amazing grace, and the fervent prayers of God's people. Again, I am so very grateful to all concerned.

Those who are in need of the healing of the memories, have access to God's healing power through the person of the Holy Spirit. It is important to reach out for help.

To sum everything up. 1 Corinthians 10:31

...whatever you do, do all to the glory of God.

Appendix

What It Means to Commit Your Life to the Lord Jesus Christ

…Choose for yourselves this day whom you will serve. (Joshua 24:15 NKJV)

And He made from one every nation of men to live on all the face of the earth, having determined allotted periods and the boundaries of their habitation, that they should seek God, in the hope that they might feel after Him and find Him. Yet He is not far from each one of us. (Acts 17:26–27 RSV)

1. **Acknowledge that you are a sinner and repent of your sin.**
   For all have sinned and fall short of the glory of God. (Romans 3:23 NIV)
   Repent therefore and be converted, that your sins may be blotted out… (Acts 3:19 NKJV)
   If we confess our sins, He is faithful and just to forgive us our sins and to cleanse us from all unrighteousness. (1 John 1:9 NKJV)

2. **Believe Christ died and rose again to save you from your sin and to give you eternal life.**
   For Christ died for sins once for all, the righteous for the unrighteous, to bring you to God. (1 Peter 3:18 NIV)
   For there is one God and one Mediator between God and men, the Man Christ Jesus. (1 Timothy 2:5 NKJV)
   For God so loved the world that He gave His only begotten Son, that whoever believes in Him should not perish but have everlasting life. (John 3:16 NKJV)

Nor is there salvation in any other, for there is no other name under heaven given among men by which we must be saved. (Acts 4:12 NKJV)

3. **Receive Christ by faith and accept the gift God has provided in His Son.**
Jesus said to him, "I am the way, the truth, and the life. No one comes to the Father, except through Me."
(John 14:6 NKJV)
Yet to all who received him, to those who believed in his name, he gave the right to become children of God.
(John 1:12 NIV)
Here I am! I stand at the door and knock. If anyone hears my voice and opens the door, I will come in and eat with that person, and they with me. (Revelation 3:20 NIV)
And this is the testimony: God has given us eternal life, and this life is in his Son. Whoever has the Son has life; whoever does not have the Son of God does not have life. I write these things to you who believe in the name of the Son of God so that you may know that you have eternal life.
(1John 5:11-13 NIV)

4. **Commit your whole life to the Lord Jesus Christ and follow Him and serve Him without reserve.**
Whoever believes in the Son has eternal life; but whoever rejects the Son will not see life, for God's wrath remains on him. (John 3:36 NIV)
...If anyone desires to come after Me, let him deny himself, and take up his cross, and follow Me.
(Matthew 16:24 NKJV)
Anyone who loves his father or mother more than Me is not worthy of Me; anyone who loves his son or daughter more than Me is not worthy of Me; and anyone who does not take his cross and follow Me is not worthy of Me.
(Matthew 10:37–38 NIV)

So He said to them, "Assuredly, I say to you, there is no one who has left house or parents or brothers or wife or children, for the sake of the kingdom of God, who shall not receive many times more in this present time, and in the age to come eternal life." (Luke 18:29–30 NKJV)

5. **Be prepared to confess Christ and to tell others that you belong to Him.**
   ...If you confess with your lips that Jesus is Lord and believe in your heart that God raised him from the dead, you will be saved. For man believes with his heart and so is justified, and he confesses with his lips and so is saved.
   (Romans 10:9–10 RSV)
   Therefore whoever confesses Me before men, him I will also confess before My Father who is in heaven. But whoever denies Me before men, him I will also deny before My Father who is in heaven. (Matthew 10:32–33 NKJV)
   For whoever is ashamed of Me and My words, of him the Son of Man will be ashamed when He comes in His own glory, and in His Father's, and of the holy angels.
   (Luke 9:26 NKJV)

6. **Acknowledge that the Lord Jesus not only died upon the Cross to give you eternal life, but that He rose again from the dead to live His life in you and through you.**
   ...Christ in you, the hope of glory. (Colossians 1:27 NIV)
   I have been crucified with Christ and I no longer live, but Christ lives in me. The life I live in the body, I live by faith in the Son of God, who loved me and gave Himself for me. (Galatians 2:20 NIV)

Your prayer of commitment of your life to the Lord Jesus Christ:

Lord Jesus, I know that I am a sinner. I turn away from my sin, in repentance, and ask You to forgive me. I believe You died on the cross for my sin and I thank You with all my heart. I now invite You to come into my heart and life. By faith, I receive You as my Savior, and make You my Lord and Master. I place my whole life in Your hands without reserve. Thank You that You not only died to give me the gift of eternal life, but that You rose again to live Your life in me and through me. I am prepared to acknowledge You as my Lord before others, and in constant dependence upon the Holy Spirit live for You, in obedience to Your promptings. Thank You that according to Your Word You have come in and made me Your child. Thank You that You have cleansed and forgiven me for my sin, and have given me eternal life.

Name:____

Date:___________________________

Essentials for Progress as a Christian

1. **Daily prayer and reading of God's Word are absolutely essential for you to grow strong spiritually.**
   You could start by reading the Gospel of John and the Psalms. Ask God the Holy Spirit to give you understanding and then thank Him that He will.
   But without faith it is impossible to please Him, for he who comes to God must believe that He is, and that He is a rewarder of those who diligently seek Him.
   (Hebrews 11:6 NKJV)
   Underline a verse when God speaks to you from it. The Bible is your guide and map.
   Your word is a lamp to my feet And a light to my path. (Psalm 119:105 NKJV)
   Do not confine prayers to "asking," but include thanksgiving and praise.
   ...With thanksgiving, let your requests be made known to God. (Philippians 4:6 NKJV)
   Praise Him for His acts of power; Praise Him for His surpassing greatness! (Psalm 150:2 NIV)

2. **Seek God's guidance in all things and expect Him to give it.**
   I will instruct you and teach you in the way you should go; I will counsel you and watch over you. (Psalm 32:8 NIV)
   He has promised to speak to us.
   My sheep hear My voice, and I know them, and they follow Me. (John 10:27 RSV)

3. **Meet regularly with other keen Christians in the church fellowship to which God leads you.**
   They devoted themselves to the apostles' teaching and to the fellowship, to the breaking of bread and to prayer.
   (Acts 2:42 NIV)
   Let us not give up meeting together, as some are in the habit of doing, but let us encourage one another—and all the more as you see the Day approaching. (Hebrews 10:25 NIV)

4. **An important method of public witness is to experience believer's baptism.**
   And as they went along the road they came to some water, and the eunuch said, "See, here is water! What is to prevent my being baptized?" (Acts 8:36 RSV)
   By baptism we make an open confession of our faith in the Lord Jesus Christ in the way in which He commanded us. *Go therefore and make disciples of all the nations, baptizing them in the name of the Father and of the Son and of the Holy Spirit. (Matthew 28:19 NKJV)*

5. **Seek opportunities to lead others to Christ.**
   ...He who wins souls is wise. (Proverbs 11:30 NIV)
   "Come, follow Me," Jesus said "and I will make you fishers of men." (Matthew 4:19 NIV)

6. **Remember that your enemy, the devil, and his demons will attack you in many ways, trying to make you sin.**
   James 4:7 says: "Therefore submit to God. Resist the devil and he will flee from you." Say, "It is written: 'He who is in you is greater than he who is in the world [the devil].'"
   (1 John 4:4 KJV)

7. **Should you fall into sin, do not be discouraged, but in repentance confess all to the Lord.**
...Let everyone who names the name of Christ depart from iniquity. (2 Timothy 2:19 NKJV)

8. **...Be filled with the Spirit (Ephesians 5:18 NKJV).**
God the Holy Spirit is a Person who wants to completely control your life, so that the Lord Jesus Christ may be made real to you, and then through you to others.

Without His control you will be a powerless, ineffective Christian.
• Surrender your will totally to God.
...the Holy Spirit whom God has given to those who obey Him. (Acts 5:32 NKJV)
• Be thorough in confession and repentance of all known sin.
He who covers his sins will not prosper, But whoever confesses and forsakes them will have mercy.
(Proverbs 28:13 NKJV)
• Ask God to fill you with His Spirit.
If you then, being evil, know how to give good gifts to your children, how much more will your heavenly Father give the Holy Spirit to those who ask Him! (Luke 11:13 NKJV)
• Believe that He will, and thank Him for doing so.
...For whatever is not from faith is sin.
(Romans 14:23 NKJV)

Allow the Holy Spirit to manifest Himself in whatever way He chooses, by being obedient to His promptings.

These conditions need to be fulfilled constantly in order to maintain the Spirit-filled life.

Copyright 1971 – Joy Dawson

Books By Joy Dawson

Available online at www.JoyDawson.com

Intimate Friendship With God – Revised Edition

This Christian Classic, best seller, explains the depth of the fear of the Lord and when applied to every area of life, releases us into the most fulfilling relationship with "the most exciting Being in the universe." Multitudes have reported it is absolutely life changing. It is published in 26 languages.

Some of the Ways of God in Healing

If you have more questions than answers about healing, then this book is for you. Joy is ruthless in her pursuit of truth from God's Word.

Intercession, Thrilling and Fulfilling

A highly inspirational manual taking the reader to greater depths and breadth in effective prayer for others in many categories – including leaders, people groups, and nations. Revival and spiritual awakening prayers are prominent.

Jesus the Model – the plumb line for Christian living

Becoming more like Jesus – radically real – we discover our greatest challenge and ultimate fulfillment.

Influencing Children to Become World Changers

Filled with wisdom, inspiration, and fascinating real-life stories, this practical book is a must-read for everyone who desires to impact children to enable them to reach their God-ordained destinities and help shape the world.

Forever Ruined for the Ordinary

This exciting book explains how to experience the adventure of hearing and obeying God's voice as a way of life. It includes 24 ways God speaks and 32 reasons why God delays answers, **and so much more.**

The Fire of God

This enlightening, very challenging book explains the price to come through the inevitable heat of life's circumstances, more like Jesus, but unscarred by the flames. It's not for wimps.

All Heaven Will Break Loose

This will happen when God's glory is on display among His people to the degree that unbelievers will say, "Wow! This is something else....and we want it!" This book clearly explains what releases God's glory in this dimension.

Booklets

Knowing God

How to understand His character and His ways. An essential read for serious disciples of the Lord Jesus.

How to Pray for Someone Near You who is Away From God

Powerful keys that work.

The Character of the One Who Says "Go"

Joy explains how amazing, faithful, just, powerful, generous, etc Jesus is when He tells us to "Go into all the world" and witness to others about Him.

Many vital taped messages (audio and video) are also available on www.JoyDawson.com

In my bedroom I have four glass framed Scripture groupings on my walls, as follows:

1. All my springs
are in You. Psalm 87:7

You are Complete in Him.
Colossians 2:10

2. Jesus
Altogether Lovely
Song of Solomon 5:16
Chiefest among Ten Thousand
Song of Solomon 5:10

3. As Your days
So shall
Your strength be.
Deuteronomy 33:25

4. The Faithful God
Deuteronomy 9:9
Has He Said,
and
Shall He Not Do It?
Numbers 23:19

Endnotes

Pg 32, 329, 399. Joy Dawson "ALL HEAVEN WILL BREAK LOOSE" When We Make The Priorities Of Jesus Our Priorities" ©2014 by Chosen Books.

Pg 44, 94, 325, 395. Joy Dawson "INTIMATE FRIENDSHIP WITH GOD" ©2008 by Chosen Books.

Pg 77, 396. Joy Dawson "SOME OF THE WAYS OF GOD IN HEALING" ©1991 by Y.W.A.M. Publishing.

Pg 136. Brother Andrew "GOD'S SMUGGLER" ©2015 by Chosen Books.

Pg 136. Loren Cunningham "IS THAT REALLY YOU GOD?" ©2011 by LorenCunningham.com.

Pg 140, 197. John Dawson "TAKING OUR CITIES FOR GOD" How To Break Spiritual Strongholds" ©2001 by Charisma House.

Pg 207, 354, 398. Joy Dawson "FOREVER RUINED FOR THE ORDINARY" ©2001 by Thomas Nelson Publishers.

Pg 222, 399. Joy Dawson "Knowing God" Teaching Article in the "WOMEN OF DESTINY STUDY BIBLE" Women Mentoring Women Through The Scriptures" ©2000 by Thomas Nelson Publishers.

Pg 245, 286, 342, 353, 396. Joy Dawson "INTERCESSION, THRILLING AND FULFILLING" ©1997 by Y.W.A.M. Publishing.

Pg 281. Graham Kendrick “SHINE JESUS SHINE” ©1987 by Make Way Music.

Pg 297. Don Richardson “PEACE CHILD” ©2005 by Regal Books.

Pg 341. Bob Sorge “THE FIRE OF DELAYED ANSWERS” ©1996 by Oasis House Publishers.

Pg 354, 397. Joy Dawson “THE FIRE OF GOD” ©2005 by Destiny Image.

Pg 367. Scott G. Bauer “THE NEW CHURCH ON THE WAY” ©2002 by The Church On The Way.

Pg 395. Vonette Bright “THE GREATEST LESSON I’VE EVER LEARNED” ©1990 by Here’s Life Publishers.

Pg 396. Joy Dawson “JESUS THE MODEL” ©2007 by Charisma House.

Pg 398. Joy Dawson “INFLUENCING CHILDREN TO BECOME WORLD CHANGERS” ©2003 by Thomas Nelson.

My Journey With Jesus

Taken From My Journals

- Ministry In Indonesia
- A "Waiting" Marathon
- Big Transition
- July 1972
- A Strategic Nation
- A Unique Privilege
- Unusual Tests
- Meeting Brother Andrew
- Just Having Fun
- A Castle For Sale
- A Vow Made And Kept
- Early Days Y.W.A.M. Lake View Terrace
- God Wowed Me
- Brazil
- My First Spiritual Leadership Conference In The U.S.A.
- The Saga At The London Airport
- Jesus The Winner
- Calcutta, India
- Having Fun
- A Challenging Missionary Assignment
- A Warning
- My Brothers
- Montreal Olympics
- Having Fun
- A Significant Day
- Unique Witnessing Opportunity
- Significant Times With Little David
- The National Prayer Committee
- An Unexpected Visitor
- Even More Fun
- Return Visit
- Brazil
- Y.W.A.M. Property In Solvang
- Radical Witnessing
- Glimpses Into The Unseen World

- Sydney, Australia
- Having Fun
- The Refugees

The 1980s

- Time For Expansion
- Cause For Rejoicing
- Wonderful Counselor
- A One Time Only Test
- Worth Waiting For
- Arnie Abraham
- Enjoyable And Fulfilling
- Harpenden, England
- Great Contrasts
- Some Wild Fun!!
- Bondage Breaking
- Ministry Trips To China
- Friday August 10th 1984
- Diverse Ministry Assignments
- Our Greatest Need
- Multi And Diverse Ministries
- Randers, Denmark
- Significant Times During Teaching Sessions
- A Hilarious Crisis in Hong Kong
- More Lessons to Learn
- Teen Challenge U.S.A.
- Some Of The Price
- Gordon Conwell Theological Seminary
- Argentina
- On The Streets In Durban, South Africa
- Before Apartheid
- Europe And The U.S.A.
- Encouraging Encounters
- CFNI And The Murchinsons

- Jim's Heart Surgery
- 9 Historic Days
- God's Faithfulness
- Korea Olympics
- My Mother's Suffering
- White House Visits
- The Power Of Unity
- A Unique Experience
- My Rave Review On God

The 1990s

- Revival And Spiritual Awakenings!
- A Cloudburst Of Genuine Revival
- A Surprise Visitation
- The Baltic States
- A Historic Event
- Latvia And England
- Argentina And Chile
- Billy Graham Retreat Center
- A Different Setting
- Taipei
- South Island Of New Zealand Roadtrip
- A Surprise Ending
- August 1992
- A Typical Ministry Day
- God's Personal Announcements
- The Road Becomes Rough
- September 1993
- A Pivotal Time
- Mario Murrilo
- God Will Prevail Over The Enemy
- Reporting On My Condition By Letter
- Expressed Gratitude
- God In Diversities

www.ingramcontent.com/pod-product-compliance
Lightning Source LLC
Chambersburg PA
CBHW041828090426
42811CB00010B/1139
9780578957098